DESIGNING BETTER ENGINEERING EDUCATION THROUGH ASSESSMENT

DESIGNING BETTER ENGINEERING EDUCATION THROUGH ASSESSMENT

A Practical Resource for Faculty and Department Chairs on Using Assessment and ABET Criteria to Improve Student Learning

Edited by Joni E. Spurlin, Sarah A. Rajala, and Jerome P. Lavelle

Foreword by Richard M. Felder

STERLING, VIRGINIA

Published by Stylus Publishing, LLC
22883 Quicksilver Drive
Sterling, Virginia 20166-2102

Library of Congress Cataloging-in-Publication-Data
Designing better engineering education through assessment : a practical resource for faculty and department chairs on using assessment and ABET criteria to improve student learning / Edited by Joni E. Spurlin, Sarah A. Rajala, and Jerome P. Lavelle.
     p.   cm.
    Includes index.
    ISBN 978-1-57922-212-3 (hardcover : alk. paper)—
    ISBN 978-1-57922-213-0 (pbk. : alk. paper)
    1. Engineering—Study and teaching (Continuing education)   I. Spurlin, Joni E.   II. Rajala, Sarah A. III. Lavelle, Jerome P.
    T65.3.D45   2008
    620.0071′5—dc22   2007021786

EAN: 978-1-57922-212-3 (cloth)
EAN: 978-1-57922-213-0 (paper)

Printed in the United States of America

All first editions printed on acid-free paper that meets the American National Standards Institute Z39–48 Standard.

Bulk Purchases

Quantity discounts are available for use in workshops and for staff development.
Call 1-800-232-0223

First Edition, 2008

10 9 8 7 6 5 4 3 2 1

Advisory Board

Mary Besterfield-Sacre, Associate Professor and Fulton C. Noss Faculty Fellow, Department of Industrial Engineering, University of Pittsburgh

J. Joseph Hoey, IV, Vice President for Institutional Effectiveness, Savannah College of Art and Design

Michael S. Leonard, Senior Associate Dean and Professor, School of Engineering, Mercer University

Eleanor W. Nault, Director of Assessment, Office of Institutional Assessment, Clemson University

C. Dianne Raubenheimer, Director of Assessment, College of Engineering, North Carolina State University

CONTENTS

FOREWORD

An engineering instructor's life was simpler in the old days (say, before 1990). All you had to do was lecture on the topics in the syllabus, give the assignments and tests, and assign grades. If the syllabus was covered, the course was considered successful, regardless of whether or not anyone learned anything. Conversations in the faculty lounge were about research budgets and the football coach's salary and the impossibility of finding parking on campus after 9 A.M.; words like "learning outcomes," "professional skills," and "Bloom's taxonomy" never entered the picture. If the term "assessment" was heard in an engineering school corridor, it was almost certainly spoken by a social scientist who had wandered into the wrong building.

That system did not work well as far as student learning is concerned. Students who dropped out of engineering in the first two years were academically indistinguishable from those who stayed in (several prominent research studies confirm this statement). Some of the dropouts had skills that many of the retained students lacked—critical thinking, creative thinking, and entrepreneurship, to name just three—that could have made them outstanding engineers, but those skills were neither taught nor assessed nor valued in engineering curricula and usually went unrecognized. The correlation between academic performance in engineering school (as measured by GPA) and success in engineering practice (as measured by promotions, salaries, and employer ratings) was found to be close to zero in several other research studies. In survey after survey, employers of engineers complained that while their new employees were fine at solving equations, they were seriously deficient in other skills such as teamwork; communication; and, yes, critical thinking, creative thinking, and entrepreneurship.

People in industry had been complaining about those deficiencies in engineering graduates for decades, but only toward the end of the 1980s did academicians begin to hear the complaints and take them seriously. In the period that followed, growing numbers of engineering school administrators and faculty members initiated curriculum reforms designed to equip students with a broad array of new skills, and the National Science Foundation began to put serious money into promoting those reforms. In the most dramatic sign of change, the Accreditation Board for Engineering and Technology (ABET) switched to an outcomes-based program evaluation and accreditation system. The switch began on a pilot basis in 1996 and became universal in 2001.

Once the new accreditation criteria were in play, engineering educators found themselves confronting an array of terms brand new to the vocabulary of the profession, such as "program educational objectives," "outcome indicators," "lifelong learning," and "closing the loop" (as applied to teaching, not process control). Under the new system, a program was no longer evaluated based on what the faculty was teaching—how many credits of "engineering science," how many of "engineering design," etc.—but rather on what the students were learning. Engineering programs now had to define in concrete terms the knowledge, skills, and values they wanted their graduates to have and then prove that the graduates in fact were getting them. To get the proof, the program instructors had to come up with ways to measure those attributes—which is to say, they suddenly found themselves neck deep in the business of assessing learning outcomes.

Most of us on engineering faculties were uncomfortable with this situation. Some of the outcomes we had to deal with were familiar—mathematical problem-solving ability, engineering laboratory and design skills, skills in computer applications, etc.—and we believed we knew how to teach and assess them. Other outcomes were problematic, however, including awareness of professional and ethical responsibilities, communication skills, ability to work in multidisciplinary teams, and understanding of the global and societal impact of engineering decisions. Nobody ever taught us those things in engineering school or anywhere else, and we weren't sure exactly what they were, let alone how to teach and assess them.

What engineering training *did* equip us to do, however, was solve problems, and learning how to define and assess unfamiliar outcomes is just another problem. Since the late 1990s, many engineering professors have invented solutions in efforts to prepare for their next ABET visit. Most of the inventors were unaware, however, that education professionals have addressed similar problems for years, in some cases quite effectively. Engineering professors generally do not read the education literature, and even if they do, that literature is so filled with jargon that attempting to penetrate it often leads to more frustration than illumination. What has been missing is a resource that takes effective assessment techniques developed by social scientists, education scholars, and statisticians and recasts them in terms that are both clear and clearly relevant to engineering education.

Designing Better Engineering Education Through Assessment is clearly intended to be such a resource. In my opinion, it succeeds admirably. It introduces and overviews the fundamentals of educational assessment, surveys the range of proven tools and methods that can be used to assess engineering courses and programs, and clearly lays out the barriers to successful engineering program assessment and offers practical guidance on ways to overcome them.

Part one of the book, "Basics of Assessment," answers such questions as these:

- What is educational assessment? What functions does it serve in designing and improving curricula? What are the meanings of all those terms that always show up in discussions of assessment and ABET accreditation—learning outcomes, outcome indicators, program educational objectives, course learning objectives, and so on?
- What are the principal methods of assessing learning outcomes? What are their strengths and weaknesses? How do you implement them effectively?
- How should assessment data be interpreted once they have been collected? How can the results be used to evaluate and improve instructional programs and individual courses?
- Which assessment methods are particularly useful for graduate education?

Part two of the book, "Barriers and Challenges," fills a vitally important function for engineering educators. The literature on assessment can sometimes lead readers into a naïve belief that simply putting an assessment program in place automatically leads to improved teaching and learning. As anyone who attempts to introduce systematic assessment in an engineering department quickly learns, designing and initiating an assessment program is the easy part; the trick is getting faculty buy-in. The two chapters in part two discuss the nature and causes of faculty resistance to assessment, how to avoid common mistakes that are made in assessment design and implementation, and how to achieve the faculty trust and buy-in that are essential to the success of an assessment program. I believe this part of the book should be required reading for every engineering educator and administrator.

Part three, "Learning Along the Continuum of the Educational Experience," offers guidance on assessment in first-year engineering programs, individual courses at any level, and the capstone course in a curriculum, and outlines how assessment can be used to improve instructional program quality. Part four, the last chapter of the book, reviews the current state of assessment in engineering education and speculates on future directions, basing the speculation on strong parallels between the evolution of assessment of learning in engineering education and that of the more advanced field of quality assessment in industry.

The chapter authors include some of the most knowledgeable and respected engineering educators in the profession, and the writing is clearly targeted to engineering educators rather than to assessment specialists. The emphasis is on practical details of implementation and not on pedagogical theories; the chapters contain a minimum of jargon; and technical terms that show up anywhere in the book are clearly defined in the first chapter and/or in an excellent glossary at the end. Survey forms and rubrics offered as examples can easily be copied and adapted for use by any instructional program. A reader who fails to find useful ideas and resources in every chapter of the book should take another look.

The movement of engineering education to an outcomes-based approach, as embodied in the ABET Engineering Criteria in the United States and the Washington Accord in a growing number of other countries, is not likely to be reversed, and assessment lies at the heart of outcomes-based education. Engineering administrators and educators would accordingly do well to become as knowledgeable about the principles and techniques of sound assessment as they are about the principles and techniques of their disciplinary specialties. Reading *Designing Better Engineering Education Through Assessment* is an excellent first step toward gaining that expertise.

Richard M. Felder
Hoechst Celanese Professor Emeritus of Chemical Engineering
North Carolina State University

T he purpose of assessment is to systematically improve the quality of student learning through improved programs, curricula, and teaching. Assessment informs planning and decision making and provides a gauge for the quality of courses, programs, and institutions. Faculty have ownership over courses and program curricula, and therefore need to also own the assessment processes designed to improve those courses/curricula.

This book is written for engineering faculty and department chairs as a practical guide to improving the assessment processes for undergraduate and graduate engineering education in the service of improved student learning. It is written by engineering faculty and assessment professionals who have many years of experience in assessment of engineering education and working with engineering faculty interested in improving student learning. The chapters have been organized to provide a practical resource for faculty and decision makers by explaining assessment theory and giving useful examples and illustrations. Our hope is to provide a baseline for good assessment for those beginning the process, as well as to challenge some readers to consider developing and using more sophisticated assessment methods.

This reference reflects the emphasis placed on student outcomes assessment by ABET, Inc., the organization that accredits most U.S. engineering, computer science, and technology programs (ABET also provides substantial equivalency evaluations to programs internationally). Assessment practices are evolving, not static, changing to meet the needs of employers, accreditors, and society. ABET, Inc., expects an ongoing dynamic systematic assessment process to be applied to the educational enterprises that seek accreditation from them. Our goal is to reflect this in this collection of chapters. The book also is meant to reflect the demands of those who employ our graduates. These organizations need engineers with strong technical and nontechnical capabilities. By improving assessment practices we all assist in improving and defining a new engineering education paradigm that better meets the demands of employers and accreditors.

The book begins with a brief overview of assessment theory and introduces readers to key assessment resources. It goes on to illustrate—through practical examples that reflect a wide range of engineering disciplines and practices at large and small institutions, and along the continuum of students' experience, from first year to capstone engineering courses through to the dissertation—how to go about applying assessment practices to improve student learning at the course and program level and to meet accreditation criteria.

The authors cover five basic themes:

- Use of assessment to improve student learning and educational programs at both undergraduate and graduate levels
- Application of ABET criteria to accomplish differing program and institutional missions
- Illustration of evaluation/assessment activities that can assist faculty in improving undergraduate and graduate courses and programs
- Description of tools and methods that have been demonstrated to improve the quality of degree programs and maintain accreditation
- Identification of methods for overcoming institutional barriers and challenges to implementing assessment initiatives

Part One: Basics of Assessment

Part one of the book gives detailed instructions on how to conduct program assessment. The authors of this book assume that all undergraduate engineering programs have been through at least one accreditation review cycle that included outcomes assessment as defined by ABET. However, part one gives those engineering faculty and department chairs who are less familiar with assessment a good foundation. Chapter 1 begins with a brief overview of assessment theory, including discussion of best practices, and an appendix that lists other assessment books and articles. Chapter 2 discusses the overall assessment process for engineering education. It outlines the assessment phases by describing who is involved, what they must do, and how often. Included in that chapter is a template useful for operationalizing and refining ABET's required Criterion 3 outcomes a–k. Outlines for program assessment plans and reports are also given. Chapter 3 provides specific methods for assessing engineering program-level objectives and outcomes. The chapter explains what types of evidence should be collected, how to link program outcomes to course outcomes, and how to link course assessment to program outcomes assessment. Appendix examples include rubrics, sample survey questions, and methods for utilizing the Fundamentals of Engineering

Exam. Chapter 4 focuses on how to analyze the assessment evidence, once collected, then discusses how to use the analyses to improve student learning. Real examples of how engineering programs have collected, analyzed, interpreted, and used qualitative and quantitative data to understand how well students have met their program outcomes are examined. Chapter 5 focuses specifically on assessment of graduate engineering programs. Even though graduate programs tend to be taught in smaller courses, with much more individualized instruction, the purpose of assessment is still the same: to improve student learning. Assessment methods include both formative and summative assessment strategies/approaches to enhance best practices within graduate programs—not just at the end.

Part Two: Barriers and Challenges

Regardless of how well outcomes are defined or assessment methods are developed, there are times when assessment processes begin to fail. Part two discusses the barriers and challenges related to conducting effective assessment in engineering education. Without actively acknowledging that barriers exist and actively providing ways to overcome these barriers, assessment practices will become limited and ultimately may not be used for any meaningful purpose other than for superficial documentation to meet accreditation criteria. Chapter 6 outlines barriers to implementing effective assessment and describes the contextual factors that contribute to the resistance to those impediments. The chapter provides a taxonomy of barriers to assessment based around aspects of trust, and suggests ways to address these issues. Chapter 7 further discusses barriers to assessment that revolve around resistance to change. Using assessment evidence implies finding issues to change regarding student learning, teaching practices, courses requirements, and curriculum. However, "change" is a major barrier to improving student learning and programs. This chapter discusses how to overcome barriers of change through organizational change agents. Steps for recognizing why individuals or institutions are resisting change and how to counter this resistance are explained.

Part Three: Learning Along the Continuum of the Educational Experience

The third part centers on learning along the continuum of the students' educational experience. Included in this part are assessment methods and examples illustrating how to assess students' learning along that continuum. The chapters of this part discuss assessment of first-year engineering, assessment of a course, assessment within the educational experience using formative assessment methods, and assessment of the capstone experiences (capstone course in undergraduate education; thesis/dissertation at graduate level). Chapter 8 discusses assessment of the first year in engineering and specifically focuses on benchmarking and illustrating programs and assessment trends in engineering programs throughout the United States. Chapters 9 and 10 address how formative assessment can be used to help provide midcourse feedback to engineering programs as they work to continuously improve learning and teaching. Chapter 9 explores the relationship between teaching and learning. It focuses on how engineering faculty can assess and improve their own instruction and courses by using classroom assessment techniques (CATs) to gather information about student learning. Chapter 10 gives theory and engineering examples of formative assessment methods for program improvement. This chapter discusses the use of forced concept inventories, concept mapping, and rubrics, among others. Chapter 11 ends the section by discussing assessment of the end of the student's educational experience in undergraduate senior design, along with the graduate-level dissertation and thesis.

Part Four: The Future

The book concludes with a vision for the future of assessment for engineering education, including the future of assessment practices, accreditation, and their future impacts on engineering education. Chapter 12 begins by examining how the development of engineering education assessment is complementary to (but lagging behind) the development of quality measurement in industry. By looking at where quality measurement is today, better forecasts can be made about the next developments in engineering education assessment. The authors propose that as engineering educators become more expert in measuring the student outcomes, they will enter into an era where the focus will be on how to measure the various processes students use to achieve the outcomes and address engineering student cognition and dimensions of learning. The book thus ends with a call for moving toward better assessment methodologies and gives several examples of emerging assessment methodologies and tools.

Joni E. Spurlin
Sarah A. Rajala
Jerome P. Lavelle

ACKNOWLEDGMENTS

T his book has been a joint effort and vision by the editors and those who have served on the advisory board for this book. The editors wish to thank the members of the advisory board for their time and dedication to educating engineers.

The editors are also delighted to include the important contributions of many experts in the field of engineering education and assessment who wrote chapters (see Contributors section). We wish to acknowledge and thank them for their time and dedication.

The editors also acknowledge and thank all those with whom we have worked on improving engineering education through assessment activities, especially those at the North Carolina State University College of Engineering. The current and past ABET Team at NC State have spent many hours debating and discussing all the issues that are contained in this book. We have used many examples from NC State's engineering programs to help illustrate good practices.

Finally, the editors and chapter authors acknowledge and thank the following colleagues for their permission to reproduce their work; their materials are an important contribution to this book.

- ABET organization for permission to reprint the ABET *Criteria for Accrediting Engineering Programs*.
- Maury Balik, North Carolina State University. Material Science Engineering's rubric for assessing lab reports was reprinted with permission in chapter 3, Appendix 3.C.
- David Beasley, North Carolina State University. Portions of the Biological Engineering's assessment plan were reproduced with permission in chapter 2, Figure 2.3 and Appendix 2.B.
- Michael Carter, North Carolina State University. His Annotated Template for Program Outcomes was reprinted with permission in chapter 2, Appendix 2.D.
- Yusef Fahmy, North Carolina State University. The program educational objectives and rubrics used to assess outcomes were reprinted

with permission in chapter 2, Appendix 2.B; and chapter 3, Appendixes 3.B, 3.D, 3.E, and 3.F.

- Stephen Kampe, Virginia Tech. Figure 4.2 in chapter 4 is a reproduction of a quadrant chart with permission from the American Society of Engineering Education. Originally published in Pappas, E., Kampe, S., Hendricks, R., & Kander, R. (2004). An assessment analysis methodology and its application to an advanced engineering communication program. *Journal of Engineering Education, 93*(3), 233–246.

- Laura Lackey, Mercer University. The Client/Tech Advisor Team Assessment rubric used in senior design was reprinted with permission from Mercer University in chapter 3, Appendix 3.B.

- Joni Spurlin, North Carolina State University. Portions of the following paper presentation were reprinted with permission from American Society for Engineering Education Conference and Exposition. See chapter 8, Table 8.2, Table 8.4, and Appendix 8.A. Originally published in Spurlin, J., Lavelle, J., Rajala, S., & Robbins, M. (2003). Assessment of an Introduction to Engineering and Problem Solving course. In *Proceedings of American Society for Engineering Education Conference and Exposition.* Retrieved September 13, 2006, from http://www.asee.org/acPapers/2003-356_Final.pdf. In addition, her information about sources of information used in assessment of engineering programs including pros and cons was reprinted with permission in chapter 2, Appendix 2.E.

- Karan Watson, Texas A&M University. Her ideational map of the process of change for an individual was reprinted with permission from Women in Engineering & Advocates Network (WEPAN)/National Association of Minority Engineering Professionals Advocates (NAMEPA) in chapter 7, Figure 7.1. Originally published in Algert, N. E., & Watson, K. (2005, April 20). Systematic change in engineering education: The role of effective change agents for women in engineering. In *Proceedings: Women in Engineering & Advocates Network (WEPAN)/National Association of Minority Engineering Professionals Advocates (NAMEPA) Conference,* Las Vegas, NV.

ABET CRITERIA FOR ACCREDITING ENGINEERING PROGRAMS

Effective for Evaluations During the 2006–2007 Accreditation Cycle

These criteria are intended to assure quality and to foster the systematic pursuit of improvement in the quality of engineering education that satisfies the needs of constituencies in a dynamic and competitive environment. It is the responsibility of the institution seeking accreditation of an engineering program to demonstrate clearly that the program meets the following criteria.

I. GENERAL CRITERIA FOR BASIC LEVEL PROGRAMS

Criterion 1. Students

The quality and performance of the students and graduates are important considerations in the evaluation of an engineering program. The institution must evaluate student performance, advise students regarding curricular and career matters, and monitor student's progress to foster their success in achieving program outcomes, thereby enabling them as graduates to attain program objectives.

The institution must have and enforce policies for the acceptance of transfer students and for the validation of courses taken for credit elsewhere. The institution must also have and enforce procedures to assure that all students meet all program requirements.

Criterion 2. Program Educational Objectives

Although institutions may use different terminology, for purposes of Criterion 2, program educational objectives are broad statements that describe the career and professional accomplishments that the program is preparing graduates to achieve.

Each engineering program for which an institution seeks accreditation or reaccreditation must have in place:

(a) detailed published educational objectives that are consistent with the mission of the institution and these criteria

(b) a process based on the needs of the program's various constituencies in which the objectives are determined and periodically evaluated

(c) an educational program, including a curriculum that prepares students to attain program outcomes and that fosters accomplishments of graduates that are consistent with these objectives

(d) a process of ongoing evaluation of the extent to which these objectives are attained, the result of which shall be used to develop and improve the program outcomes so that graduates are better prepared to attain the objectives.

Criterion 3. Program Outcomes and Assessment

Although institutions may use different terminology, for purposes of Criterion 3, program outcomes are statements that describe what students are expected to know and be able to do by the time of graduation. These relate to the skills, knowledge, and behaviors that students acquire in their matriculation through the program.

Each program must formulate program outcomes that foster attainment of the program objectives articulated in satisfaction of Criterion 2 of these criteria. There must be processes to produce these outcomes and an assessment process, with documented results, that demonstrates that these program outcomes are being measured and indicates the degree to which the outcomes are achieved. There must be evidence that the results of this assessment process are applied to the further development of the program.

Engineering programs must demonstrate that their students attain:

(a) an ability to apply knowledge of mathematics, science, and engineering

(b) an ability to design and conduct experiments, as well as to analyze and interpret data

(c) an ability to design a system, component, or process to meet desired needs within realistic constraints such as economic, environmental, social, political, ethical, health and safety, manufacturability, and sustainability

(d) an ability to function on multi-disciplinary teams

(e) an ability to identify, formulate, and solve engineering problems

(f) an understanding of professional and ethical responsibility

(g) an ability to communicate effectively

(h) the broad education necessary to understand the impact of engineering solutions in a global, economic, environmental, and societal context

(i) a recognition of the need for, and an ability to engage in, life-long learning

(j) a knowledge of contemporary issues

(k) an ability to use the techniques, skills, and modern engineering tools necessary for engineering practice.

In addition, an engineering program must demonstrate that its students attain any additional outcomes articulated by the program to foster achievement of its education objectives.

Criterion 4. Professional Component

The professional component requirements specify subject areas appropriate to engineering but do not prescribe specific courses. The faculty must ensure that the program curriculum devotes adequate attention and time to each component, consistent with the outcomes and objectives of the program and institution. The professional component must include:

(a) one year of a combination of college level mathematics and basic sciences (some with experimental experience) appropriate to the discipline

(b) one and one-half years of engineering topics, consisting of engineering sciences and engineering design appropriate to the student's field of study. The engineering sciences have their roots in mathematics and basic sciences but carry knowledge further toward creative application. These studies provide a bridge between mathematics and basic sciences on the one hand and engineering practice on the other. Engineering design is the process of devising a system, component, or process to meet desired needs. It is a decision-making process (often iterative), in which the basic sciences, mathematics, and the engineering sciences are applied to convert resources optimally to meet these stated needs.

(c) a general education component that complements the technical content of the curriculum and is consistent with the program and institution objectives.

Students must be prepared for engineering practice through the curriculum culminating in a major design experience based on the knowledge and skills acquired in earlier course work and incorporating appropriate engineering standards and multiple realistic constraints.

Criterion 5. Faculty

The faculty is the heart of any educational program. The faculty must be of sufficient number; and must have the competencies to cover all of the curricular areas of the program. There must be sufficient faculty to accommodate adequate levels of student–faculty interaction, student advising and counseling, university service activities, professional development, and interactions with industrial and professional practitioners, as well as employers of students.

The program faculty must have appropriate qualifications and must have and demonstrate sufficient authority to ensure the proper guidance of the program and to develop and implement processes for the evaluation, assessment, and continuing improvement of the program, its educational objectives and outcomes. The overall competence of the faculty may be judged by such factors as education, diversity of backgrounds, engineering experience, teaching experience, ability to communicate, enthusiasm for developing more effective programs, level of scholarship, participation in professional societies, and licensure as Professional Engineers.

Criterion 6. Facilities

Classrooms, laboratories, and associated equipment must be adequate to accomplish the program objectives and provide an atmosphere conducive to learning. Appropriate facilities must be available to foster faculty–student interaction and to create a climate that encourages professional development and professional activities. Programs must provide opportunities for students to learn the use of modern engineering tools. Computing and information infrastructures must be in place to support the scholarly activities of the students and faculty and the educational objectives of the program and institution.

Criterion 7. Institutional Support and Financial Resources

Institutional support, financial resources, and constructive leadership must be adequate to assure the quality and continuity of the engineering program. Resources must be sufficient to attract, retain, and provide for the continued professional development of a well-qualified faculty. Resources also must be sufficient to acquire, maintain, and operate facilities and equipment appropriate for the engineering program. In addition, support personnel and institutional services must be adequate to meet program needs.

Criterion 8. Program Criteria

Each program must satisfy applicable Program Criteria (if any). Program Criteria provide the specificity needed for interpretation of the basic level criteria as applicable to a given discipline. Requirements stipulated in the Program Criteria are limited to the areas of curricular topics and faculty qualifications. If a program, by virtue of its title, becomes subject to two or more sets of Program Criteria, then that program must satisfy each set of Program Criteria; however, overlapping requirements need to be satisfied only once.

Reproduced with permission. ABET. (2006). Criteria for accrediting engineering programs. Retrieved January 30, 2007, from http://www.abet.org/Linked%20Documents-UPDATE/Criteria%20and%20PP/ E001% 2006-07%20EAC%20Criteria%205-25-06.pdf

PART ONE

BASICS OF ASSESSMENT

I

UNDERSTANDING THE NATURE AND PURPOSE OF ASSESSMENT

Linda Suskie

This chapter provides an overview of the nature of assessment, some of the key reasons why the higher education community is being called to rethink and expand its approaches to assessment, and the fundamental characteristics of effective assessment. The chapters that follow apply the generic principles presented in this chapter to the specific context of engineering.

The Fundamentals of Assessment

What is assessment? While definitions abound (e.g., Angelo, 1995), perhaps the most straightforward way to understand assessment is to put it into the context of a dynamic teaching–learning–assessment cycle, composed of four steps as shown in Table 1.1 (Middle States Commission on Higher Education, 2006).

The first step of the cycle is developing clearly articulated written statements of expected learning outcomes. Assessment is a bit like planning a road trip; one can't plot a route without knowing the eventual destination. Assessment thus requires clear statements of exactly what students should know and be able to do as a result of their learning experience.

Effective statements of student learning outcomes may be a bit different from the "objectives" noted on many course syllabi. To be of maximum value in the assessment process, learning outcomes statements should:

TABLE 1.1
The Four Steps of the Teaching–Learning–Assessment Cycle

1. Develop clearly articulated written statements of expected learning outcomes.
2. Design learning experiences that provide intentional, purposeful opportunities for students to achieve those learning outcomes.
3. Implement appropriate measures of student achievement of key learning outcomes.
4. Use assessment results to improve teaching and learning.

- Focus on the most important things that students will learn. Often it is less important that students understand key concepts than that they can use their understanding to analyze and solve real-life problems.
- Use action words that describe not what students will know but what they will be able to do as a result of their learning. A statement that students will *explain* or *describe* key concepts is clearer, for example, than a statement that students will *understand* key concepts, and makes an appropriate assessment strategy easier to discern.
- Reflect the outcomes of a course or program—what students will be able to do *after* they have successfully completed the course or program—not the activities that happen *during* the course or program. A statement that students will write four lab reports is not a statement of learning outcomes; the learning outcome is what the lab reports are preparing the student to do, perhaps write clear, complete, and accurate summaries of laboratory research.
- Be developed for entire programs as well as individual courses. A good academic program is more than a collection of courses; it is designed to focus on outcomes that are emphasized repeatedly, in multiple courses, throughout the students' studies.

The second step of the cycle is designing learning experiences that provide intentional, purposeful opportunities for students to achieve those learning outcomes. Students learn what we value when they have plentiful and well-designed opportunities to do so. Suppose, for example, that one of the goals of an academic program is for students to make effective oral presentations on their work. Students will be more likely to achieve this goal if the curriculum is designed to include oral presentation assignments at multiple points in the program. Students will also be more likely to achieve this goal if faculty design their pedagogies or teaching methods to help students learn how to make effective oral presentations, with carefully designed opportunities for practice and feedback.

The third step of the cycle is implementing appropriate measures of student achievement of key learning outcomes. While faculty frequently see this as the most challenging step of the cycle, in reality it can be the easiest if the first two steps of the cycle are executed carefully and thoughtfully. Once expected learning outcomes are clearly articulated and curricula and pedagogies are carefully designed to help students achieve them, appropriate assessments become almost self-evident.

The final and most important step of the teaching–learning–assessment cycle is using assessment results to improve teaching and learning. There is not much point in assessing student learning if the results are simply filed away. Assessment results can be used in two ways: If the evidence is that students are indeed learning what we want them to learn, results can be used to garner support and resources for the institution and the program from benefactors, employers, legislators, board members, and the like. If the results are disappointing, they can be used to promote the improvement of student learning by launching, as appropriate, modifications to expected learning outcomes, curricula, pedagogies, and/or assessment strategies and tools.

The Call to Rethink Approaches to Assessment

Faculty have been evaluating student work and assigning grades for centuries. Why, then, are accreditors, legislators, and government agencies calling for new approaches to assessment? While several factors have come into play, two are perhaps most significant. First, a college education is increasingly becoming an essential need, not an option. The United States no longer leads the world in the rate of college completion (Suskie, 2006a), especially in the education of scientists and engineers. As a result, the United States has been overtaken by other countries in the proportion of the population with a postsecondary education, as other countries increasingly recognize that postsecondary education is essential to sustained economic development. While it was possible a generation or two ago to earn a good living with a high school diploma, those jobs are rapidly vanishing, and today most people need some form of postsecondary education in order to earn a comfortable living. These people look on a college education as an economic investment in their future, and they want solid assurance that their investment will give them the knowledge and skills they need for successful careers.

Second, while American higher education is the best in the world, there is growing recognition that it could—and needs to—be better. Most college professors are largely self-taught when it comes to curricular design, pedagogical techniques, addressing diverse student learning styles, and assessing student learning. Despite their best efforts, their tests and assignments often do not reflect key student learning goals, focus too much on memorized knowledge rather than thinking skills, and are unclear or otherwise of poor quality. Many faculty persist in teaching through traditional lectures, even though extensive research (e.g., Angelo, 1993; Chickering & Gamson, 1987; Mentkowski & Associates, 2000; Pascarella & Terenzini, 2005; What research says, 1996) has shown that engaging students actively in their learning is a far more effective pedagogical strategy.

In short, there are increasing calls both within and outside the academy to do all we can to ensure that students graduate with the knowledge, skills, and competencies they need for successful careers and rich, fulfilling lives. We in higher education are responding by embarking on nothing less than a radical transformation of what and how we teach our students. Assessment is a vital tool for understanding student learning, developing and implementing improvements in our teaching, and documenting successes to an increasingly demanding society.

Principles of Good Practice in Assessing Student Learning

What is "good" assessment? Several statements of principles of good practice in assessment have been put forth in recent years (e.g., American Association for Higher Education, 1991; American Productivity and Quality Center, 1999; Association of American Colleges and Universities, 2002; Banta, 2002; Bresciani, 2003; Council of Regional Accrediting Commissions, 2004; Driscoll & Cordero de Noriega, 2006; Greater Expectations Project on Accreditation and Assessment, 2002, 2004; Huba & Freed, 2000; Joint Committee on Standards for Educational Evaluation, 1994; Joint Committee on Testing Practices, 2004; Middle States Commission on Higher Education, 2005; National Council on Measurement in Education, 1995; National Research Council, 1993; Palomba & Banta, 1999; Suskie, 2000, 2004). They may be summarized, as shown in Table 1.2, into five key characteristics (Suskie, 2006b).

TABLE 1.2
What Are the Key Characteristics of "Good" Assessments?

1. Good assessments are used.
2. Good assessments are cost-effective, especially in terms of time.
3. Good assessments yield reasonably accurate and truthful results.
4. Good assessments are valued.
5. Good assessments focus on and flow from clear and important goals.

Good Assessments Are Used

Assessments leading to results that wind up collecting dust somewhere are a waste of everyone's time. Good assessment efforts and results are therefore used to inform important decisions, especially those to improve curriculum and pedagogy but also those regarding planning, budgeting, and accountability. Assessments that are used have a number of characteristics:

1. Assessments that are used start with a clear understanding of why you are assessing. The most effective assessments are designed with a clear purpose and clear audience in mind. First, consider who will want to see and use the assessment results. Possible audiences for assessment results include not only faculty and administrators but also current students, prospective students and their families, employers of graduates, board members, legislators and government officials, and accreditors. Next, consider what questions your audiences will want the assessment to answer. What decisions will the assessment help them make? The following are examples of questions that might be answered by assessments:
   - Are students meeting institutional and programmatic standards for academic achievement?
   - How do students compare with their peers?
   - Are students' knowledge, skills, and competencies growing and improving while they are enrolled at our institution and in our program?
   - Are the changes that have been made to curricula and teaching methods having the desired effects on student learning?

2. Assessments that are used focus on clear and important goals. The most effective assessments are part of the purposeful, coherent process described earlier, in which curricula and pedagogies are explicitly designed to achieve key student learning outcomes; assessments are designed to evaluate student achievement of those key learning outcomes; and assessment results are used appropriately to improve teaching and learning.

3. Assessments that are used involve the active participation of those with a stake in decisions stemming from the results. Banta (2002) notes that assessment should "involve stakeholders . . . from the outset to incorporate their needs and interests" (p. 262), while the Council of Regional Accrediting Commissions (2004) encourages institutions to use "broad participation in reflection about student learning outcomes as a means of building a commitment to educational improvement." It is particularly important that faculty have ownership of the assessment process, as they have ownership of the curricular and pedagogical decisions that assessment results inform.

4. Assessments that are used are communicated widely and transparently. The National Council on Measurement in Education (1995) states that assessment results should be communicated to appropriate audiences in a fair, complete, understandable, and timely manner. It certainly makes sense that if decision makers don't receive the results or can't easily understand them, the results will not be used to inform decisions.

5. Assessments that are used are used fairly, ethically, and responsibly (Suskie, 2000). The fastest way to kill any assessment effort is to base a major decision on the results of only one assessment, especially if the results are used punitively, such as reacting to disappointing assessment results by eliminating a program or denying promotion or tenure to the faculty involved.

Good Assessments Are Cost-Effective, Especially in Terms of Time

Assessments should yield value that justifies the time and expense we put into them (Suskie, 2004). They should not take so much time that they detract from other essential activities such as teaching. Assessments with the greatest "bang for the buck" have a number of characteristics:

1. Cost-effective assessments focus on clear and important goals. The prospect of assessing a long list of learning outcomes in the coming

semester is naturally daunting. Instead, begin by assessing a subset of goals and grow assessment efforts from there. Some faculty begin with the learning outcomes that they have identified as most impor- tant (and the discussion that identifies the most important goals is a valuable one in its own right). Others begin with those outcomes that they believe, through anecdotal evidence or gut instinct, they are most successful in instilling in their students. The "start with suc- cesses" approach can create a "win-win" situation: Faculty get solid evidence of student achievements that they can use to attract future students and gain support for the program. When they then move on to assess other areas where they are not as confident of success, they will know that any disappointing results will be viewed in light of the successes that they have documented.

2. Cost-effective assessments start with what you have. Do a quick in- ventory of assessment information already on hand, such as certifica- tion and licensure examination scores, surveys, field experience supervisors' evaluations of students, and reviews of capstone research projects. You may find that you already have a great deal of informa- tion, and perhaps after giving current assessment tools a bit of tweak- ing, you need not develop any new ones.

3. Cost-effective assessments are kept as simple as possible and have minimal paperwork. Assessment efforts can quickly drown under paper or computer files, so carefully scrutinize everything you have planned and continually look for ways to streamline and simplify what you are doing. One way to keep things simple is to use samples (see Suskie, 2004, for information on calculating sample sizes). An- other way is to use simple, easy-to-use assessment tools such as ru- brics (Walvoord & Anderson, 1998) and minute papers (Angelo & Cross, 1993). Yet another strategy is to keep assessment tools as short as possible. A ten-page alumni survey will yield ten pages of results that faculty and administrators must tabulate, analyze, and discuss, while a two-page survey, though not yielding the same breadth of information, will take far less time to implement, summarize, share, and use.

   Also keep in mind that assessments can be staggered over time. Faculty might develop a rolling three-year cycle, for example, in which research papers are reviewed in the first year, alumni surveys are conducted in the second year, and interviews with graduating seniors are conducted in the third. Assessments that have yielded satisfactory results are especially suitable for moving to a staggered schedule, while assessments that have identified problem areas may be subject to more frequent monitoring to see if planned improvements are having their desired effect.

Finally, do all you can do to minimize the burden of preparing reports on assessment efforts. As Bresciani (2006) points out, if assessment results are not recorded, they cannot be shared, discussed, and used, so periodic reports on assessment efforts and results are needed. The burden of preparing them can be minimized, however. The shorter and simpler the expectations for reporting, the less faculty will resent having to provide requested information and the more likely they will be to comply, so strip down reporting requirements to the bare essentials. When you see signs that a culture of assessment has become embedded in a particular department—that the report itself is no longer part of what motivates the faculty to engage in assessment—reward the department's faculty by moving them from an annual to a biennial reporting schedule.

4. Cost-effective assessments have realistic expectations. Rather than ask everyone to use a particular rubric or submit a report by a particular date, be flexible; doing so will give faculty a sense of empowerment and promote their engagement in assessment. Recognize that some important learning outcomes, especially those related to attitudes, values, and dispositions, may be difficult if not impossible to assess accurately. Continue to value them as important goals, but focus energies, at least initially, on more assessable goals. And recognize that you will not get everyone on board with and engaged in assessment. Work around the hard-core resisters, and focus energies instead on getting the reluctant but "winnable" people involved.

Good Assessments Yield Reasonably Accurate and Truthful Results

The key word here is "reasonably." Assessment is a form of "action" research, not as carefully designed or executed as laboratory research but rather planned simply with an eye to yielding locally useful results (Upcraft & Schuh, 2002). Most faculty do not have the time, skills, or inclination to conduct major validation studies, although any faculty who wish to design assessments that can lead to a dissertation, journal article, or conference presentation should of course never be discouraged from doing so. Instead, simply aim for assessments that are of good enough quality that they can be used with confidence to make decisions about curriculum and pedagogy. Most faculty, even those without formal training in educational research methods, have a good instinct for what is "good enough," such as how many papers they should review in order to draw a reasonably accurate conclusion about student writing skills.

1. Assessments yielding reasonably accurate and truthful results flow from clear and important goals. Of the types of validity evidence identified by educators and psychometricians (e.g., construct validity, criterion-related validity), the most important when assessing student learning in higher education is content-related validity, which is simply how closely the assessment tool aligns with your particular goals for student learning (Gay, Mills, & Airasian, 2005). A writing test that focuses on grammar skills, for example, would not be a valid writing test if your primary goals are to improve students' skills in writing well-organized papers with well-reasoned arguments. A quantitative reasoning test that focuses on arithmetic skills would not be a valid test to evaluate students' use of calculus to solve engineering dilemmas.

2. Assessments yielding reasonably accurate and truthful results use a variety of approaches, including direct evidence of student learning. Because any one assessment tool or strategy has inherent imperfections and is not equally appropriate for every situation, use a variety of assessment approaches and corroborate or triangulate results (Campbell & Fiske, 1959). Depending on your goals, students' needs, and institutional culture, assessments may be quantitative and/or qualitative and may look at teaching-learning processes as well as outcomes. To have credibility, however, any assessment effort should include direct (clear and compelling) evidence of student learning, such as that demonstrated through examinations, papers, projects, portfolios, and the like.

3. Assessments yielding reasonably accurate and truthful results represent a balanced sample of key outcomes, including multidimensional, integrative thinking skills. Assessment efforts in higher education increasingly use "capstone" experiences: papers, projects, examinations, or field experiences in which students pull together and integrate many of the concepts and skills they have learned over a course or program. Capstone assignments evaluating student achievement of

multiple outcomes should represent a balanced sample of key outcomes, not just the ones that are most easily assessed. A simple and
effective way to ensure balanced attention is to use a rubric or test
blueprint (Suskie, 2004) to design the assessment.

In many cases, key outcomes are for students not just to learn concepts but to be able to use them in real-world situations. In these
cases, "authentic" assessments (those that focus on "messy," real-
world problems with more than one acceptable solution) provide the
most meaningful picture of student learning.

4. Assessments yielding reasonably accurate and truthful results recognize diverse approaches to teaching, learning, and assessment. In assessment, one size does not fit all. Suskie (2000) notes that "students
   learn and demonstrate their learning in many different ways. Some
   learn best by reading and writing, others through collaboration with
   peers, others through listening, creating a schema or design, or
   hands-on practice. . . . Because all assessments favor some learning
   styles over others, it's important to give students a variety of ways to
   demonstrate what they've learned" (p. 8).

5. Assessments yielding reasonably accurate and truthful results assess
   teaching-learning processes as well as outcomes. While assessment
   outcomes tell you *what* your students have learned, they don't tell
   you *why*. In order to understand assessment results, look at information on teaching-learning processes as well as outcomes (Pascarella,
   2001; Suskie, 2004). Sources such as transcripts, course syllabi, and
   student surveys can provide information on teaching-learning processes and practices such as the true alignment of goals, curricula, and
   assessments; the degree of emphasis on thinking and performance
   skills as opposed to rote learning; and opportunities for active and
   collaborative learning.

6. Assessments yielding reasonably accurate and truthful results are developed thoughtfully. Good assessments do take time and careful de-
   liberation. Often assessments must be tested on a small scale and then
   revised before they can be used with confidence in larger settings.

7. Assessments yielding reasonably accurate and truthful results are
   looked upon as perpetual works in progress. Assessments are neither
   static nor once-and-done; as students, their needs, and the needs of
   employers and society all evolve, assessments must evolve as well.
   Plan to periodically review your assessment efforts and be willing to
   adapt them to changing circumstances.

Good Assessments Are Valued

Perhaps the most important way that an institution values assessment efforts is by using them to inform important decisions, as discussed earlier. But there are other ways in which an institution can develop a climate that values assessment efforts.

1. Valued assessment results inform important decisions on important goals. Assessment efforts thrive at institutions whose culture is to base decisions on systematic, compelling evidence; they struggle at institutions whose culture is to base decisions on whim or anecdote. If assessment results are to be used, standards, goals, and results should all be expressed in ways that are transparent (i.e., clear and understandable) to faculty, administrators, students, and other stakeholders.

2. Valued assessment efforts are recognized and honored through meaningful incentives and rewards. Some institutions provide grants or stipends to faculty who undertake extraordinary assessment efforts. Others recognize such faculty with events, awards, or letters of commendation from institutional leaders.

3. Valued assessments are part of an institutional climate in which innovation, risk taking, and efforts to improve teaching and learning are recognized and honored through meaningful incentives and rewards. The primary purpose of assessment, after all, is to improve student learning, so assessment results will not be used if there is no incentive to improve one's teaching. Curricular improvement grants and other mechanisms that encourage risk taking and innovation encourage assessment efforts as well.

4. Valued assessments are supported with appropriate resources, including time. Faculty intrigued by assessment are often nonetheless concerned about how they will find the time to engage in it, given their already overfull plates of teaching, advisement, scholarship, service, and other activities. Because there are only a finite number of hours in each day, the only way to help faculty find the time for assessment is to help them stop doing something else. Perhaps some committee work can be put on hold, for example, while assessments are planned and launched. Perhaps a temporary moratorium can be placed on new courses or programs.

5. Valued and used assessments are supported with guidance, support,

and feedback. Just as students learn best when they are given clear guidelines for their assignments and feedback on their work, so do faculty and staff do their best assessment work when they are provided with clear expectations, overall guidance and coordination, and constructive feedback on their efforts. Faculty committees can be charged with reviewing reports on assessment efforts and providing written feedback on what faculty are doing well and what they might consider improving. A rubric is an effective way to provide this feedback (e.g., Suskie, 2004, pp. 68–69).

Good Assessments Focus on and Flow From Clear and Important Goals

A recurring theme through the four characteristics of effective assessment discussed on pages 8–10 is that assessments focus on and flow from clear and important goals. Assessments that do so are used, are cost-effective, yield reasonably accurate and truthful results, and are valued. Assessments that focus on and flow from clear and important goals have clear, appropriate standards for acceptable and exemplary student performance.

Meeting Accreditors' Expectations for Assessment

There are dozens of federally recognized accreditors and, while their accreditation standards and processes vary, nearly all have two requirements in common: They expect periodic, intensive, thorough self-examination, and they expect to see evidence of student learning. The key to meeting these expectations efficiently and effectively is to prepare for the accreditation process, especially in terms of assessment, in an ongoing, systematic way rather than as a once-and-done activity. Faculty who assess student learning regularly will have a good body of evidence that they need merely summarize by the time they prepare for an accreditation review. In contrast, those who engage in assessment only when preparing for an accreditation review face a huge project on top of all the other things that must be done. Chances are that what was done for the last accreditation effort has been lost or forgotten, so extra time is spent reinventing the assessment wheel. Slow and steady is clearly the better assessment course to take.

Keeping the Momentum Going

While it may seem easier to keep assessment efforts going once the initial burst of activity gets everyone on board, in fact the opposite can be true:

Momentum can flag as assessment work becomes routine, even mundane, and attention will turn to other initiatives. Suskie (2003) offers four tips for keeping assessment thriving, summarized in Table 1.3:

1. Continue to emphasize keeping assessment efforts useful, cost-effective, and valued. Review practices and procedures periodically to make sure that they support rather than impede assessment and are not excessively burdensome.
2. Be flexible. Be willing to bend local rules to smooth the path for those who have trouble keeping assessment going. Perhaps the due date for the annual report can be adjusted, for example, or perhaps one department need not fit its assessment data into the online template that the institution provides.
3. Revisit policies, guidelines, and standards regularly. Ask if they still make sense, if they are still appropriate, and if they still meet the faculty's, program's, and institution's needs.
4. Continue to provide support for assessment efforts. Suskie (2003) notes that "while workshops, consultants, and other resources can help spur assessment efforts, providing one-on-one assistance is more effective" (p. 9). This is especially true for faculty who have been working on assessment for a few years and now have specialized questions that cannot be addressed through generic resources such as a workshop, website, or newsletter.

The Future of Assessment

Is assessment a fad that will soon fade away? Without a crystal ball, no one can tell for sure, but while other issues may move to the forefront, it is likely that assessment expectations will remain high for the foreseeable future. Pub-

TABLE 1.3
Tips for Keeping Assessment Thriving

1. Keep assessment efforts useful, cost-effective, and valued.
2. Be flexible.
3. Revisit policies, guidelines, and standards regularly.
4. Continue to support assessment efforts.

lic pressures for quality, access, and affordability are simply too strong to anticipate otherwise.

So where might the higher education assessment community focus its attention over the next few years? Four areas that seem particularly worthy of attention are listed in Table 1.4 and discussed here.

1. Learning outcomes: Developing clear statements of expected learning outcomes throughout the curriculum is an art, not a science, as effective goals must strike a carefully nuanced balance, neither so specific that they are copious or trivial nor so broad that they are vague platitudes. Developing a clearer sense of exactly what we want our students to learn will doubtless consume faculty attention over the coming years, especially in some general education and liberal arts disciplines that historically haven't given this much thought.

2. Faculty development: Many faculty in today's colleges and universities are well educated about the subject they teach but have little or no formal training in curricular design, effective teaching strategies, neuroscience research on how people learn . . . or how to assess student learning. For some faculty, changing what and how they teach to reflect current pedagogical research means taking a 180-degree turn from what they have been doing for many years. This is a difficult, threatening prospect, and faculty need help and support as they work their way through these changes.

3. Technological innovation: Electronic tools such as online examinations, electronic portfolios, and computerized scoring of writing samples hold great promise for improving both the efficiency and quality of assessment efforts, but they take time, research, and resources to develop.

4. Collaborative efforts: Many hands make light work, and it only

TABLE 1.4
Possible Future Areas of Emphasis in Assessment

1. Learning outcomes
2. Faculty development
3. Technological innovation
4. Collaborative efforts

makes sense for faculty to work collaboratively with colleagues from peer institutions to articulate common learning goals and develop shared assessment tools such as rubrics and test questions. One of the greatest strengths of American higher education is its diversity, so it won't be possible to develop just one test or rubric that is relevant and applicable to every program in the country. But disciplinary associations and institutional consortia can sponsor the development of "banks" of learning goals and assessment tools from which faculty can choose those most relevant to their program's aims and needs.

Appendix 1.A is an annotated list of seminal readings on principles and practices for assessing student learning that constitute a good start for an assessment library.

References

American Association for Higher Education. (1991). *Principles of good practice for assessing student learning.* Sterling, VA: Stylus.

American Productivity and Quality Center. (1999). *Measuring institutional performance outcomes: Consortium benchmarking study best-in-class report.* Houston, TX: Author.

Angelo, T. A. (1993, April). A "teacher's dozen": Fourteen general, research-based principles for improving higher learning in our classrooms. *AAHE Bulletin, 45*(8), 3–7, 13.

Angelo, T. A. (1995). Reassessing (and redefining) assessment. *AAHE Bulletin, 48*(3), 7–9.

Angelo, T. A., & Cross, K. P. (1993). *Classroom assessment techniques: A handbook for college teachers* (2nd ed.). San Francisco: Jossey-Bass.

Association of American Colleges and Universities. (2002). *Criteria for recognizing "good practice" in assessing liberal education.* Washington: Author. Retrieved July 5, 2006, from http://www.aacu-edu.org/paa/assessment.cfm

Banta, T. W. (2002). Characteristics of effective outcomes assessment: Foundations and examples. In T. W. Banta & Associates, *Building a scholarship of assessment.* San Francisco: Jossey-Bass.

Bresciani, M. J. (2003). Expert-driven assessment: Making it meaningful. *Educause Center for Applied Research (ECAR) Research Bulletin, 2003*(21).

Bresciani, M. J. (with contributions by Anderson, J. A., & Allen, J.). (2006). *Outcomes-based undergraduate academic and co-curricular program review: A compilation of institutional good practices.* Sterling, VA: Stylus.

Campbell, D. T., & Fiske, D. W. (1959). Convergent and discriminate validation by the multitrait-multimethod matrix. *Psychological Bulletin, 56*(2), 81–105.

Chickering, A. W., & Gamson, Z. (1987). Seven principles for good practice in undergraduate education. *AAHE Bulletin, 39*(7), 5–10.

Council of Regional Accrediting Commissions. (2004). *Regional accreditation and student learning: A guide for institutions and evaluators.* Atlanta, GA: Southern Association of Colleges and Schools. Retrieved July 5, 2006, from http://www.sacscoc.org/pdf/handbooks/GuideForInstitutions.PDF

Driscoll, A., & Cordero de Noriega, D. (2006). *Taking ownership of accreditation: Assessment processes that promote institutional improvement and faculty engagement.* Sterling, VA: Stylus.

Gay, L. R., Mills, G. E., & Airasian, P. W. (2005). *Educational research: Competencies for analysis and applications* (8th ed.). New York: Prentice Hall.

Greater Expectations Project on Accreditation and Assessment. (2002). *Criteria for recognizing "good practice" in assessing liberal education as collaborative and integrative.* Washington, DC: Association of American Colleges and Universities.

Greater Expectations Project on Accreditation and Assessment. (2004). *Taking responsibility for the quality of the baccalaureate degree.* Washington, DC: Association of American Colleges and Universities.

Huba, M. E., & Freed, J. E. (2000). Applying principles of good practice in learner-centered assessment. In M. E. Huba & J. E. Freed (Eds.), *Learner-centered assessment on college campuses: Shifting the focus from teaching to learning* (pp. 65–90). Needham Heights, MA: Allyn & Bacon.

Joint Committee on Standards for Educational Evaluation. (1994). *The program evaluation standards: How to assess evaluations of educational programs* (2nd ed.). Thousand Oaks, CA: Sage.

Joint Committee on Testing Practices. (2004). *Code of fair testing practices in education.* Washington, DC: Author.

Mentkowski, M., & Associates. (2000). *Learning that lasts: Integrating learning, development, and performance in college and beyond.* San Francisco: Jossey-Bass.

Middle States Commission on Higher Education. (2005). *Assessing student learning and institutional effectiveness: Understanding Middle States expectations.* Philadelphia: Author.

Middle States Commission on Higher Education. (2006). *Characteristics of excellence in higher education: Eligibility requirements and standards for accreditation* (12th ed.). Philadelphia: Author.

National Council on Measurement in Education. (1995). *Code of professional responsibilities in educational measurement.* Washington, DC: Author. Retrieved July 5, 2006, from http://www.natd.org/Code_of_Professional_Responsibilities.html

National Research Council. (1993). *Leadership statement of nine principles on equity in educational testing and assessment.* Washington, DC: Author. Retrieved May 25, 2006, from http://www.ncrel.org/sdrs/areas/issues/content/cntareas/math/ma1newst.htm

Palomba, C. A., & Banta, T. W. (1999). *Assessment essentials: Planning, implementing, improving.* San Francisco: Jossey-Bass.

Pascarella, E. T. (2001). Identifying excellence in undergraduate education: Are we even close? *Change, 33*(3), 19–23.

Pascarella, E. T., & Terenzini, P. T. (2005). *How college affects students: A third decade of research.* San Francisco: Jossey-Bass.

Suskie, L. (2000). Fair assessment practices: Giving students equitable opportunities to demonstrate learning. *AAHE Bulletin, 52*(9), 7–9.

Suskie, L. (2003). Assessment at Towson University: Lessons learned on keeping assessment thriving. *Assessment Update, 15*(3), 8–9.

Suskie, L. (2004). *Assessing student learning: A common sense guide.* Bolton, MA: Anker.

Suskie, L. (2006a). Accountability and quality improvement. In P. Hernon, R. E. Dugan, & C. Schwartz (Eds.), *Revising outcomes assessment in higher education.* Westport, CT: Libraries Unlimited.

Suskie, L. (2006b). *What is "good" assessment? A new model for fulfilling accreditation expectations.* Paper presented at the NASPA International Assessment and Retention Conference, Phoenix, AZ.

Upcraft, M. L., & Schuh, J. H. (2002). Assessment vs. research: Why we should care about the difference. *About Campus, 7*(1), 16–20.

Walvoord, B., & Anderson, V. J. (1998). *Effective grading: A tool for learning and assessment.* San Francisco: Jossey-Bass.

What research says about improving undergraduate education. (1996). *AAHE Bulletin, 48*(8), 5–8.

ANNOTATED RESOURCES

American Association for Higher Education. (1991). *Principles of good practice for assessing student learning.* Sterling, VA: Stylus.

This is the most widely quoted set of principles of good practice for student learning assessment, including keeping assessment ongoing rather than episodic, and involving representatives from across the educational community.

Barr, R. B., & Tagg, J. (1995). From teaching to learning: A new paradigm for undergraduate education. *Change, 27*(6), 12–25.

This classic article was one of the first to propose a student-centered approach in which faculty accept greater responsibility for student learning.

Bresciani, M. J. (with contributions by Anderson, J. A., & Allen, J.). (2006). *Outcomes-based undergraduate academic and co-curricular program review: A compilation of institutional good practices.* Sterling, VA: Stylus.

This book presents good practices for effective program-level assessment drawn from a plethora of institutional case studies. It includes many specific models, templates, and examples plus a chapter on overcoming barriers to assessment.

Chickering, A. W., & Gamson, Z. (1987). Seven principles for good practice in undergraduate education. *AAHE Bulletin, 39*(7), 5–10.

This classic article proposes seven good practices, including encouraging active learning, giving prompt feedback, emphasizing time on task, communicating high expectations, and respecting diverse ways of learning.

Dolence, M. G., & Norris, D. M. (1995). *Transforming higher education: A vision for learning in the 21st century.* Ann Arbor, MI: Society for College and University Planning.

This highly readable book speaks clearly and succinctly to the need for higher education to transform to meet the needs of the "Information Age" and offers specific suggestions on how to do so, including reframing curricula and pedagogies.

Huba, M. E., & Freed, J. E. (2000). *Learner-centered assessment on college campuses: Shifting the focus from teaching to learning.* Needham Heights, MA: Allyn & Bacon.

This short and clearly written book focuses on assessment tools that support a "learner-centered" approach to teaching, with particular attention to articulating learning outcomes and using rubrics and portfolios as assessment tools.

Joint Committee on Testing Practices. (2004). *Code of fair testing practices in education.* Washington, DC: Author.

While this statement was developed for those developing and using published tests, much of it applies to anyone engaged in any form of assessment of student learning. The code emphasizes fair and ethical assessment practices.

Mentkowski, M., & Associates. (2000). *Learning that lasts: Integrating learning, development, and performance in college and beyond.* San Francisco: Jossey-Bass.

This book documents extensive research at Alverno College on practices that promote deep, lasting learning and offers models for engaging in the scholarship of teaching and assessment.

Middle States Commission on Higher Education. (2003). *Student learning assessment: Options and resources.* Philadelphia: Author.

This short guide gives the novice assessment practitioner many principles and tips for planning and conducting assessments.

National Council on Measurement in Education. (1995). *Code of professional responsibilities in educational measurement.* Washington, DC: Author.

While this statement, like that of the Joint Committee on Testing Practices, was developed for those developing and using published tests, much of it applies to anyone engaged in any form of assessment of student learning. Like the Joint Committee's statement, this code emphasizes fair and ethical assessment practices.

Palomba, C. A., & Banta, T. W. (1999). *Assessment essentials: Planning, implementing, improving.* San Francisco: Jossey-Bass.

This highly regarded assessment primer addresses "the essentials of successful assessment" including developing goals and plans, selecting methods and approaches, and reporting and using assessment results.

Shavelson, R. J., & Huang, L. (2003). Responding responsibly to the frenzy to assess learning in higher education. *Change, 35*(1), 10–19.

The authors offer six propositions for assessing learning responsibly, including encouraging "real dialogue and greater agreement on the content of assessments" and recognizing that "what we test and make public will greatly influence what is taught and what is learned" (p. 18).

Steen, L. A. (1992, May). 20 questions that deans should ask their mathematics department (or, that a sharp department will ask itself). *AAHE Bulletin, 44*(9), 3–6.

While this article is directed toward mathematics departments, many of the questions it raises (e.g., Does your curriculum meet the postgraduation needs of your students?) are applicable to other departments as well.

Suskie, L. (2000). Fair assessment practices: Giving students equitable opportunities to demonstrate learning. *AAHE Bulletin, 52*(9), 7–9.

This article presents seven principles for making assessments as fair as possible to students, including matching assessments to what is taught and vice versa, helping students learn how to do the assessment task, and interpreting assessment results appropriately.

Suskie, L. (2004). *Assessing student learning: A common sense guide.* Bolton, MA: Anker.

This is a soup-to-nuts primer that introduces assessment novices to virtually all aspects of assessment, including some rarely addressed elsewhere, such as choosing a published instrument, writing multiple-choice tests, and communicating assessment results.

Walvoord, B. E. (2004). *Assessment clear and simple: A practical guide for institutions, departments, and general education.* San Francisco: Jossey-Bass.

This simply written book has just four chapters—one for everyone—for institution-wide planners, for departments and programs, and for general education—filled with practical tips.

What research says about improving undergraduate education. (1996). *AAHE Bulletin, 48*(8), 5–8.

This article expands Chickering and Gamson's (1987) list of 7 principles of good practice into 12 attributes of quality undergraduate education, including requiring coherence in learning, ongoing practice of learned skills, and synthesizing experiences.

2

ASSESSING STUDENT LEARNING

Ensuring Undergraduate Students Are
Learning What We Want Them to Learn

Joni E. Spurlin, Sarah A. Rajala, and Jerome P. Lavelle

The purpose of assessment is to improve student learning. The challenge is in deciding what constitutes learning and how best to measure it. This chapter focuses on assessment as a process and develops a structure for measuring the degree to which our students are learning what we want them to learn.

In some ways student learning is a simple concept: We know it when we see it. We know when the lightbulb goes off in a student's head and he or she finally grasps a complex problem for the first time. We feel the excitement as students design their first engineering system and it actually functions as designed. But going through the process of assessment—to prove to others that students are learning and that their learning has improved—is tedious and artificial to many faculty. This, however, is both the essence and the challenge of assessment.

The Assessment Process

Many experts in the field have provided a "definition" of assessment (e.g., Huba & Freed, 2000; Palomba & Banta, 1999, 2001; Upcraft & Schuh, 1996). Through our work with faculty in the College of Engineering at North Carolina State University, we have identified a few definitions that have proven most useful:[1]

- "Assessment is an ongoing process aimed at understanding and improving student learning. It involves making our expectations explicit and public; setting appropriate criteria and high standards for learning quality; systematically gathering, analyzing, and interpreting evidence to determine how well performance matches those expectations and standards; and using the resulting information to document, explain, and improve performance. When it is embedded effectively within larger institutional systems, assessment can help us to focus our collective attention, examine our assumptions, and create a shared academic culture dedicated to assuring and improving the quality of higher education" (Angelo, 1995, p. 7).
- "Assessment is the systematic collection, review and use of information about educational programs undertaken for the purpose of improving student learning and development" (Palomba & Banta, 1999, p. 4).
- Assessment is a process that focuses on student learning, a process that involves reviewing and reflecting on student performance—what students can do—and focuses on curriculum and group performances in a planned, deliberate, and careful way (Ewell, 2002, 2004; Ewell & Rice, 2000).

From these definitions, it is easy to see that assessment is as much a process as it is a product. Chapters 2 through 4 outline the basic process of assessment and the products that engineering faculty can use to provide evidence of what and how well engineering students are learning. This chapter addresses how to define what we want students to learn.

Figure 2.1 shows the assessment process in three cycles: the program educational objectives cycle (1a), the program outcomes cycle (1b), and the course outcomes cycle (1c). In addition, it specifies where these cycles overlap (1d). The figure loops (1a–1c) all involve defining/refining, planning/implementation, data collection, assessment/evaluation, and decision making. Loop 1d shows how the other loops are connected from an assessment system perspective. On the whole, the process describes who does what and when. This process is not new, and each institution describes it in a different way to meet the needs of the institution, but the basic steps and execution are common across most assessment systems.

Figure 2.1 (1a) outlines the assessment cycle for program educational objectives (PEOs) as defined by ABET Criterion 2. These reflect "broad

FIGURE 2.1
Assessment Processes

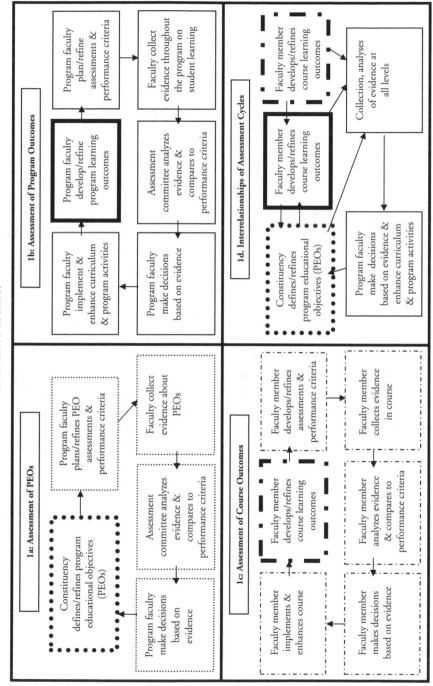

1a: Assessment of PEOs

Constituency defines/refines program educational objectives (PEOs)

Program faculty plans/refines PEO assessments & performance criteria

Faculty collect evidence about PEOs

Assessment committee analyzes evidence & compares to performance criteria

Program faculty make decisions based on evidence

1b: Assessment of Program Outcomes

Program faculty plan/refine assessments & performance criteria

Faculty collect evidence throughout the program on student learning

Program faculty develop/refine program learning outcomes

Assessment committee analyzes evidence & compares to performance criteria

Program faculty implement & enhance curriculum & program activities

Program faculty make decisions based on evidence

1c: Assessment of Course Outcomes

Faculty member develops/refines assessments & performance criteria

Faculty member collects evidence in course

Faculty member develops/refines course learning outcomes

Faculty member analyzes evidence & compares to performance criteria

Faculty member implements & enhances course

Faculty member makes decisions based on evidence

1d: Interrelationships of Assessment Cycles

Faculty member develops/refines course learning outcomes

Collection, analyses of evidence at all levels

Faculty member develops/refines course learning outcomes

Constituency defines/refines program educational objectives (PEOs)

Program faculty make decisions based on evidence & enhance curriculum & program activities statements that describe the career and professional accomplishments that the program is preparing graduates to achieve" (ABET, 2006). The PEO assessment cycle spans the longest time frame, because these are the broadest and least changing elements of the educational program, typically covering a two- to four-year period. ABET requirements ask that constituencies, most often including faculty members, students, alumni, and/or employers, define and assess the PEOs. Whatever model is used, it is critical that each constituency help define PEOs (initially), then determine whether the PEOs have been met and refine them, if needed, after assessment results have been gathered. Employers and alumni are often asked to assess the PEOs through the use of surveys. Advisory boards, with representation from industry, alumni, and/or other academic institutions, often participate in the establishment and review of PEOs. Further details on how to assess PEOs can be found in chapter 3.

Figure 2.1 (1b) shows the assessment cycle for program learning outcomes. ABET Criterion 3 defines program outcomes as "statements that describe what students are expected to know and be able to do by the time of graduation. They relate to the skills, knowledge and behaviors that students acquire in their matriculation through the program" (ABET, 2006). The involvement of faculty in the assessment of outcomes is very critical. Input from students, alumni, and employers may also be a part of the process. Depending on the size of the faculty, programs may establish one or more committees to oversee the assessment process. At a minimum, one person should be assigned the responsibility for the program's assessment process. Possible formats for departmental assessment teams include the following:

- Using the current course and curriculum committee
- Establishing three- to four-person faculty teams, with each team responsible for a few program outcomes
- Involving the entire faculty in assessment decisions
- Developing an assessment committee with representations from the faculty

The assessment committee(s) is responsible for all of the following:

- Ensuring that an assessment plan is developed and followed
- Obtaining assessment data from faculty and other resources
- Providing an initial interpretation of the data

- Discussing its interpretation of the data with the faculty at large
- Documenting the findings, interpretations, and follow-up actions
- Sending appropriate recommendations to a curriculum committee or faculty as a whole

Each faculty member is responsible for ensuring that her or his course outcomes map to one or more of the program outcomes and for providing data, as applicable, for the assessment of those outcomes. Not every faculty member will need to provide assessment data on every course for every semester; however, every course should teach to one or more outcomes. Individual faculty members should know what their role is, that is, to assess specific identified course material and provide summary data. Ideally faculty will also use this data to improve their own courses. Chapter 3 provides examples of how to use student work for program improvements; chapter 9 provides examples of how to use student work for course improvements.

The program assessment cycle is usually on a semester or annual basis. This does not mean that every outcome needs to be assessed every semester or even every year. However, every year, some outcomes assessment should be occurring. Appendix 2.A provides a sample timeline. In considering the assessment cycle, program faculty should devote one meeting each year (or each semester if on that timeline) to a discussion of the findings from the assessment process. This will allow for any recommended changes to courses to be implemented during the following year, and for changes in the overall program (curriculum) to be implemented over an appropriate time period (given the constraints imposed by the university in terms of developing new courses and curricular changes).

Figure 2.1 (1c) outlines the assessment cycle for a course that occurs within one semester. Not all courses need to be evaluated at this level, but for those that do, this cycle can be very useful. The faculty member(s) who teaches the course defines the learning outcomes, some of which map to the program learning outcomes. To improve the course, the faculty develops assessments for the outcomes. The faculty may also provide the results from the course-based assessment for use in assessing the program outcomes; see the links in Figure 2.1 (1d). The faculty can make course improvements based on evidence from the course and/or program assessments. Changes to the course should be communicated to the entire faculty, and the program's curriculum committee should ensure continued mapping of the course to the overall curriculum (see Figure 2.2 for mapping of the curriculum to outcomes). Felder and Brent (2003) provide a methodology and examples of how to develop course outcomes that relate to program outcomes. They also provide a step-by-step integrated process for addressing the a–k outcomes through course- and program-level assessment activities.

Figure 2.1 (1d) shows the interrelationships of the previous three processes (PEOs, program outcomes, and course assessments). This figure is a macroview of the important connections of these processes. Notice the important linkage of course-to-outcome-to-PEO assessment. For example, assessment results of the outcomes should also be considered when refining program PEOs. PEO and outcomes assessments are conducted separately, but this linkage provides an important way to add to the data in terms of assessment. The results from the assessments should be fed into the assessment committee process, the program's curriculum committee, and college- or university-level curriculum committees—as well any university assessment processes. Documentation is also a key to the process, as discussed later in this chapter.

Because every educational institution must also develop assessment processes for regional accreditation, it is important that the processes developed for meeting ABET requirements also satisfy any university assessment requirements. The engineering faculty should develop a process that is of value to the engineering faculty and their programs, meets regional and programmatic accreditation needs, and is consistent with the institutional assessment and program review processes.

What Do We Want Engineering Students to Know?

Assessment asks "what and how well" students learn. ABET has defined both program educational objectives and a set of 11 outcomes that students in every engineering program must meet (i.e., ABET's Criteria 3.a–k). But what does this really mean for any specific engineering program? Has ABET defined all we need to think about in terms of what we want our students to know? If everyone uses the same outcomes, then can programs differentiate themselves? In fact, the very nature of these statements encourages programs to provide specific definitions for both the PEOs and outcomes.

At your next faculty meeting, take 20 minutes to brainstorm the attributes of a student who is graduating from your program: What does your graduate "look like"? What skills, knowledge, ability, and "sensibilities" does that person have? What words and verbs best describe this student? Then take another 20 minutes and match these attributes with your PEOs and program learning outcomes. How well do they match? Are your current

PEOs reflective of what you think the career and professional accomplishments of recent graduates, three to five years out, should be? Are your current outcomes reflective of what you think a student at the time of graduation should be able to do and know? Do your current outcomes reflect what you value, as a program and as an institution? See Appendix 2.B for examples of PEOs from two engineering programs at North Carolina State University. Although we assume most programs have already developed at least one set of PEOs, it may be helpful to review the process for establishing PEOs, as outlined by Carter, Brent, and Rajala (2001).

How can you improve on how you have written your outcomes? The outcomes can relate to any type of learning; many faculty refer to Bloom's taxonomy to help clarify the level of learning (Bloom, 1956).[2] Think about the different types of outcomes:

- Cognitive outcomes: What the student knows; thinking skills
- Affective outcomes: Attitudinal, personal, and social dimensions
- Skill outcomes: What students can do, such as write, use a computer, use design technology; ability to design

Many programs around the country have developed outcomes other than ABET's 3.a–k, and have mapped them back to a–k. Examples of these other types of outcomes are given in Appendix 2.C. It is nevertheless important that however outcomes are defined and measured, the program be able to identify their relationship to ABET a–k outcomes. ABET evaluators will be looking for evidence of student abilities related to a–k outcomes. Those who want to adopt the more traditional ABET a–k outcomes should take the next step, which is to operationalize what each of these outcomes means to their program. To make this process easier, Dr. Michael Carter, professor of English at North Carolina State University, developed a template for the 17 undergraduate engineering programs at NC State to use. Most of these programs chose to use the ABET a–k outcomes and then used this template to expand on each outcome for their program. See Appendix 2.D for the template; further information can be found on NC State's website: www.engr.ncsu.edu/abet/. Please be aware that any program with specific program criteria specified in ABET's Criterion 8 (ABET, 2006) will also need to develop outcomes that address those criteria.

To further define what we want our students to know, the program educational objectives and program learning outcomes must be directly linked to the curriculum and to course outcomes and objectives (see the relationship in Figure 2.1 [1d]). Each course in the program will typically have three to five course learning outcomes/objectives related to one or more of the program outcomes. Although not the direct subject of this book, it is important to consider how to teach students to acquire the skills implicit in these outcomes. Felder and Brent (2003) discuss specific instructional methods that relate to a–k outcomes.

Not all courses will be mapped to *all* program outcomes. A graphical mapping of the relationship is useful: One side of the grid lists the program outcomes, the other side of the grid lists the courses within the program, and inside the grid is the relationship of the course to the outcome. Some programs' maps of the curriculum to outcomes tend to map this relationship by marking an "X" where the course teaches to that outcome. However, an "X" does not really explain the relationship. Following are other examples that provide more information about the relationship of the course to the outcome. To show in which courses student work will be used for course-based assessment, an "A" can be added to the grid to indicate assessment will be taken in that course. To show which courses implement (or teach to) an outcome, an "I" can be added. Many institutions use a numerical system as shown in Figure 2.2. Using a numerical system has the advantage of allowing rows to be "added together," which provides insight into the amount of emphasis that has been placed on each outcome. Faculty can then assess the curriculum by discussing the relationship of an outcome that has "11 points" versus one that has "27 points." (See tables 2 and 3 in Felder and Brent [2003] for other examples of mapping systems.) The Rose-Hulman Institute also has an interesting mapping system in which each course objective is mapped to each program objective using three questions:

1. Is the objective explicitly stated as a learning objective for this course?
2. Are students asked to demonstrate their competence on this objective through homework, projects, tests, etc.?
3. Are students given formal feedback on their performance on this objective? (G. Rogers, personal communication, April 8, 2001)

In Criterion 3, ABET has prescribed the 11 a–k outcomes, and these are often viewed by programs as the "ending point" of their outcomes assessment definition. ABET, on the other hand, views these a–k outcomes as the starting point whereby individual programs are free (and encouraged), not

FIGURE 2.2
Curriculum Mapping to Outcomes

Example of Curriculum Mapping to Outcomes 3.a–k
Fictitious University

Major (4): Topics are fully introduced, developed, and reinforced throughout the course in course lectures, labs, homework assignments, tests, exams, projects; an "application knowledge"

Moderate (2): Topics are introduced and further developed and reinforced in course lectures, labs, assignments, tests, etc.; a "working knowledge"

Minor (1): Topics are introduced in course lectures, labs, homework, assignments, etc.; a "talking knowledge" or "awareness"

(0): Does not relate

Course/outcome	150	210	225	289	305	329	345	425	465	499	TOTALS
a	2	2	4	2	0	0	4	4	4	4	26
b	0	1	1	1	2	1	2	2	4	1	15
c	4	1	2	1	1	4	4	4	2	4	27
d	0	4	0	4	0	0	4	1	0	4	17
e	0	2	2	2	1	1	4	2	4	4	22
f	0	1	2	1	0	1	2	2	0	2	11
g	4	4	1	1	2	4	4	1	2	4	27
h	0	4	1	2	2	4	2	4	2	4	25
i	1	1	0	0	1	4	1	1	1	2	12
j	0	1	2	2	2	2	1	1	1	1	13
k	1	1	2	2	2	4	4	2	4	4	26

only to define outcomes a–k, but to both expand them and make them "local" to the program. If outcomes are true reflections of the planned-for student skills, it is natural to assume that over time these skills will shift and change in some regards. For example, a student may be expected to be skilled in reading and interpreting blueprints in one era, and proficient in creating detailed 3-D solid models in another. What the outcome assessment model helps faculty do is to be very explicit about what those fundamental skills are, and then to implement processes to see if students are exhibiting those traits. Taking the system apart, we see that course data focuses the faculty on both course-level learning and program-level achievements. The course-level view stresses both defining what students learn (via student learning outcomes/objectives) and mapping of how these relate to the bigger assessment picture. When data suggest that refinements at the course level are due, implementation decisions should acknowledge both the learning outcomes/objectives and mapping components of change.

The outcomes-based assessment approach is a dynamic and living process. At the stage of system initiation, outcomes are designed to illuminate student learning, document a–k achievement, and link to PEOs in meaningful ways. Over time, as PEOs change and/or as it becomes clearer which outcomes best reflect knowledge about student learning, the way outcomes are assessed may need to be modified. As an example, a program may decide to use a combination of exam questions, Fundamentals of Engineering (FE) Exam results, and student survey data to measure a particular student outcome. Perhaps a metric is formed that combines these data into a single measure, or maybe these are looked upon as a group. If the program finds that the FE results are not measuring the intended outcome, this element may be dropped from the metric or as an individual consideration in the future. Alternatively, exam questions may need to be changed to better reflect the outcomes being measured. ABET's outcomes-based assessment process is a living framework that will change over time.

How Do We Know if Students Are Learning What We Want Them to Learn?

The assessment process is designed to determine what and how well students are learning. Once the PEOs and outcomes have been established, then the next step in the assessment process is to select the most appropriate assessment methods (see Figure 2.1). Other experts have described how to develop assessment methods in many other disciplines (e.g., Huba & Freed, 2000; Palomba & Banta, 1999, 2001; Upcraft & Schuh, 1996). Appendix 2.E provides sources of information that can be used in assessment of engineering programs. ABET emphasizes the importance of including "direct assessment" of program outcomes. Assessment methods that are "direct" are those that judge student work, projects, and portfolios developed as a result of the learning experiences; some consider this "authentic assessment." "Indirect" assessment uses students' or others' opinions to provide evidence about students' abilities. Appendix 2.E also lists some pros and cons for using each method. Many times we worry about not having the perfect assessment method, but matching the correct assessment method to the outcome is more important than having a perfect, well-controlled assessment method. As stated by Tukey (1962), "Far better an approximate answer to the right question . . . than an exact answer to the wrong question" (pp. 13–14).

More detailed information about assessment is given later in this book. Chapter 3 discusses various assessment methods for using student work in assessing ABET outcomes a–k. Chapter 4 discusses how to use these methods to know how well students are learning.

Documenting the Process

Documentation of the assessment process is important to show continuous improvement of education. Each program's assessment processes and assessment plan should be documented, publicly available to all faculty within the department as well as deans of engineering, and implemented through the program's assessment committee. Each program should diagram the process in a way similar to that in Figure 2.1. A documented, published assessment plan should include the following elements:

- Program educational objectives (PEOs): The broad statements that describe the career and professional accomplishments that the program is preparing graduates to achieve.
- Plan for data collection: A brief description of how each PEO will be assessed, who will collect the data, and how it is expected to be used. More specifically, define the following in the plan:
  - Who is being assessed (typically alumni) and who will judge that assessment (e.g., constituencies)
  - What method is being used
  - When assessment will take place (typically every 2 to 4 years)
  - Where (in which course or in what time frame) the assessment will occur
  - Other descriptions as needed
- Program outcomes: Outcomes describe what the academic department intends for students to know (cognitive), think (affective, attitudinal), or do (behavioral, performance, psychomotor) when they have completed a given educational program. Each outcome's relationship to the program's educational objectives should be shown.
- Implementation: Each program should describe how/where it will im-

plement or teach the concepts related to each outcome. (A curriculum map is a good way to show these relationships.)

- Plan for data collection: A brief description of how each outcome will be assessed, who will collect the data, and how it is expected to be used. More specifically, define the following in the plan:
  - ○ Who is being assessed (typically students) and who will judge that assessment (e.g., assessment committees, faculty at large, constituencies)
  - ○ What method is being used
  - ○ When assessment will take place (each outcome should be assessed at least every two years)
  - ○ Where (in which course or in what time frame) the assessment will occur
  - ○ Other descriptions as needed
- Relationships: Clearly specify how the designed program outcomes relate to ABET Criteria 3 and 8.

Each year, the results from the outcomes assessment need to be documented. An annual documented "results report" for *each* assessed PEO and outcome could include the following:

- Summary of results: It is important that the documentation include a summary of the major findings from the data and what they suggest; it should not simply be pages of data. It is recommended that the summary reflect the program outcomes or program educational objectives defined in the assessment plan and how well each met its performance criteria. For *each* PEO or outcome assessed that year, include (1) the assessment method actually used, (2) a summary of findings, and (3) the location of the data (e.g., in a file cabinet in the dean's office, on a common computer drive, on a website).
- Proposed modifications to the curriculum or program: Based on the summary of results, a decision should be made on whether modifications to the curriculum or program are needed. The documentation should clearly articulate:

  1. Modifications made during the reporting period: Describe any actions taken based on the assessment data; list modifications according to outcomes/objectives.
  2. Modifications planned for the coming year: Describe any ac-

tions to be taken based on the assessment data; list modifications according to outcomes/objectives.

3. Modifications to the assessment plan: Describe any decisions to delete assessment methods and why; describe any modifications to the assessment process.

One way to facilitate sustainability is to keep the assessment data organized. Faculty responsibilities change over time, and some faculty are more organized than others. A website is one alternative, but keeping data in a notebook in a central location can also work well. The key is ensuring all faculty know about the location of the data.

A program or college of engineering may develop Web-based tools to allow for streamlining the process. A simple website can be established with the help of computer science students. An example of a simple database is the NC State College of Engineering assessment database website (www.engr.ncsu.edu/assessment), which stores each program's assessment plan, summary data, assessment results, and changes to the program. The website is accessible to all faculty at all times. A syllabus tool and upload features allow faculty to enter data onto the Web without the need for a webmaster to add the documentation. By having a website where individual faculty can enter course findings, anyone (with security access) can see an overview of the program assessment at any time. See Figure 2.3 for an example for one outcome from the Department of Biological Engineering at NC State.

To date, there is no commercial software for assessment specific to engineering. However, several institutional assessment products are available. The following are examples of some of this software:

- eLumen, www.elumen.info/
- Tk20, www.tk20.com/home/index.html
- TracDat (Nuventive), www.nuventive.com/products_tracdat.html
- TrueOutcomes and TrueCurriculum, www.trueoutcomes.com/
- Weaveonline, www.weaveonline.net/welcome/

Whatever approach one chooses, the keys to success include organization, a known storage location, and up-to-date information.

Conclusion

The focus of this chapter was on assessment as a process. Although there is no single correct model that will ensure program improvement and meet the

FIGURE 2.3
Example of an Online Assessment Report Form

Academic Year: 2005–2006

Outcome 3(j) To demonstrate that graduates possess knowledge of contemporary issues.

Course: BAE100—Introduction to Biological Engineering

Course Objectives	Implementation	Assessment Methods and Goals	Findings
2. Explain what distinguishes biological engineering from other branches of engineering	Students in BAE 100 will complete written exercises exploring technical areas within Biological Engineering. Reports will include a discussion of self-identified contemporary issue.	The lectures and homework will emphasize contemporary issues in agricultural, bioprocess, and environmental engr. Dr. XX will evaluate. Outcome will be met if 80% of the students score an 80%.	

Course: BAE315—Properties of Biological Engineering Materials

Course Objectives	Implementation	Assessment Methods and Goals	Findings
1. Describe the unique characteristics of biological materials that distinguish their engineering properties from those of conventional materials	Students in BAE 315 will select and research a contemporary issue using the scientific literature.	Assessment will be conducted by Dr. YY. The topics selected, oral and written assignments, and literature cited will be the basis for judgment. Outcome will be met if instructor concludes that topic coverage is adequate, and 90% of the students have cited an adequate body of literature.	

Course: BAE451—Engineering Senior Design I

Course Objectives	Implementation	Assessment Methods and Goals	Findings
4. Discover and develop creative talents	Students in BAE 451 are expected to gain a familiarity with patents and other types of intellectual property.	Students are assigned to do a patent search and other related exercises by conducting an online search at the U.S. Patent and Trademark office. Outcome is met if 90% of the students complete with a satisfactory grade.	

NOTE: Each faculty responsible (listed under assessment method) enters "findings" at end of course.

Reproduced by permission, Dr. David Beasley, North Carolina State University needs of engineering accreditation, the defined structure will need to measure the degree to which our students are learning what we want them to learn. Defining program educational objectives and program outcomes enables us to describe to ourselves and to students what we want them to learn.

Working on assessment does not have to be a solitary activity. Consulting with other engineering faculty at your institution, with others in similar programs at other institutions, and with those with assessment expertise will facilitate the process. A list of leaders in engineering education besides the authors of this book can be found at http://www.engrng.pitt.edu/~ec2000/. Here are some examples of others who may have assessment expertise at your institution:

- Assessment or evaluation professionals (i.e., anyone with "assessment" in his or her title)
- Faculty with assessment or evaluation background (e.g., psychology, education, sociology)
- Other assessment committees at department, college, or institutional levels
- Institutional research or planning office
- Registrar/admissions
- Centers for faculty development on teaching

Search your institution's website to see who is associated with these terms: *survey, assessment, planning, benchmark, performance indicators, goals,* and *outcomes.*

Notes

1. For those interested in a history of the development of assessment, see Peter Ewell's writings, including chapter 1 in *Building a Scholarship of Assessment,* 2002.

2. Many of the leaders in engineering education have worked together to connect Bloom's taxonomy with ABET a–k outcomes. Their work can be found at the University of Pittsburg's engineering education website: http://www.engrng.pitt .edu/~ec2000/. Other examples of how to use Bloom's taxonomy for developing outcomes can be found at the following websites: www.nwlink.com/~donclark/hrd/bloom.html; http://faculty.washington.edu/krumme/guides/bloom1.html

References

ABET. (2006). Criteria for accrediting engineering programs. Retrieved May 30, 2006, from http://www.abet.org/Linked%20Documents-UPDATE/Criteria%20and%20PP/E001%2006-07%20EAC%20Criteria%205-25-06-06.pdf

Angelo, T. (1995). Reassessing (and redefining) assessment. *AAHE Bulletin, 48*(3), 7–9.

Bloom, B. S. (1956). *Taxonomy of educational objectives, handbook I: The cognitive domain.* New York: David McKay.

Carter, M., Brent, R., & Rajala. S. (2001). EC 2000 Criterion 2: A procedure for creating, assessing, and documenting program educational objectives. *Proceedings of the 2001 American Society for Engineering Education Annual Conference.* Retrived July 20, 2006 from http://www4.ncsu.edu/unity/lockers/users/f/felder/public/Pa pers/ABET_paper(RB).pdf

Ewell, P. (2002). An emerging scholarship: A brief history of assessment. In T. Banta & Associates (Eds.), *Building a scholarship of assessment.* San Francisco: Jossey-Bass.

Ewell, P. (2004). Assessment that matters: Creating authentic academic cultures of evidence. Retrieved April 2, 2006, from http://www.usna.edu/CTL/DeptPosters/ PostersPPT/Ewell.pps

Ewell, P., & Reis, P. (2000). Assessing student learning outcomes: A supplement to measuring up. National Center for Public Policy and Higher Education. Retrieved July 20, 2006, from http://measuringup2000.highereducation.org/assessA.html

Felder, R. M., & Brent, R. (2003). Designing and teaching courses to satisfy the ABET Engineering Criteria. *Journal of Engineering Education, 92*(1), 7–25. Re-trieved July 20, 2006 from http://www4.ncsu.edu/unity/lockers/users/f/felder/ public/Papers/ABET_Paper_(JEE).pdf

Huba, M. E., & Freed, J. E. (2000). *Learner-centered assessment on college campuses.* Needham Heights, MA: Allyn & Bacon.

Palomba, C. A., & Banta, T. W. (1999). *Assessment essentials: Planning, implement-ing, and improving assessment in higher education.* San Francisco: Jossey-Bass.

Palomba, C. A., & Banta, T. W. (2001). *Assessing student competence in accredited disciplines.* Sterling, VA: Stylus.

Tukey, J. (1962). *Annals of Math Statistics, 33*, pp. 1–67.

Upcraft, M. L., & Schuh, J. H. (1996). *Assessment in student affairs.* San Francisco: Jossey-Bass.

APPENDIX 2.A

EXAMPLE OF A SIX-YEAR CYCLE OF ASSESSMENT ACTIVITIES

Fall 2003   ABET visit

Spring 2004   Senior Survey conducted
              Collect course-based assessment data on outcomes a, c, e

Fall 2004   Collect course-based assessment data on outcomes b, d, f, j, k

Spring 2005   Assessment of PEOs through Alumni Survey

Fall 2005   Discuss Alumni assessment results on PEOs with constituencies; make revisions as needed to PEOs

Spring 2006   Collect course-based assessment data on outcomes a, c, e

Fall 2006   Faculty retreat to review data collected last three years on outcomes; make revisions to assessment processes as needed
              Collect course-based assessment data on outcomes b, d, f, j, k

Spring 2007   Collect course-based assessment data on outcomes a, g, h, i
              Senior Survey conducted

Fall 2007   Write Self-Study; ensure have data on all outcomes and PEOs
              Summarize outcomes data in light of PEOs and bring to constituencies; make revisions as needed to PEOs

Spring 2009   Complete Self-Study

Fall 2009   ABET visit

EXAMPLES OF PROGRAM EDUCATIONAL OBJECTIVES

North Carolina State University
Program: Biological Engineering

The BAE faculty, in concert with program constituencies, have developed the following undergraduate program educational objectives for the BE degree.

Graduates of this program, within the first few years following graduation, will be:

1. Prepared to establish successful careers in engineering, as related to one of the specialized program focus areas: Agricultural, Bioprocessing and Environmental.
2. Able to grasp and apply engineering principles, procedures, and time management skills needed to solve complex, real-world problems especially as related to the fields of man–machine systems, greenhouse and animal structures, agricultural water and waste management, and unit operations in food and biological systems.
3. Professionally responsible in their work ethic while performing engineering tasks at a high level of expertise and willing to accept the ethical responsibility for the social and environmental impacts of engineering practices.
4. Able to communicate effectively with diverse audiences and able to work effectively in today's integrated team environments.
5. Broadly educated engineers and life-long learners, with a solid background in the biological sciences, engineering sciences and mathematics; an understanding and appreciation for the arts, humanities, and social sciences; and, a desire to seek out further educational opportunities.
6. Knowledgeable of current advances in engineering practice and re-

search; prepared for opportunities in graduate engineering education and making progress towards registration as a professional engineer.
7. Capable of contributing to the future economic and social well-being of citizens of North Carolina, the nation and the world.

Program: Engineering with a Concentration in Mechatronics

The Mechatronics Engineering Program prepares engineers to achieve the following career/professional accomplishments:

1. Apply mechanical engineering and electrical engineering knowledge and skills to problems and challenges in the area of mechatronic engineering.
2. Integrate and use systems or devices incorporating modern micro-electronics, information technologies and modern engineering tools for product design, development and manufacturing.
3. Demonstrate professional interaction, communicate effectively with team members and work effectively on multi-disciplinary teams to achieve design and project objectives.
4. Engage in lifelong learning in their profession and practice professional and ethical responsibility.

Reprinted with permission, Dr. David Beasley and Dr. Yusef Fahmy, North Carolina State University

EXAMPLES* OF OTHER TYPES OF OUTCOMES THAT RELATE TO ABET CRITERIA

- Draw on knowledge of mathematics, science, and engineering to critically evaluate, analyze, and solve problems at the interface of engineering and science by using appropriate tools. (ABET Criteria 3.a, 3.b, 3.e, 8)
- Ability to apply fundamental science and engineering of permanent value. (ABET Criteria 3.a, 3.b, 3.e, 3.k)
- Ability to apply in-depth knowledge of one or more specializations within our specialized field of engineering (ABET Criterion 3.a)
- Design and conduct experiments of our engineering processes and systems. (ABET Criteria 3.a, 3.b)
- Identify contemporary issues and be able to discuss potential engineering experimental and design solutions. (ABET Criteria 3.a, 3.e, 3.j, 8)
- Design and model engineering materials, systems, and/or devices. (ABET Criteria 3.a, 3.c, 3.e, 3.k, 8)
- Design and conduct experiments to test hypotheses and to make measurements on and interpret data from systems. (ABET Criteria 3.b, 3.e, 8)
- Ability to apply knowledge of rate and equilibrium processes to identify, formulate, and solve engineering problems. (ABET Criteria 3.c, 3.e)
- Work effectively in multidisciplinary teams to complete projects. (ABET Criterion 3.d)
- Ability to participate in creative, synthetic, integrative activities of several fields of engineering and design. (ABET Criteria 3.c, 3.e)
- Assess, evaluate, and reference peer-reviewed technical literature. (ABET Criteria 3.g, 3.i)
- Use modern engineering tools to communicate ideas with others within the engineering discipline. (ABET Criteria 3.g, 3.k)
- Ability to express ideas persuasively, in written and oral form, to multiple audiences. (ABET Criterion 3.g)

*Examples are taken from various engineering programs from around the country. The specific engineering program identifications have been eliminated.

- Articulate, identify, and evaluate contemporary ethical issues in engineering and their impact on society. (ABET Criteria 3.f, 3.h, 3.j)
- Demonstrate a desire for learning through postgraduate career plans. (ABET Criterion 3.i)
- Understand and articulate their responsibility to their profession and society in a global context and prepare for and realize the importance of lifelong learning. (ABET Criteria 3.i, 3.j)
- Use the techniques, skills, and modern tools of engineering effectively and correctly in engineering practice: engineering analysis tools, engineering design and manufacturing tools, Internet and library information resources, mathematical computing and analysis tools. (ABET Criteria 3.a, 3.i, 3.k, 8)
- Ability to apply spreadsheets, computer modeling programs, and other computer-based methods to solve engineering-specific problems. (ABET Criteria 3.c, 3.e, 3.k, 8)

ANNOTATED TEMPLATE
FOR PROGRAM OUTCOMES

This template has been created to give you a solid starting point for generating program outcomes, so that you don't have to start from nothing. Each of the general outcomes a–k has been given a generic operational definition. More annotations, comments and advice can be found on North Carolina State University's ABET website: www.engr.ncsu.edu/abet/

(a) To demonstrate that graduates have an ability to apply knowledge of mathematics, science, and engineering, they should:

- show that they can employ general principles, theories, concepts, and/or formulas from mathematics, science, and engineering in the solution of problems in their field of engineering. For a particular problem, students should demonstrate that they can:
  - define and describe the pertinent principle, theory, concept, and/or formula,
  - explain why it is appropriate to the problem, and
  - demonstrate how it has been applied in the solution of the problem;
- respond positively, after they have been on the job, to the instruction and guidance they received at NC State in applying knowledge of mathematics, science, and engineering to the particular engineering problems they encounter at work;
- achieve a positive rating from their employers regarding their ability to apply general principles of mathematics, science, and engineering to particular engineering situations.

(b) To demonstrate that graduates have an ability to design and conduct experiments as well as analyze and interpret data, they should:

- show that they can take an experimental problem and develop a hypothesis, define the pertinent dependent and independent variables, and establish a sound experimental method that will allow them to measure the variables and test the hypothesis;

- show that they can conduct an experimental procedure, use laboratory materials properly and safely, carefully note observations in a laboratory notebook, and describe the procedure clearly for others;
- show that they can measure and record raw experimental data and analyze those data for the purposes of understanding and explaining the data. Graduates should be able to represent data in both verbal and visual forms (equations, tables, graphs, figures, etc.) in a way that is both an accurate and an honest reflection of the data;
- show that they can render the data meaningful by discussing the data in the context of the hypothesis and appropriate theories and principles and by stating, clearly and concisely, conclusions that can be drawn from the experiment.

(c) To demonstrate that graduates have an ability to design a system, component, or process to meet desired needs, they should:

- show that they can engage productively and creatively in the process of design. Design is a multi-dimensional act that requires a balance of opposing characteristics: divergent and convergent thinking, synthesis and analysis, aesthetic and utilitarian sensibilities. The process itself is flexible and recursive; that is, designers often find it necessary to skip around among the different phases of the process. It is helpful to think of the design process as defined by the following phases:
  - establishing the goal of the design project, the outcome that must be attained,
  - defining the project,
  - brainstorming for alternative possibilities,
  - choosing the best of the possible solutions,
  - creating a prototype or model that embodies or represents the chosen solution;
  - testing the prototype or model against the criteria for the project, and
  - choosing and justifying to an appropriate audience the final system, component, or process;
- respond positively, after they have been on the job, to the training and guidance in design process they received at NC State;
- achieve a positive rating from their employers regarding their ability to engage productively and creatively in the process of design.

(d) To demonstrate that graduates have an ability to function on multi-disciplinary teams, they must:

- possess a conceptual understanding of group dynamics, that is, how to make groups work effectively. This conceptual understanding includes:
  ○ how to create a group climate that encourages success,
  ○ how to recognize and make effective use of power resources in group activities, and
  ○ how to use communication strategies for dealing productively with conflict;
- show that they can participate effectively as team members in long-term group projects: working cooperatively with others, accepting divergent views, encouraging active participation of others, dealing productively with conflict, and taking leadership roles as the need arises to accomplish the group's objective;
- show that they can work successfully with people who are in other fields and those who perform a variety of functions within a group. This means that they must:
  ○ exhibit respect for these people and the diversity they bring to the group,
  ○ accept and incorporate, where appropriate, ideas from people with different perspectives, and
  ○ explain pertinent engineering principles and applications to people who have no training in those principles and applications but who need to make use of them;
- report, upon graduation, positive experiences related to the work they have done in teams. And if those experiences have been negative they should show that they know what they could have done to make their teams work more productively;
- respond positively, after they have been on the job, to the training and guidance they received at NC State in working in teams.

(e) To demonstrate that graduates have an ability to identify, formulate, and solve engineering problems, they should:

- show that they can identify engineering problems. Problem identification entails two procedures:
  ○ the ability to recognize an engineering problem. An engineering problem is an opportunity for change in which engineering solu-

tions can be applied to improve on existing or anticipated conditions and

○ the ability to define an engineering problem. Defining a problem means describing, in concrete and specific terms, the existing or anticipated condition that creates the opportunity for change and the goal state(s) that provides the direction and end-point for change;

• show that they can analyze problems, that is, isolate and describe the important components of a problem: what is given (design specifications, availability of materials, performance requirements, testing standards, etc.); what is known from previous experience relevant to the problem; and what the unknowns are;

• show that they can represent a problem in a form that makes finding solutions more efficient and effective. Such representations are typically visual, such as a model, flow chart, diagram, or table. This visualization should represent the components of the problem in a way that leads to the construction of a solution;

• show that they can apply engineering principles and mathematics to find the unknowns and arrive at appropriate solutions to the problem;

• respond positively, after they have been on the job, to the training and guidance they received at NC State in solving engineering problems;

• achieve a positive rating from their employers regarding their ability to solve engineering problems.

(f) To demonstrate that graduates have an understanding of professional and ethical responsibility, they should:

• show that they can apply an understanding of ethical responsibility to a design project. This means demonstrating that they can
  ○ identify the ethical issues pertinent to a project,
  ○ generate ethical criteria related to the project,
  ○ incorporate those criteria in the justification of the final outcome of the project, and
  ○ argue effectively for the responsibility of the engineer for that particular design project in maintaining the optimal balance between the contending forces of utility, cost, and risks;

• respond positively, after they have been on the job, to the preparation in professional and ethical responsibility they received at NC State;

- achieve a positive rating from their employers regarding their professional and ethical responsibility.

(g) To demonstrate that graduates have an ability to communicate effectively, they should:

- exhibit a mastery of the forms of discourse appropriate to the profession of engineering: oral and written project proposal, oral and written progress report, technical report, technical presentation, etc. Depending on the form that is used, students should demonstrate that they can:
  - describe the context (institutional and/or technological) of a problem and the significance of that problem within that context (introduction),
  - describe clearly and precisely the procedures used to solve the problem (methods),
  - report both verbally and visually the findings (results), interpret the findings in a way that is appropriate to the audience (discussion), and
  - propose recommendations for a solution to the problem and justify that solution persuasively (conclusion).
- show that they can summarize technical material in a way that is appropriate to a particular audience. Graduates should demonstrate that they can synthesize their own work and the work of others in the form of abstracts, executive summaries, and literature surveys;
- show that they can communicate successfully for obtaining and maintaining productive employment. For getting employment, graduates should show that they can write résumés and letters of application and perform capably in a job interview situation. For maintaining employment, graduates should show that they can write competent memos, letters, e-mail messages, and various reports (progress, personnel, maintenance, sales, trip, etc.) and give effective oral presentations to a variety of audiences;
- express confidence, upon graduation, of their ability to communicate effectively in their engineering careers and satisfaction with the guidance and instruction they received in writing and speaking;
- respond positively, after they have been on the job, to the usefulness and appropriateness of the preparation they received at NC State in oral and written communication;

- achieve a positive rating from their employers regarding their ability to communicate effectively.

(h) To demonstrate that graduates have the broad education to understand the impact of engineering solutions in a global and societal context, they should:

- express satisfaction, upon graduation, that their education at NC State has helped them to understand the impact of engineering solutions in a global and societal context;
- respond favorably, after they have been on the job, to the broad education they received at NC State and the way it has helped them to understand the impact of engineering solutions in a global and societal context.

(i) To demonstrate that graduates recognize the need for and possess the ability to engage in life-long learning, they should:

- show that they can use the critical information-seeking tools that enable engineers to continue to stay up to date in their profession: internet resources, engineering journals, U.S. and foreign patent materials, standards, etc.;
- show that as long as they continue to be employed as engineers, they are actively involved in the profession: membership in an engineering society, achievement and maintenance of technical registration for engineers, involvement in continuing education, etc.;
- express, upon graduation, both a full appreciation for the need for and the motivation to pursue further education and training, both engineering and otherwise, over their lifetimes;
- show that after graduation they have continued to seek opportunities for further education and training, both engineering and otherwise.

(j) To demonstrate that graduates possess a knowledge of contemporary issues, they should:

- show that they have taken and performed adequately in a variety of university courses that are concerned with contemporary issues and/or the context for understanding those issues, including courses in the humanities, arts, and social sciences, and those that combine one or more fields of study, such as science, technology, and society;

- respond favorably, after they have been on the job, to the quality of education in contemporary issues they received at NC State.

(k) to demonstrate that graduates possess an ability to use the techniques, skills, and modern engineering tools necessary for engineering practice.

Because the identification of techniques, skills, and modern engineering tools is peculiar to each field, there is no attempt here to come up with a general outcome. One good strategy is to do some brainstorming to generate a list that is appropriate to your field. Think about what special skills students ought to have to be effective as professionals in the field. What kinds of software should they be able to manage? What kind of special knowledge do they need? Are there any particular techniques they must master? What are the modern engineering tools of your field? What kinds of professional attributes should they exhibit?

After you have developed your list, determine which elements on it are the most important and then divide those remaining elements into categories. Each of these groups may provide the basis for a bullet for your operational definition.

APPENDIX 2.E

SOURCES OF INFORMATION TO BE USED IN ASSESSMENT OF ENGINEERING PROGRAMS, INCLUDING PROS AND CONS

Student Learning Data

Information About Student Learning

- From course work, embedded, or authentic assessment (direct assessment methods)
  - ○ Tests, including pre-post, entry, and exits
  - ○ Graded homework
  - ○ Ratings or rubrics judging quality of papers, reports, projects
  - ○ Tests, rubrics on paper, projects from capstone course experience
  - ○ Concept mapping or knowledge mapping
  - ○ Expert's judgment of work
  - ○ Criteria, rating, rubrics judging thesis, dissertation work
  - ○ Qualifying exams for graduate work
- From longitudinal, cross-sectional, or cross-course comparisons including student portfolios (direct assessment methods)
  - ○ Rubrics judging quality of work across time, sections, or courses
  - ○ Comparison of best examples of student learning
  - ○ Reflections by students about their learning
- From internships/coop experiences
  - ○ Surveys completed by intern/coop advisors/faculty about student's abilities (direct assessment method)
  - ○ Survey, interview, focus groups about satisfaction with student's performance (indirect assessment method)
- From employers/potential employers
  - ○ Surveys to employers about student's abilities (direct assessment methods)
  - ○ Survey of those who interview for employment purposes about perceived students' abilities

- ○ Survey, interview, focus groups about satisfaction with student's performance
- • From outside evaluations (direct assessment methods)
  - ○ Experts judge overall major/program quality of students' abilities
  - ○ Experts judge performance outside of course work
- • From nationally normed tests (direct assessment methods)
  - ○ Fundamentals of Engineering Exam (seniors)
  - ○ SAT, GRE
  - ○ Professional licenses requirements or exams

Information About Student's Satisfaction, Attitudes (Indirect Assessment Method)

- • Surveys, interviews, or focus groups about satisfaction with learning environment, faculty, courses, curriculum, their learning and equipment/tools from prospective, current, graduating and withdrawn students and alumni
- • Inventories about students' attitudes; monitor attitude changes over time

Information About Faculty's Satisfaction (Indirect Assessment Method)

- • Surveys, interviews, or focus groups about satisfaction with learning environment, incoming students' ability, courses, curriculum, amount of student learning, equipment/tools

Other Data (not to be used instead of direct and indirect measures of student learning)

Information About Students

- • Calculate enrollment headcount
- • Calculate retention trends
- • Determine number of transfer credits
- • Compute institutional, programs', and courses' gender and ethnicity numbers and ratios
- • Identify membership in student professional organizations
- • Use specific studies conducted by institution's institutional research office

- Calculate alumni job placement, graduate school acceptance rates
- Track alumni honors/awards

Information About Faculty

- Determine number of faculty/student credit hours for each semester—by department, course, or instructor
- Calculate number of full-time and part-time faculty—by rank, by headcount, ethnicity, and gender
- Analyze student–faculty ratio
- Estimate workload of faculty
- Compare salary ranges for faculty by specific ranks, gender, and ethnicity
- Use specific studies conducted by institution's institutional research office

Information About Courses and Curriculum

- Transcript analysis or degree audit of courses students actually take
- Surveys about quality from students, alumni, and faculty
- Student development transcripts analysis (record of cocurricular experiences)
- Accreditors' or outside experts' judgment about quality of curriculum
- Specific studies conducted by institution's institutional research office

Information About Learning Environment

- Surveys from users about quality
- Quantity of types of spaces
- Numbers of participants in offerings in cocurriculum
- Space utilization study
- Teaching-learning experts' observations using predetermined criteria

Information About Equipment/Tools

- Survey users about quality
- Track use of equipment, tools, software, books
- Count quantity by type and by learning space (i.e., classroom, labs)

Information About Technology Tools Related to Student Learning

- Surveys about usage, quality, attitudes (faculty, students, alumni)
- Specific software tools usage through the software: e.g., learning man-

agement systems may track amount of use of discussion boards or pages of content
- How technology was used (taxonomy of functional uses)

Benchmarking Information—Comparison to Other Institutions

- National surveys (e.g., ETS, Educause, National Survey of Student Engagement)
- Published studies from national sources (e.g., *US News & World Report*, Association of Research Libraries, Educause, American Association of University Professors)
- Specific studies conducted by institution's institutional research office

Pros and Cons of Assessment Methods on Student Learning

Example Assessment Methods on Student Learning	Pros of Method	Cons of Method
• From course work (embedded, course-based) (direct assessment methods)	• In general, students take embedded course work seriously; therefore work has a good chance of reflecting actual abilities • Reflects program or department's course and curriculum, and program outcomes	• In general, biases of the data over years and instructor or departmental differences can influence the results • Reluctance of faculty to share results with entire faculty membership
• Tests, including pre-post, entry and exits	• Inexpensive • Comprehensive • Pre-post testing allows for "value added" assessment	• Developing appropriate test questions that reflect learning outcomes and complex levels of learning takes time and skill • For pre-post testing, it's difficult to design tests that are comparable at different times
• Graded homework	• Reflects students' ability when they have access to resources	• Does not assess students' ability or overall learning as typically defined
• Ratings or rubrics judging quality of papers, reports, projects	• Can be used by others besides instructor, to assess quality	• Developing accurate rubric dimensions that reflect learning outcomes and levels of learning takes time and skill
• Tests, rubrics on paper, projects from capstone course experience	• Allows for assessment of higher cognitive abilities such as synthesis and evaluation of knowledge • Can assess in-depth knowledge • Allows creativity • Assessment of integration of learning	• Labor intensive for both faculty and students • Because course and project are high-stakes, it may produce student anxiety that may result in assessment reflecting lesser ability than actual ability
• Concept mapping or knowledge mapping	• Unique technique to understand connections of concepts within students' knowledge base • Assessment of complex relationships	• Difficult to compare across students • Difficult to obtain objective judgment on abilities
• Expert's judgment of performance (e.g., art, drama, healthcare)	• Improves face validity of assessment activities	• Obtaining appropriate experts' time

(continued)

Pros and Cons of Assessment Methods on Student Learning (Continued)

Example Assessment Methods on Student Learning	Pros of Method	Cons of Method
• Criteria, rating, rubrics judging thesis, dissertation work	• Allows for judgment about overall graduate program across several students	• Difficult to define rubric dimensions that relate to multiple thesis or dissertations
• Qualifying exams for graduate work	• Developing exam questions across several graduates allows for better assessment of the graduate program	• Oral presentations may be a challenge for those with language difficulties • Difficult to define questions that relate to several students
• From longitudinal, cross-sectional or cross-course comparisons including student portfolios (direct assessment methods)	• In general, shows longitudinal trends with rich detail • Assessment becomes an integral part of students' learning process	• In general, validity depends on how work is collected • Can overload assessment committees with too much information
• Rubrics judging quality of work across time, sections, or courses	• Highlights students' strengths and weaknesses in comprehensive manner	• Developing accurate rubric dimensions that reflect learning outcomes and levels of learning takes time and skill • Content may vary widely by student
• Comparison of best examples of student learning	• Students do the work of providing the assessment "data" by supplying their best examples	• Student's judgment of "best examples" may not actually reflect faculty's judgment of "best examples"
• Reflections by students about their learning	• Provides opportunity for students to synthesize own work • Identifies strengths and weaknesses	• Difficult to judge objectively
• From internships/coop experiences	• Supervisors typically provide feedback to students anyway	• Ratings and criteria of supervisor may not reflect program outcomes
• Surveys completed by intern/coop advisors/faculty about student's abilities (direct assessment method)	• Based on actual work experience that may reflect future career	• May obtain information only on a small number of outcomes • Limited observation time
• Survey, interview, focus groups about satisfaction with student's performance (indirect assessment method)	• Provides information about other outcomes besides competencies such as attitude	• Satisfaction with performance may not be reflective of student's ability

Example Assessment Methods on Student Learning	Pros of Method	Cons of Method
• From employers/potential employers	• In general, improves face validity of assessment activities	• Difficult to identify where alumni are employed • Sensitive information for both employer and program/department
• Surveys to employers about student's abilities (direct assessment methods)	• Provide information about student's abilities needed by employers	• Difficult to get direct supervisors to respond to surveys
• Survey of those who interview for employment purposes about perceived students' abilities	• Best person to compare quality of one institution's graduates to other institutions' graduates	• May only be able to assess a small number of general outcomes such as communication skills
• From outside evaluations experts judge overall major/program quality of students' abilities (direct assessment methods)	• Improves face validity of assessment activities	• Obtaining appropriate experts' time
• From nationally normed tests (direct assessment methods)	• Ability to compare from year to year or to other groups • National standard can be used for program's performance criteria • Convenient • Well-developed test • National or commercial surveys have reliability and validity information	• May not reflect program or institution's curriculum or outcomes • Limited faculty ownership • Costly to institution or student
• Information about student's satisfaction, attitudes (indirect assessment method)	• Important to hear from student's viewpoint • Conduct comparison of different groups of students on same outcomes/questions	• In general, students' perception of their ability may not relate to their actual ability • In general, alumni are more satisfied than graduating seniors who tend to be more satisfied than sophomores, etc.
• Surveys about satisfaction with learning environment, faculty, courses, curriculum, their learning, equipment/tools from prospective, current, graduating, withdrawn students and alumni	• Easy to administer • Low cost • National or commercial surveys have reliability and validity information	• Usefulness is based on good design of survey questions

(continued)

Pros and Cons of Assessment Methods on Student Learning (Continued)

Example Assessment Methods on Student Learning	Pros of Method	Cons of Method
• Interviews or focus groups about satisfaction with learning environment, faculty, courses, curriculum, their learning, equipment/tools from prospective, current, graduating, withdrawn students and alumni	• Can provide rich data, personal perspectives; can go into depth about a particular aspect or factor • Other factors may arise that relate to academics such as pedagogy, class size, etc. which not expected or asked about.	• Those who participate tend to have either very positive or very negative opinions, which is a selection bias • Fear of retributions may bias respondents' answers
• Inventories about students' attitudes; monitor attitude changes over time	• Commercially available instruments provide reliability and validity information	• Usefulness depends on how related to program outcomes
• Information about faculty's satisfaction (indirect assessment method) through survey, interviews, or focus groups	• Important to hear from faculty's view • Factors may arise that relate to academics such as pedagogy, class size, etc.	• Usefulness is based on good design of questions

Table copyright © Joni E. Spurlin, 2006; reprinted with permission.

3

ASSESSMENT METHODS USED IN UNDERGRADUATE PROGRAM ASSESSMENT

Joni E. Spurlin

"The value of knowledge lies not in its accumulation, but in its utilization."

—Anonymous

Chapter 2 talked about knowing what we want students to learn; this chapter discusses how we can tell how well students are learning this material. In this context the assessment questions are: How can we show that students are achieving the desired outcomes? What is the overall quality of the program? and What are specific methods or tools we can use to gather evidence that indicates what needs to be improved and what does not? Looking at the model in Figure 2.1 (p. 25), we see that faculty members and assessment committees are responsible for developing and collecting assessment data, but what are the best methods? This chapter presents various methods for assessing engineering program-level objectives and outcomes, and explains what types of evidence should be collected, how to link program outcomes to course outcomes, and how to link course assessment to program outcomes assessment. Chapter 4 addresses how to analyze the evidence, once collected.

In discussing assessment methodology, the level of analysis must be identified. Is the assessment for an individual student, a course, a program, or an institution? Traditionally, assessment is about aggregate information—students as a group within courses, programs, or institutions. The methods discussed in this chapter specifically address assessment at the program level, including how to use assessment from courses to provide input into the program-level assessment. Chapter 10 discusses specific ways to assess classrooms and courses.

There are many resources that detail good assessment methodology for any educational discipline and include detailed discussion of the pros and cons of each method. A few of these resources include Palomba and Banta's (1999) *Assessment Essentials: Planning, Implementing, and Improving Assessment in Higher Education*, Suskie's (2004) *Assessing Student Learning: A Common Sense Guide*, and *Assessment Clear and Simple: A Practical Guide for Institutions, Departments, and General Education* by Walvoord (2004).

ABET requires each program to develop measures and evidence that indicate the degree to which each of the program outcomes is achieved. Each program must document assessment results and how the results are used. It is required that programs assess each of their program outcomes, that they gather the assessment evidence on a regular and ongoing basis, and that each outcome has a metric goal.

What does "evidence" mean? What is acceptable and what is not? Evidence includes appropriate data of what and how well students are learning. Evidence should be collected through a variety of methods and from multiple sources. The training provided to ABET evaluators states that the assessment methodology should include student work and direct assessment rather than rely solely on indirect assessments such as students' opinion of their own abilities. This means faculty need to identify student work that documents the extent to which students have acquired the stated outcomes.

Direct assessment methods are those that judge student work, projects, or portfolios developed as a result of the learning experiences; direct methods include rubrics, final exams, national exams, portfolio review, and external reviewers. Some educators label this "authentic" assessment. Indirect methods include conducting surveys or interviews to indicate student abilities, as well as calculating retention, transfer rates, and time to degree. Other sources of data for making decisions are listed in Appendix 2.E (in chapter 2).

One of the first considerations in choosing an assessment method is to consider how well the method matches the program's educational objectives or learning outcomes. In addition, the assessment method needs to match the level of analysis (i.e., student, course, or program level). Most methods can be used at any level. The more complex the level of analysis, the more complex the assessment method becomes. A student survey for a course can be very focused, while a survey distributed to all students within an academic program addresses broader questions, covering a wider range of topics. An exam for a specific course that tests a specific concept is easier to develop than an exam that assesses all senior students' ability on the same outcome.

While there are many appropriate assessment methods, there are only a few inappropriate methods. Inappropriate assessment methods generally include course grades, grade point averages (GPAs), curriculum tracking, and demographic data. Course grades are not considered appropriate for program assessment because course grades reflect not only student performance but also requirements such as classroom participation. In addition, course grades are too inconsistent from section to section and year to year (e.g., Rogers, 2003; Suskie, 2004). In *Student Learning Assessment: Options and Resources*, the Middle States Commission on Higher Education (2003) states that grades do not serve as direct evidence of student learning because letter or number grades do not describe "the content of what students have learned" (p. 37).

However, course grades can be used if—this is a big "if"—the faculty of a program rigorously determine and agree upon methods for scoring student achievement in their course grading system. Walvoord and Anderson (1998) have written an excellent resource that explains how to develop course grades for assessment purposes. GPAs and demographic data are not appropriate assessment methods because they don't give any indication of how programs can be improved. If a student has a low GPA, is that because the program needs improvement? Maybe. However, what specifically should be improved is impossible to tell from GPA or demographic data. Finally, although it is tempting to track which courses students take as an indicator of their learning, this is the old "input" model and not outcomes-based assessment. Just because students take a specific course does not mean they have learned the material. Even if students make an "A" in a specific course, it does not mean that these students have met the program's specific outcomes.

Characteristics of Good Assessment Methods

Before we discuss specific methods, we will consider the characteristics and features of good assessment methods. Figure 3.1 outlines features of good assessment methods. The following section discusses a few of these points in detail.

Prior to developing an assessment methodology, appropriate outcomes need to be defined. How to develop appropriate outcomes was discussed in chapter 2. The next step is to define a target, performance criterion, or met-

FIGURE 3.1
Characteristics of Best Practices Regarding
Assessment Methods for Program Outcomes

Measurable Outcomes
- Clearly defined outcomes
- Outcomes prescribe behaviors/benchmarks that provide criteria for evaluation
- Identifiable metric used to define outcome attainment

Effective, Meaningful
- Evidence illuminates issues surrounding outcomes
- Assessment embedded within the curriculum

Pragmatic, Efficient
- Evidence is useful for decision making
- Same methods and evidence used for a variety of purposes: program assessment, program accreditation, institutional accreditation
- Balances the value of the assessment evidence with the effort or resources involved in gathering the evidence

Systematic, Ongoing
- Systematic approach—organized instead of haphazard
- Continual evaluation process
- Both formative and summative

Multifaceted
- Assessed using multiple methods—more than one method for an outcome and measured at more than one point in time
- Cumulative—compare results, monitor progress over time
- Evidence illuminates issues surrounding objectives/outcomes
- Each program's/unit's assessment process evolves and develops based on what is learned from prior assessments

Resourced
- Time given to the data collection, analysis, and interpretation
- Faculty are fully engaged
- Needed resources obtained to ensure data collection and analyses

ric, for each outcome. A metric is a quantifiable goal of student achievement for a specific outcome. As with the program outcomes, the faculty members in the program need to come to an agreement on the level of student achievement for each outcome. Examples of performance metrics include the following:

- Eighty percent of the students will score 70 percent or higher on exam questions related to topic.
- On average, students in the civil engineering program at our institution will score higher than the national average on each subtest of the Fundamentals of Engineering (FE) Exam.
- An average score of 70 percent on an exam question shows the program has met the outcome; 50 percent indicates the outcome was partially met; lower than 40 percent indicates the outcome was not met.
- A total score of 80 percent on the entire rubric meets the outcome.
- Seventy-five percent of the class as a whole will score 3 or 4 on each dimension of the rubric.
- Eighty percent of the students will rate their preparation as "good" or higher on survey questions.

To be most meaningful, assessment needs to be ongoing. A single view of evidence at a single point in time tends to give a distorted view. Trends over time provide a more consistent and systematic view of program effectiveness related to student learning. A trend analysis will allow the faculty to determine how student learning is impacted when a course is added or modified. Developing a system of assessment that can show the effect of these changes is a best practice.

Another best practice is to develop a baseline of learning on all outcomes for one or two years, and then to periodically reassess learning on each outcome. That is, not every outcome needs to be assessed every semester or every year. Once a baseline is established, outcomes that are related to program changes should be reassessed more often, but other outcomes may be reassessed at established points in time (every two or three years). It is important that the methods be useful, but not so overwhelming that data collection will stop. An efficient system is one that has an established time line, over a four- to six-year period, with indications of who will collect which data. Ad hoc, one-time data collection is not appropriate and does not demonstrate that a program has a thoughtful and well-designed assessment process.

Another efficiency method is to use the same student work and assessment method for more than one outcome. For example, student papers written about a nuclear engineer's ethical responsibility, scored by two faculty using an established rubric, provide evidence on at least two ABET outcomes: Criterion 3.f, "An understanding of professional and ethical responsibility," and Criterion 3.g, "An ability to communicate effectively."

One of the most important characteristics of good assessment practices is that multiple assessment methods have been developed for each outcome. This method, called *triangulation*, gives an overall picture of how well students are performing on an outcome. Consider triangulating with indirect and direct assessment methodologies. For example, a program could triangulate by obtaining students' opinion of their ability with a senior survey, assessing student work with a rubric, and comparing student performance on a subtest of the FE Exam. The comparison of the evidence from these three methods will give a good picture of how students are meeting a specific outcome.

Assessment Methods for Program Educational Objectives

Based on criteria established by ABET, the program educational objectives (PEOs) must be assessed by the constituencies. The PEOs tend to be very broad statements; therefore, assessing them can be difficult. Most programs use three types of constituencies and develop surveys for these main constituencies: faculty, alumni, and employers. A program's advisory board can also be used to assess the program at a broad level. Below are some specific examples of assessment methods for PEOs.

Alumni Survey

Surveys of alumni (typically, those who have graduated within the last three to five years) can be conducted every three to five years, as needed. These should be scheduled in the overall timeline of the program's assessment process. Teaming up with other units on campus who may conduct alumni surveys (alumni association, foundation unit, planning and analysis, etc.) is also a good practice. Specific questions can sometimes be incorporated into ongoing standard alumni surveys conducted by the institution.

Because every program's PEOs are different, giving specific survey-question examples in this chapter will not be meaningful. In general, the survey questions should ask about the alumni's level of preparation and their perception of the importance of specific items to their current situation. A set of questions can ask the alumni about their preparation in relationship to their abilities as specified in the PEOs. Alumni can rate how well the institution/college or program prepared them for the topics addressed in the survey questions on a scale from 1 (poor preparation) to 5 (excellent preparation). Alumni can indicate on a five-point scale how important each area is in their current professional position, including graduate studies.

Once the data has been collected, mapping the responses back to the

PEOs provides the ability to assess each PEO separately. See Figure 3.2 for a summary of these types of results. All constituencies should then be given the opportunity to review the results for each PEO. Once the feedback is gathered from the constituencies, revisions to the PEOs can be made as needed.

Figure 3.2 shows an example of alumni survey data averaged and plotted (invented data). The figure shows a plot of the ratio of one program within a college of engineering against all the other programs. A ratio of 1 indicates that the program and collegewide responses were the same. Ratios higher than 1 indicate that the program responses were higher than the collegewide responses. The average scores could also be plotted without comparisons to other programs. The survey questions are grouped according to PEO by the dotted lines.

Employer Survey

Surveys of employers are more difficult to conduct (Kurstedt, 1999; Leonard & Nault, 2000; Nault & Marr, 2002). A few of the main obstacles to conducting employer surveys are the inability to (a) identify the employers,

FIGURE 3.2
Results of Alumni Survey for Constituencies' Review (Fictitious University)

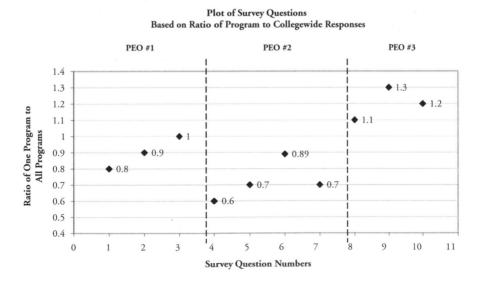

Plot of Survey Questions
Based on Ratio of Program to Collegewide Responses

(b) obtain sufficient responses from employers, and (c) obtain permission from alumni to contact their employers; and the resistance by the same employer to answering multiple surveys from multiple institutions. It may be easier to survey recruiters who come to campus than to survey actual employers. Recruiters can compare your alumni to other institutions' alumni in the same field. If employer surveys are used, it is a best practice for comparison purposes to use the same questions as with the alumni survey. Therefore, the stems for questions are essentially the same as with alumni surveys:

- Rating the performance of our graduate(s)
- Indicating the importance of that skill or knowledge in your organization or for the graduate's job
- Comparing the graduates at the same level of experience from other engineering programs to the institution's graduates

Some institutions that have developed employer surveys include Georgia Tech, Montana State University–Bozeman, University of Virginia, Northeastern University, and Stanford University. Another alternative to conducting employer surveys is to hold interviews or focus group sessions with local employers.

Advisory Board

A program's advisory board and other program constituencies can review summaries of the results from any of these methods (see Figure 3.2 for an example). Also, to add to the assessment effort, the constituencies may be asked the following questions, annually or biennially:

- Based on this data and your experience with our students and alumni, do you feel that the program is achieving its PEOs? If not, which PEOs are of concern to you?
- Based on your knowledge of new trends in the field, do you feel the PEOs address these new trends?
- Do you feel that the PEOs need to be changed? If so, what additions, deletions, or modifications do you suggest?
- What other recommendations do you have for the program?

Assessment Methods for Program Outcomes

Developing or improving the assessment methods for each outcome is the next step after carefully defining your program outcomes. See chapter 2 for a discussion of how to operationalize each of the ABET's required outcomes. (Be sure to include outcomes from ABET's Criterion 8.) The better defined the outcome, the easier it is to develop appropriate assessment methods. This book assumes that all programs have already developed some assessment methods. Many programs currently have developed adequate indirect methods (e.g., student surveys) for their assessment. Therefore, this chapter emphasizes the use of direct assessment methods (e.g., using student work).

The examples given in this section are considered good examples that have been useful to institutions around the country, but these examples are by no means all the possible examples. Many other examples can be found by searching the ABET website, the ASEE conference publications, Rose-Hulman's Best Practices Conference resources, and the University of Pittsburgh engineering education website (http://www.engrng.pitt.edu/~ec2000). Also, many of the eight engineering coalitions funded by the National Science Foundation (NSF) have worked on specific assessment processes (see the list at Foundation Coalition's website: www.foundationcoalition.org/home/foundationcoalition/engineering_coalitions. html). For convenience, this chapter pulls together in one resource at least one assessment-method example for each ABET outcome (3.a–k).

Course-based assessment, use of the FE exam, and surveys will be discussed here. (Pros and cons of various assessment methods are given in Appendix 2.E on p. 51.) Not discussed in this chapter are the uses of portfolios or assessments in senior design; however, other chapters in this book discuss the use of portfolios and examples of assessments in senior design courses, as well as other, more innovative methods such as concept mapping.

Course-Based Assessments

Course-based assessment, sometimes called embedded assessment or authentic assessment, is based on identifying and acquiring student work within specific courses that best relates to specific program outcomes. Course-based assessment is effective and efficient because it allows faculty to use actual assignments, tests, projects, and papers for program assessment.

How the student work is used for assessment purposes is the key. One way to determine which student work products to use is to consider which courses relate to the program outcomes. (Refer to chapter 2 for mapping the curriculum to the learning outcomes.) The faculty who teach the specific courses that map to specific outcomes can be asked to identify student work. For example, if a junior-level engineering course has the students write a paper on engineering design as it relates to contemporary issues, that assignment in that course could be matched to the outcome on "communication," "engineering design," and "contemporary issues."

Therefore, in order to identify specific course-based assessments, the first step is to do the curricular mapping. The second step is to identify which courses should be assessed. If there are four courses that cover an outcome called "use of modern tools," one must determine which of these courses will be best to use when assessing that program outcome. One way to decide is to participate in a faculty retreat where all faculty agree which course assignments will be used as part of the program assessment process. See Appendix 3.A for worksheets that can assist with this discussion.

Do not put all your emphasis on the senior design course—this is tempting, but this course has a great deal to accomplish. The students' work, especially the final senior design product, can give a useful global overall measure of all the outcomes. This work can be used as one of the major ends of triangulation but not as the sole course-based assessment. Two examples of rubrics to use with senior design projects are given in Appendix 3.B.

After the entire faculty membership for the program has come to consensus on which assignments to use, the final step is to develop a complete list of course-based methods for all the outcomes and who is responsible for each assessment. Remember to consider the overall program's timeline for assessment. It may not be necessary to collect course-based assessment in every course, every semester, or even every year. The overall timeline of assessment of the outcomes should dictate how often this method is used. The faculty members responsible for the identified course-based assessment data should also know how to transmit the assessment work and results to the program's assessment committee.

Once the exact assignment, test, or student work has been identified, the faculty member may provide the scoring of that work. Best practices show that a team of faculty who examine the work can provide less biased judgment. One of the ways to assess student work will be the use of rubrics. Rubrics are sets of criteria or scoring guides that define what is expected of students. There are many examples of rubrics in this chapter. Other example rubrics and tools to develop rubrics can be found online: search for "rubrics" and "rubric makers" with any search engine.

When designing or using rubrics, the dimensions within each rubric need to be defined or operationalized to relate clearly to the program outcome(s). These rubrics take skill and time to develop. Taggart, Phifer, Nixon, and Wood (2001) and Stevens and Levi (2005) have written good resources about developing and using rubrics. Rubrics can be used for more than one outcome and for similar student work in multiple courses. For example, a "lab" rubric could be designed (see Appendix 3.C). All courses that use a lab report could be designed to have a common format. Within the courses with similar lab reports, the common rubric's scores for each lab can be averaged together to provide an overall score on labs from that course, or the faculty could decide to use just the last lab report's rubric scores. By having multiple courses using the same rubric, student learning related to "writing" and "lab analyses" can be assessed across the curriculum.

Hake (e.g., 1998, 2002, 2004) has written extensively about the use of pre-post exams within courses with the use of normalized gain scores. See his work for the specific methodology on how to use pre-post exams to show program improvement.

Developing competencies tests or comprehensive exams in the field of engineering is being considered by many institutions as part of the assessment procedure. Some institutions are developing end-of-sophomore-, end-of-junior-, or end-of-senior-year exams. An example of one program is chemical engineering at Tri-State University (Wagner, Finley, & McKetta, 1999). The Foundation Coalition, one of eight engineering coalitions funded by the NSF, has information about assessment of many broad engineering concepts on its website: www.foundationcoalition.org (see Concept Assessment Inventory Tools).

Course-Embedded Assessment Examples for Each Outcome

The author studied engineering assessment plans from many programs across the country and compiled lists of assessment examples for each outcome. Although many of the examples in the appendices are from North Carolina State University (which has 17 ABET-accredited undergraduate engineering programs), many other institutions have developed good examples of assessments.

ABET Outcome Criterion 3.a: An ability to apply knowledge of mathematics, science, and engineering

Course-embedded assessment examples:

- Test questions from exams in courses such as calculus, chemistry, and physics
- Test questions from exams in advanced courses that test the interrelationship of basic science knowledge and engineering knowledge

Sometimes the engineering program needs to collaborate with other departments to gather assessment data. For example, to assess outcome 3.a, the NC State College of Engineering assessment committee has worked with the mathematics and physics programs. The mathematics program, the physics program, and the College of Engineering's engineering programs have developed common assessment procedures, including a set of common program learning outcomes that serves all these programs in their outcomes assessment. The mathematics department has developed, validated, and implemented end-of-course exam questions in each of four service courses as its assessment of the common program learning outcomes. The physics department and the College of Engineering share information about success in physics and the impact of the various pedagogical versions of the two physics service courses. The results of the common assessment process are being used to improve course offerings and student learning in mathematics, physics, and engineering. This type of cooperation may also be needed to help assess other of the outcomes, such as

3.f. An understanding of professional and ethical responsibility
3.i. A recognition of the need for, and an ability to engage in, life-long learning
3.j. A knowledge of contemporary issues

ABET Outcome Criterion 3.b: An ability to design and conduct experiments, as well as to analyze and interpret data
Course-embedded assessment examples:

- Graded laboratory reports from engineering courses with lab sections
- Specific analysis problems solved, including "open-ended" application of assumptions

If laboratory reports are to be used, it will be important to clearly indicate what subsections relate uniquely to designing experiments, conducting experiments, analyzing data, and interpreting data. See Appendix 3.C for an example of a rubric to assess lab reports. Note that some of these dimensions can also contribute to assessment of "written communication" (outcome 3.g). A good practice is to have all lab reports in all courses designed with a common format so that the same rubric can be used to assess reports from different courses.

ABET Outcome Criterion 3.c: An ability to design a system, component, or process to meet desired needs
Course-embedded assessment examples:

- Technical products from capstone courses
- Graded design projects in introduction, junior, or senior courses
- Rubrics to judge design ability based on student presentations; judging done by visitors from industry
- Experimental task that includes components of 3.c within

ABET Outcome Criterion 3.d: An ability to function on multi-disciplinary teams
Course-embedded assessment examples:

- Observation of faculty, advisors, industry experts on teams
- Team members' assessment of other team members

The main issue that arises from this outcome is how to define "multi-disciplinary." Institutions with only a few engineering programs may want to provide experiences across engineering disciplines. Some disciplines can assign multi-disciplinary teams within their discipline: For example, for civil engineering, team members can represent structural, environmental, construction management, geotechnical, and hydrological engineering. Other programs may define "multi-disciplinary" by providing teams with roles for each member, such as team leader, financial manager, construction manager, technical consultant, quality assurance leader, test leader, and document writer. Appendix 3.D gives an example of a rubric for students' self-assessments of teamwork experiences. The Foundation Coalition has information about assessment of teamwork on its website: www.foundationcoalition.org. Ohland, Pomeranz, and Feinstein (2006) at Clemson University have developed an online instrument called the Comprehensive Assessment of Team Member Effectiveness (CATME). Another teamwork-related tool is the *Team Developer* (now the *Professional Developer*) (e.g., McGourty & De Meuse, 2000; McGourty, Reynolds, Besterfield-Sacre, Shuman, & Wolfe, 2003; McGourty, Sebastian, & Swart, 1998; McGourty, Shuman, Chimka, Besterfield-Sacre, & Wolfe, 2001).

ABET Outcome Criterion 3.e: An ability to identify, formulate, and solve engineering problems
Course-embedded assessment examples:

- Test questions on exams related to ability to identify and formulate design tasks
- Rubrics used to score specific engineering problems
- California Critical Thinking rubric

ABET Outcome Criterion 3.f: An understanding of professional and ethical responsibility
Course-embedded assessment examples:

- Technical reports from capstone courses
- Professional portfolios consisting of materials from a course
- Testing of professional code of ethics and application of code of ethics
- Reports/testing based on case studies: see University of Michigan's engineering assessment website: www.engin.umich.edu/teaching/assess _and_improve/handbook/direct/casestudy.html
- Rubrics used to score essays from ethics courses or from courses/seminars that discuss ethics issues
- Faculty observation of ethical behavior of students; signed contracts with students related to ethical behaviors

ABET Outcome Criterion 3.g: An ability to communicate effectively
Course-embedded assessment examples:

- Scored assignments in any course that require students to provide written work, oral presentations, communication of graphical skills
- Rubrics on written work—judged for technical ability and written skills
- Rubrics used when viewing student presentations
- Rubrics used by industry experts, especially in senior-design final-project presentations and reports

As has been illustrated for other outcomes, this outcome needs to be further refined to describe communication in terms of students' ability in oral, written, graphical, and other methods of communication. See Appendix 3.C for a lab rubric that contains dimensions related to written communication skills. See Appendix 3.E for an example of an oral presentations rubric. Many programs use judgments by faculty as well as by student peers and experts in the field. Using rubrics designed by faculty, student peers can assess each other's written, oral, and graphic abilities. Bennett (1986, 1993) has developed the *Intercultural Development Inventory* (IDI) to measure cultural sensitivity.

ABET Outcome Criterion 3.h: The broad education necessary to understand the impact of engineering solutions in a global, economic, environmental, and societal context

Course-embedded assessment examples:

- Scored paper by students that describes what they are learning from their engineering education and that shows their understanding of the global nature of engineering as well as social, political, and/or economic issues
- Graded discussion of current events in engineering and changes to analysis/design procedures

ABET Outcome Criterion 3.i: A recognition of the need for, and an ability to engage in, life-long learning

Course-embedded assessment examples:

- Assessment of student's ability to search the Internet or library resources and distinguish quality resources
- Scored work of students entered into national design competitions; judgment of work by national competition judges

The concern of many engineering faculty with this example is what defines lifelong learning. It is important that each program first define what lifelong learning means. Once defined, it is much easier to determine a method for assessing it. Many engineering programs interpret lifelong learning in terms of information literacy skills (see a detailed example of how to instruct and assess information literacy in engineering from NC State Libraries: www.lib.ncsu.edu/instructiontoolkit/). The *Self Directed Learning Readiness Scale* (SDLRS) is another type of assessment tool related to measuring lifelong learning (Litzinger, Lee, & Wise 2004; Litzinger, Wise, & Lee, 2005). Many programs use job placement and graduate school acceptances as ways to assess outcome 3.i. The latter are useful indicators but should not be the only means of assessing this outcome.

ABET Outcome Criterion 3.j: A knowledge of contemporary issues
Course-embedded assessment examples:

- Related portions of a rubric used to assess a senior design project or course paper
- Test questions in which students have proposed solutions to contemporary engineering problems
- Graded homework on contemporary issues modules

To facilitate assessment of this outcome, some thought needs to be given to where information about contemporary issues will be taught in the curriculum. To facilitate assessment, many programs add an assigned paper or project to an upper-level course. The paper may ask students to discuss how a specific engineering problem relates to contemporary issues or to address how and why contemporary technical and nontechnical issues were taken into account during a design process. Examples of contemporary issues include patent law, environmental concerns, and health issues. See Appendix 3.F for an example of a rubric related to contemporary issues used with papers written in the mechatronics program at NC State.

ABET Outcome Criterion 3.k: An ability to use the techniques, skills,
and modern engineering tools necessary for engineering practice
Course-embedded assessment examples:

- Tools used in field assessed by faculty, industry experts
- Graded assignments that incorporate assessment of student's ability to use tools, such as analytical software, design tools, CAD programs, robotics
- Project assessment that incorporates assessing student's ability to apply tools appropriately

The assessment of this outcome is also linked with other outcomes in student work that is assessed, including using tools to

3.a. Apply knowledge of mathematics, science, and engineering
3.b. Design and conduct experiments, as well as to analyze and interpret data
3.c. Design a system, component, or process to meet desired needs

Fundamentals of Engineering Exam

Many engineering programs require or highly recommend that seniors take the Fundamentals of Engineering (FE) exam. FE exam results can be found at the local state's Board of Examiners for Engineers and Surveyors (see www.ncees.org/exams/fundamentals for information about the exam and for specification of materials covered on the exam).

If a program has more than 60 percent of its seniors taking the exam, the following method for examining the data may be useful. Joni Spurlin (editor of this book) and Jim Nau, a professor of civil engineering, developed the following trend analysis methodology for use by engineering programs at North Carolina State University. The purpose of the trend analysis is to ensure that the engineering program uses data from multiple test administrations prior to making decisions about the quality of its program. By examining the trends of each test administration over time, interpretations can be made about how well students are performing overall. Examine Table 3.1, which has fictitious data that is similar to what institutions receive. Should a program only report the average pass rate over the four years, or would it be better to examine the trends as they relate to curricular changes?

The more interesting analysis, however, comes from an evaluation of each of the subtests. We can relate the subtests to specific ABET a–k outcomes. This analysis can be used for both the morning and afternoon exams. See Figure 3.3 for an example of averages on the FE Exam for a fictitious engineering program. Since one cannot average the averages, which is what is reported to each institution, it is necessary to calculate the number of possible correct questions based on the number of students who took the exam. This number can then be added up, and one can derive an average either for each academic year or for four years overall. An example of the calculation is shown in Appendix 3.G. Using the method shown, an average can be calculated for the year or for several years (see Figure 3.3).

Surveys Related to Outcomes

Senior surveys. Most programs use a survey of their graduating seniors as an assessment method. This is useful for triangulation but should not be used as the sole assessment method. Surveys may ask graduating seniors to rate how balanced the program is in terms of its coverage of specific skills, competencies, and outcomes. Surveys provide a perception-based assessment of all the outcomes, especially the outcomes that are not easily addressed otherwise. The best use of survey results is to develop trends analysis, not to define

TABLE 3.1
Example of Pass Rates on Fundamentals of Engineering Exam (Fictitious Engineering Program)

Test Date	Fictitious Engineering Program A, Institution B			State C Students			National Students		
	Number Take	Number Pass	Percent Pass	Number Take	Number Pass	Percent Pass	Number Take	Number Pass	Percent Pass
Oct. 2002	35	34	97	43	34	79	1075	786	73
Apr. 2003	36	27	75	48	31	65	890	620	70
Oct. 2003	45	33	73	51	36	71	864	591	68
Apr. 2004	42	42	100	70	49	70	1544	1100	71
Oct. 2004	36	29	81	48	31	65	902	626	69
Apr. 2005	40	34	85	52	46	88	1560	1196	77
Oct. 2005	70	64	91	84	69	82	1443	1090	76
Apr. 2006	50	41	82	53	38	72	899	660	73
Totals	**234**	**199**	**85**	**312**	**227**	**73**	**6835**	**4919**	**72**

FIGURE 3.3

Averaging Subscores for Fundamentals of Engineering Examination

Engineering Program: Fictitious Engineering Program X (FEPX)

Averages for Eight Administrations From October 2002 Through April 2006

	Fictitious Engineering Program X, Institution Y			State Z Students Fictitious Engineering Program X			National Students Fictitious Engineering Program X			Carnegie Research/Doc Extensive Fictitious Engineering Program X		
	Number Take	Number Pass	Percent Pass	Number Take	Number Pass	Percent Pass	Number Take	Number Pass	Percent Pass	Number Take	Number Pass	Percent Pass
Total	318	281	88.4%	401	298	74.3%	8287	5956	71.9%	2307	1828	79.2%

The chart above can be calculated by averaging numbers of students who take the exam over each administration. However, the chart that follows requires care in calculating averages. See Appendix 3.G for explanation on how to calculate averages.

FIGURE 3.3 (Continued)

Averages for Eight Administrations From October 2002 Through April 2006

AM Exam

Subject	Number of Exam Qstns	FEPX Inst. Y Average Percent Correct	National FEPX Average Percent Correct	Inst. Y/ National	Carnegie Extensive FEPX Average Percent Correct	Inst. Y/ Carnegie
CHEMISTRY	11	66.7	61.5	108.5%	66.0	101.2%
COMPUTERS	7	77.2	60.4	127.7%	67.6	114.2%
DYNAMICS	9	65.0	57.5	113.1%	60.9	106.7%
ELECTRICAL CIRCUITS	12	47.9	45.2	106.0%	47.7	100.5%
ENGIN ECON	5	56.7	63.4	89.4%	68.3	83.0%
ETHICS	5	65.5	73.0	89.7%	71.6	91.5%
FLUID MECHANICS	8	55.3	58.6	94.3%	61.8	89.5%
MAT SCI/STR MATTER	8	60.3	55.2	109.3%	57.8	104.3%
MATH	24	64.5	59.5	108.3%	63.1	102.2%
MECH OF MATERIALS	8	61.9	58.1	106.7%	64.6	95.8%
STATICS	12	66.1	58.2	113.6%	61.0	108.4%
THERMODYNAMICS	11	72.3	48.1	150.2%	51.1	141.4%

PM Exam

Subject	Number of Exam Qstns	FEPX Inst. Y Average Percent Correct	National FEPX Average Percent Correct	Inst. Y/ National	Carnegie Extensive FEPX Average Percent Correct	Inst. Y/ Carnegie
CHEMISTRY	5	69.4	46.1	150.5%	50.6	137.4%
COMPUTERS	3	40.2	56.4	71.2%	62.2	64.6%
DYNAMICS	5	56.2	40.3	139.5%	41.7	134.9%
ELECTRICAL CIRCUITS	6	57.1	35.7	160.1%	36.4	157.0%
ENGIN ECON	3	49.7	43.6	113.9%	48.1	103.3%
ETHICS	3	80.2	75.0	106.9%	73.6	108.9%
FLUID MECHANICS	4	56.7	46.2	122.7%	52.7	107.6%
MAT SCI/STR MATTER	3	54.8	52.7	104.1%	54.5	100.7%
MATH	12	58.5	55.0	106.4%	60.0	97.5%
MECH OF MATERIALS	4	51.3	45.3	113.1%	47.2	108.7%
STATICS	6	60.9	56.2	108.3%	57.1	106.7%
THERMODYNAMICS	6	58.6	40.3	145.3%	48.1	121.7%

a single point in time. Consider how much the students' perceptions change over the years. If the program made some improvements, do the students' perceptions change to match the improvements made? Seniors may also be interviewed as they exit. They can comment on their general experience in the program. Examples of survey items by Criterion 3 outcomes a–k are given in Appendix 3.H.

Faculty surveys. Faculty can give their opinion on how well the seniors in any one year are performing. Again, this method should not be the only method, but it can be an important tool to use every five or six years to compare faculty opinions to student opinions. See Appendix 3.I for an example of a faculty survey.

Use of Assessment Evidence

Regardless of how effective your method is, if the results are not used and actions not taken on them, they are not effective. Chapter 4 goes into detail about how to interpret assessment evidence, once collected, and make decisions.

The final step is to document the process, assessment results, and decisions. Documentation of assessment evidence should indicate the outcome, how well the performance metric was met, a summary of the evidence, interpretation of the evidence, and decisions made. Appendix 3.J gives an exercise that can be used by an assessment committee to help determine what results show. Estell (2004, 2006) has presented a way to report course-based assessment through a *Faculty Course Assessment Report* (FCAR). Although he discusses the use of course grades (see above for why these may not be appropriate for assessment), the report format is worth reviewing.

References

Bennett, M. J. (1986). A developmental approach to training for intercultural sensitivity. *International Journal of Intercultural Relations, 10*(2), 179–195.

Bennett, M. J. (1993). Towards ethnorelativism: A developmental model of intercultural sensitivity. In M. Paige (Ed.), *Education for the intercultural experience*. Yarmouth, ME: Intercultural Press.

Estell, J. (2004, February). The faculty course assessment report. *Proceedings of the Best Assessment Processes VI Symposium. Terre Haute, IN: Rose-Hulman Institute of Technology.*

Estell, J. (2006). *Streamlining the assessment process with the Faculty Course Assessment Report.* Retrieved December 15, 2006, from http://www.ece.ufl.edu/secedha/meetings/2006/Estelle.pdf

Hake, R. R. (1998). Interactive engagement versus traditional methods: A six thousand student survey of mechanics test for introductory physics courses. *American Journal of Physics, 66,* 64–74.

Hake, R. R. (2002, December). Assessment of physics teaching methods. *Proceedings of the UNESCO-ASPEN Workshop on Active Learning in Physics.* Sri Lanka: University of Peradeniya.

Hake, R. R. (2004, August 19). Re: Pre-post testing in assessment. Message posted to POD, archived at http://listserv.nd.edu/cgi-bin/wa?A2=ind0408&L=pod&P=R9135&I=-3

Kurstedt, P. (1999, November). Lessons learned from piloting an employer feedback process for gathering EC 2000 Criteria a–k. *Proceedings of the Frontiers in Education Conference,* San Juan, Puerto Rico.

Leonard, M., & Nault, E. (2000, February). *Employer input for program improvement: Inviting business to the table.* 13th Annual South Carolina Association of Institutional Research Conference, Myrtle Beach, SC.

Litzinger, T. A., Lee, S. H., & Wise, J. C. (2004). Assessing readiness for self-directed learning. *Proceedings of the 2004 American Society for Engineering Education Conference and Exposition.* Retrieved January 15, 2007, from http://www.a-see.org/acPapers/2004-649_Final.pdf

Litzinger, T. A., Wise, J. C., & Lee, S. H. (2005). Self-directed learning readiness among undergraduate engineering students. *Journal of Engineering Education, 94*(2), 215–221.

McGourty, J., Sebastian, C., & Swart, W. (1998). Development of a comprehensive assessment program in engineering education. *Journal of Engineering Education, 87*(4), 355–361.

McGourty, J. M., & De Meuse, K. (2000). *The team developer: An assessment and skill building program.* New York: J. Wiley.

McGourty, J. M., Reynolds, J., Besterfield-Sacre, M., Shuman, L. J., & Wolfe, H. (2003). Using multi-source assessment and feedback processes to develop entrepreneurial skills in engineering students. *Proceedings of the 2003 American Society for Engineering Education Annual Conference and Exposition.* Retrieved January 15, 2007, from http://www.asee.org/acPapers/2003-1082_Final.pdf

McGourty, J. M., Shuman, L. J., Chimka, J., Besterfield-Sacre, M., & Wolfe, H. (2001). Multi-source feedback processes and student learning styles: Measuring the influence on learning outcomes. *Proceedings of the 2001 American Society for Engineering Education Conference and Exposition.* Retrieved January 15, 2007, from http://www.asee.org/acPapers/00715_2001.pdf

Middle States Commission on Higher Education. (2003). *Student learning assessment: Options and resources—A handbook.* Philadelphia: Author.

Nault, E., & Marr, J. (2002, June). *Structuring and unifying employer feedback.* Presentation at SUCCEED Annual Conference, Montreal.

Ohland, M., Pomeranz, H. R., & Feinstein, H. W. (2006, June). The comprehensive assessment of team member effectiveness: A new peer evaluation instrument. *Proceedings of the American Society for Engineering Education Annual Conference and Exposition,* Chicago.

Palomba, C. A., & Banta, T. W. (1999). *Assessment essentials: Planning, implementing, and improving assessment in higher education.* San Francisco: Jossey-Bass.

Rogers, G. (2003). Do grades make the grade for program assessment? Communications Link, ABET, INC. Retrieved December 15, 2006, from http://www.abet.org/Linked%20Documents-UPDATE/Assessment/Assessment%20Tips4.pdf

Stevens, D., & Levi, A. (2005). *Introduction to rubrics.* Sterling, VA: Stylus.

Suskie, L. (2004). *Assessing student learning: A common sense guide.* Bolton, MA: Anker.

Taggart, G., Phifer, S., Nixon, J., & Wood, M. (2001). *Rubrics: A handbook for construction and use.* Lanham, MD: Scarecrow Press.

Wagner, J. R., Finley, D., & McKetta, J. J. (1999, June). Development of a dynamic curriculum assessment examination. *Proceedings of the American Society for Engineering Education Annual Conference and Exposition,* Charlotte, NC.

Walvoord, B. E. (2004). *Assessment clear and simple: A practical guide for institutions, departments, and general education.* San Francisco: Jossey-Bass.

Walvoord, B., & Anderson, V. J. (1998). *Effective grading: A tool for learning and assessment.* San Francisco: Jossey-Bass.

APPENDIX 3.A

ASSESSMENT PLAN WORKSHEET

Team Worksheet to Determine Course-Based Assessment Methodology

(Team consists of faculty members who teach the courses identified as strongly related to this outcome in the curriculum/outcome matrix.)

Program Outcome Number: _____

Briefly paraphrase the Program Outcome: _____

Step 1: For each course identified under this outcome (see curriculum/outcome matrix), come to consensus on 1–3 course outcomes that best match the program outcome.

Step 2: Determine how to assess each of these 1–3 course outcomes in order to give a complete assessment of the program outcome (team should come to a consensus on the method, with agreement by the faculty member who teaches the course or is in charge of the course).

Course #	Paraphrase course outcome here	Assessment Method: Be as specific as possible	Assessment Process: Who will collect assessment, who will process assessment, and where will data be kept?	Assessment Standard: How will the faculty know if the outcome has been met?	Can this data be used for another program outcome? If so, which one?

(continued)

Team Worksheet to Determine Course-Based Assessment Methodology (Continued)

Examples

Program Outcome Number: 3c

Briefly paraphrase the Program Outcome: To demonstrate that graduates have an ability to design a system, component, or process to meet desired needs

Course #	Paraphrase course outcome here	Assessment Method: Be as specific as possible	Assessment Process: Who will collect assessment, who will process assessment, and where will data be kept?	Assessment Standard: How will the faculty know if the outcome has been met?	Can this data be used for another program outcome? If so, which one?
CIL 361	Integrate basic science and engineering knowledge to effectively solve technical problems	Test 3 will cover this outcome; 5 topics will be covered with 3 or more questions on each topic; 3 topics will involve solving technical problems with 2 topics dealing with basic science and engineering knowledge.	Test given in class and score for each question by individual students will be kept for database by [name]. Data will be summarized to note the number of students who get questions correct on each topic.	Excellent: 86% or more of the students get 2 or more questions correct on specific topic Average: 70–85% of students get 2 or 3 questions correct on topic Poor: fewer than 70% of students get 2 or 3 questions correct on topic Outcome met if 4 out of 5 topics have at least an "average"	No

Program Outcome Number: 3c

Briefly paraphrase the Program Outcome: To demonstrate that graduates have an ability to design a system, component, or process to meet desired needs

Course #	Paraphrase course outcome here	Assessment Method: Be as specific as possible	Assessment Process: Who will collect assessment, who will process assessment, and where will data be kept?	Assessment Standard: How will the faculty know if the outcome has been met?	Can this data be used for another program outcome? If so, which one?
CIL 451	2. Define the design project 5. Identify possible solutions to a design problem 7. Communicate the design project	Oral presentation of capstone project Use of rubric to judge each part of the design process as well as oral communication	Step 1: Faculty team to define the rubric to be used Step 2: Faculty make and keep videotapes of oral presentations of capstone project Step 3: Review of videotapes by panel of four reviewers each January and May Step 4: Keep spreadsheet of rubric scores on database	Each topic on rubric will be met by at least 85% of the students.	3·g—oral communication

APPENDIX 3.B

EXAMPLES OF RUBRICS FOR SENIOR DESIGN PROJECTS

Example 1: Rubric Used by Mercer University Bachelor of Science in Engineering

The following team assessment form is used by project clients (typically from industry) and technical advisors (faculty members). This form refers to a Written CDR (Critical Design Review), which specifies the details of the final review of senior design projects.

Client/Tech Advisor Team Assessment

1. Please circle the rating that best describes your perceptions of the team for each of the three questions below.

a. As far as you could tell, did all members of the group share in the team's responsibilities?

Some members did no work at all.	A few members did most of the work.	The work was generally shared by all members.	Everyone did an equal share of the work.

b. Which of the following best describes the level of conflict that you observed among group members at meetings?

Open warfare: still unresolved	Disagreements were resolved with considerable difficulty	There were disagreements, but they were easily resolved	No conflict, everyone seemed to agree on what to do

c. From your perspective, how productive was the team overall?

Accomplished some but not all of the project's requirements	Met the project requirements but could have done much better	Efficiently accomplished goals that we set for ourselves		Went way beyond what we had to do, exceeding even our own goals

2a. Please rate the written Critical Design Review on the students' ability to Develop a Test Plan.

Unacceptable		Acceptable		Excellent
1	2	3	4	5

Did the team finish building such that some or all testing could occur (i.e., was the Test Plan Implemented)?

YES NO

If YES, please answer questions 2b and 2c.

2b. Please rate the written Critical Design Review on the students' ability to CONDUCT experiments in the test plan.

Unacceptable		Acceptable		Excellent
1	2	3	4	5

2c. Please rate the written Critical Design Review on the students' ability to ANALYZE results obtained from execution of test plan.

Unacceptable		Acceptable		Excellent
1	2	3	4	5

3. Write a brief description of the problems you encountered in working with this group and how they were resolved.

Example 1: Rubric Used by Mercer University Bachelor of Science in Engineering (Continued)

4. Over all, how effective would you say this team has been at working together, based on your experience with other project teams?

Very ineffective	Ineffective	Effective	Very effective
1	2	3	4

5. Please distribute 100 points among the members of the team, based on your perceptions of each member's contribution to the team's efforts. Use integers only. No two people should receive the same number of points.

Name:	# of Points
Total	**100**

6. Please rate the overall oral <u>Critical Design Review</u> on the students' ability to communicate to a specialized audience (technical personnel in their field).

Unacceptable		Acceptable		Excellent
1	2	3	4	5

(continued)

7. Please rate the overall written Critical Design Review on the students' ability to communicate to a specialized audience (technical personnel in their field).

Unacceptable		Acceptable		Excellent
1	2	3	4	5

8. Please rate the executive summary of Critical Design Review on the students' ability to communicate to a generalized audience (general public).

Unacceptable		Acceptable		Excellent
1	2	3	4	5

9. Please rate the executive summary of Critical Design Review on the students' ability to communicate to a generalized audience (nontechnical management in their organization).

Unacceptable		Acceptable		Excellent
1	2	3	4	5

Reprinted with permission from Mercer University

Example 2: Senior Design Project Rubric Used by Mechatronics Engineering Program at NC State

Dimension	Poor (1 point)	Average (2 points)	Excellent (3 points)	Score
Introduction	• No attempt to explain context in which project was done • Paper does not indicate why design process is important	• Discussion of why design process is important is disorganized or missing some issues	• Clearly explains purpose of the design project within the context of the course • Clearly organized discussion of why design process is important	
Problem Identification & Working Criteria	• Too broad, not specific objectives • Few criteria • Contradictory, incomplete, or confused criteria	• Somewhat specific, but not clear objectives • Several criteria • Some criteria detailed, but missed one or more criteria	• Clear, explicit, and measurable objectives • Many criteria • Complete and logical criteria clearly detailing mechatronic problem	
Research Sources	• Reported only one source, or few sources of one type • Reported irrelevant or not credible sources	• Reports only a few sources (of few types) • Most sources are relevant and credible, but not all	• Report many sources (of varying types) • Sources are relevant and credible	
Summarize Research Findings	• Lack of or poor summary	• Summary too broad, not precise, or some irrelevant statements	• Summary is accurate, precise, and relevant	
Project Management Team	• Lack or poor description of team structure and/or individual roles and responsibilities • Lack of or poor description of scheduling and tasks	• Describes some but not all aspects of team structure and/or individual roles and responsibilities • Incomplete description of scheduling and tasks	• Clearly and completely describes team structure and individual roles and responsibilities • Clearly and completely describes issues related to scheduling and completion of tasks	

Project Management: Resources	• Poor description of acquisition of materials, tools, and other resources required • Lack of or sketchy budget included	• Description of the acquisition of materials, tools, and other resources required is missing some details • Budget includes some details, but is not complete	• Clearly and completely describe the acquisition of materials, tools, and other resources required • Detailed budget included	
Identification of Feasible Alternatives	• One idea identified • Process to identify alternative mechatronic designs not described • Minimal connection between research and alternatives identified	• Few or very similar ideas identified • Process to identify alternative mechatronic designs not fully described • Refers to research, but connection between research and alternatives not established	• Multiple ideas of different types identified • Process to identify alternative mechatronic designs fully described • Alternatives clearly based on research	
Analytical Method	• Did not use math, physics or other science to examine mechatronic problem • Did not incorporate computer-based tools to illustrate analysis	• Used a math, physics or other science, but did not explain well how it related to the mechatronic problem • Incorporated a poor example of the principle with computer-based tools	• Explained well how math, physics, mechanics, electronics, or other science and engineering principles were appropriate to the mechatronic problem • Used computer-based tools to show a good example of this principles relationship to problem	
Selection and Analysis of Alternatives	• Process is not described • No evidence of planning • No decision • No connection between analysis and working criteria	• Process is not fully described • Some evidence of planning • Two alternatives chosen • Some connection between analysis and working criteria, but unclear	• Clearly explains process for narrowing number of alternatives • One alternative chosen • Clear and documented connection between analysis and working criteria	

(continued)

Example 2 (Continued)

Dimension	Poor (1 point)	Average (2 points)	Excellent (3 points)	Score
Develop Project	• Description of construction of mechatronic device lacks detail; not replicable	• Detailed description of construction of mechatronic device but lacks some key details	• Detailed description of construction of mechatronic device • Clear step-by-step description • Can be replicated	
Component Selection	• Did not successfully select any components best suited to perform desired tasks	• Successfully selected some, but not all, components best suited to perform desired tasks	• Successfully selected all components best suited to perform desired tasks	
Project Testing	• Limited or no testing described • No description of what worked and what did not work and why	• Confused or only one type of test described • Described partly what worked but not all details about what worked, did not work and why	• Multiple types of testing • Described well what worked and what did not work and why	
Analysis of Results	• No summary of final design • Limited strengths and weaknesses outlined • Does not explain how results compared to original design	• Final design explained • Emphasis on strengths or weaknesses, but not both • Does not explain well how results compared to original design	• Key components of final design are detailed • Both strengths and weaknesses detailed • Explained well how results compared to original design	

Conclusion	• No lessons learned summarized • Does not explain whether project met design objectives		• Few lessons learned are outlined, but are not tied to specific aspects of the project or research • Summarization is unclear and/or disorganized • Little attempt to describe whether project met design objectives	• Lessons learned both positive and negative are outlined, and are tied to specific aspects of the process or research • Summarization is clear, organized, and the degree to which project met design objective is clearly and completely explained
Project Schedule	• Tasks and deadlines are not synchronized		• Tasks are not adequately delineated • Some deadlines are reasonable	• Detailed task statements and reasonable deadlines
Design Drawings	• No design solution, or draws solution that is unsupported by design needs.		• Drawing is incomplete or inaccurate	• Draws accurate solutions supported by design needs
Overall Design Process	• Paper shows students did not follow or did not understand the design process		• Paper shows students understood most but not all steps in design process	• Paper show students clearly understood and used the design process
Focus and Flow of Paper	• No transition between sections • Organization within most sections lacks coherence; ideas not clear; and writing not focused		• Some transition between sections • Writing clear in some sections, but not all, and some sections are focused, but others ramble	• Transition between sections is clear and natural • Organization of ideas within all sections and between sections is clear • Within sections writing is focused and supportive

(continued)

Example 2 (Continued)

Dimension	Poor (1 point)	Average (2 points)	Excellent (3 points)	Score
Style	• Sentence structure is too simple or monotonous and does not place emphasis on important ideas; word choice is clichéd, dull, inconsistent, or unsuitable to audience or purpose	• Sentences are clear and incorporate proper emphasis; they are written at a level appropriate to the audience; word choice is suitable to the audience and purpose and avoids wordiness and redundancy	• Sentence structure is varied and highly readable; the choice of words is fresh and interesting, making the ideas memorable and powerful	
Grammar	• The kind and number of grammatical and mechanical errors seriously impede the progress of the reader and undermine the credibility of the writer • Sources are documented inadequately	• Reader is not impeded by grammatical and mechanical errors • Writing demonstrates general mastery of Standard Written English • Sources are documented adequately, using a documentation that is appropriate to the audience	• Writing has virtually no problems with grammar or mechanics, demonstrating a mature command of Standard Written English	
Ethics	• Did not identify and evaluate ethical ramifications related to design project	• Moderately identified and evaluated ethical ramifications related to design project	• Identified and evaluated ethical ramifications related to design project	
Professional Responsibilities	• Professional responsibilities were not included in design criteria	• Professional responsibilities were somewhat included in design criteria	• Professional responsibilities were included in design criteria	

The capstone project demonstrated engineering practice that shows students' ability to effectively manage the following issues:	Sufficiently Demonstrated	NOT Sufficiently Demonstrated
Economic issues related to project		
Environmental issues related to project		
Sustainability of product or process		
Manufacturability of product or process		
Ethical concerns related to project		
Health and safety concerns of project		
Social impact of project		
Political impacts of project		

Developed by Spurlin, Fahmy, Alderman for Mechatronic Engineering Program, NCSU.

Adapted from Spurlin, Robbins, Lavelle, NCSU, College of Engineering. Reprinted with permission.

APPENDIX 3.C

RUBRIC FOR ASSESSING LAB REPORTS

Assign "1, 2, 3, or 4" for each category in the first column.

	1 Beginning or incomplete	2 Developing	3 Accomplished	4 Exemplary	Score
Abstract/Summary	Several major aspects of the experiment are missing; student displays a lack of understanding about how to write an abstract	Abstract misses one or more major aspects of carrying out the experiment or the results	Abstract references most of the major aspects of the experiment; some minor details are missing	Abstract contains reference to all major aspects of carrying out the experiment and the results; well written	
Introduction	Very little background information provided or information is incorrect	Some introductory information, but still missing some major points	Introduction is nearly complete, missing some minor points	Introduction complete and well written; provides all necessary background principles for the experiment	
Experimental procedure	Missing several important experimental details or not written in paragraph format	Written in paragraph format; still missing some important experimental details	Written in paragraph format; important experimental details are covered; some minor details missing	Well-written in paragraph format, all experimental details are covered	

Results: data, figures, graphs, tables, etc.	Figures, graphs, tables contain errors or are poorly constructed; have missing titles, captions, or numbers; units missing or incorrect; etc.	Most figures, graphs, tables OK; some still missing some important or required features	All figures, graphs, tables are correctly drawn, but some have minor problems or could still be improved	All figures, graphs, tables are correctly drawn, are numbered, and contain titles/captions
Discussion	Very incomplete or incorrect interpretation of trends and comparison of data indicating a lack of understanding of results	Some of the results have been correctly interpreted and discussed; partial but incomplete understanding of results is still evident	Almost all of the results have been correctly interpreted and discussed; only minor improvements are needed	All important trends and data comparisons have been interpreted correctly and discussed; good understanding of results is conveyed
Conclusions	Conclusions missing or missing the important points	Conclusions regarding major points are drawn, but many are misstated, indicating a lack of understanding	All important conclusions have been drawn; could be better stated	All important conclusions have been clearly made; student shows good understanding
Spelling, grammar, sentence structure	Frequent grammar and/or spelling errors; writing style is rough and immature	Occasional grammar/spelling errors; generally readable with some rough spots in writing style	Less than 3 grammar/spelling errors; mature, readable style	All grammar/spelling correct and very well-written
Appearance and formatting	Sections out of order, too much handwritten copy, sloppy formatting	Sections in order, contains the minimum allowable amount of handwritten copy; formatting is rough but readable	All sections in order; formatting generally good but could still be improved	All sections in order; well-formatted, very readable

Reprinted with permission from Maury Balik, Materials Science and Engineering Program, North Carolina State University

APPENDIX 3.D

RUBRIC FOR TEAMWORK EVALUATION

Use the following criteria as the basis for evaluating yourself and your team members. Place a score (1, 2, or 3) for each dimension in the table below.

	Dimension	Poor (1 point)	Average (2 points)	Excellent (3 points)
I	Effort	• Did little, almost no work or did all the work • Did not support team members	• Did average amount of work, but could have done more • Supported team members, but could have helped others more	• Did fair share of work • Supported others in their share
II	Contribution to Discussions and Decisions	• Made little contribution to team discussions and decisions • Contribution was of poor quality	• Made average contributions to team discussions and decisions • Contribution was of average quality	• Contributed beyond average to the team discussions and decisions • Contribution was of high quality
III	Team Spirit	• Removed from commitment to the team effort, or overbearing and inconsiderate of team members	• Respected team members, considerate and cooperative, more than half of the time	• Exceptionally helpful, respectful, and considerate of other team members
IV	Dependability	• Unreliable, skipped many meetings or arrived late • Generally poorly prepared	• Dependable, attended most team meetings, generally punctual • Prepared more than half of the time	• Exceptionally dependable, always attended meetings on time • Fully prepared

V	**Communication**	• Team member continuously talking or never talks • Argues inappropriately	• Most of the time listens and speaks appropriately • Rarely argues inappropriately	• Always listens and speaks appropriately • Never argues inappropriately
VI	**In-class Presentations and Discussion**	• Little, if any, participation in class presentation and discussion	• Contributed fair share to class presentation and discussion, but could have done more	• Exceptionally valuable contribution to the team success in planning and presenting results to class and a major contributor to successful discussion
VII	**Overall Evaluation**	• Poor • I would not work with this person again	• Desirable • I probably would work with this person again	• Outstanding • I would definitely work with this person again

NAMES OF TEAMMATES	I	II	III	IV	V	VI	VII
(*Self*)							

This rubric, reprinted with permission, was modified for the Bachelor of Science in Mechatronics Engineering, North Carolina State University, from the rubric found on this website during January 2003: http://www-geology.ucdavis.edu/~hnr094/HNR_094_PeerEval.html

Robert J. Twiss, HNR 094-5: Science and Pseudo-Science, Davis Honors Challenge, University of California–Davis, Spring 1997.

APPENDIX 3.E

RUBRIC FOR ORAL PRESENTATIONS

Ref #	Dimension	Poor (1 point)	Average (2 points)	Excellent (3 points)	Score
1	Organization	• Sequence of information is difficult to follow • Lacks beginning or ending or beginning or ending inappropriate • Does not move smoothly from one idea to the next	• Student presents information in logical sequence which audience can follow • Uses an appropriate beginning or ending • Moves smoothly from one idea to the next some of the time	• Information in logical, interesting sequence that audience can follow • Uses an engaging beginning and/or thoughtful ending • Moves smoothly from one idea to the next all of the time	
2	Content Depth	• Student does not have grasp of information • Cannot answer questions	• Student is able to demonstrate basic concepts • Can answer questions, but not fully	• Student demonstrates full knowledge • Can answer questions fully and accurately	
3	Content Accuracy	• Information included is sufficiently inaccurate that the listener cannot depend on the presentation as a source of accurate information	• Enough errors are made to distract a knowledgeable listener, but some information is accurate	• Information is correct and accurate	
4	Grammar and Spelling	• Presentation has three or more spelling and/or grammatical errors	• Presentation has no more than two misspellings and/or grammatical errors	• Presentation has no misspellings or grammatical errors	
5	Connection to Audience	• Level of presentation is too elementary or too sophisticated	• Level of presentation is generally appropriate	• Level of presentation is appropriate to the audience	

6	Graphics and Communication Aids	• Superfluous graphics or no graphics	• Graphics relate to text and presentation and contribute to the quality of the presentation • Some material may not be supported by communication aids	• Graphics explain and reinforce screen text and enhance the presentation
7	Visual Impact of Slides	• Font is too small to be easily seen • Too much information is included • Unimportant information is highlighted	• Font is appropriate for reading but could be larger for better • Most of the information is appropriate • Unimportant information or too much detail was included	• Font is large enough to be seen by all • Details are minimized so that main points stand out • No unimportant information was included
8	Context	• No discussion of application and relevance	• Some discussion of application and relevance	• Thorough discussion of application and relevance
9	Professionalism	• Personal appearance is inappropriate for the occasion and audience • No members of the team were on time • The team members handled any technical difficulties unprofessionally • No acknowledgment of sources of support	• Personal appearance is somewhat inappropriate for the occasion and audience • One member of the team was not on time • The team members handled some part of the presentation unprofessionally • Some acknowledgment of sources of support	• Personal appearance is completely appropriate for the occasion and the audience • All members of the team were ready on time • The team members handled the entire presentation professionally, even if there were technical difficulties • Full acknowledgment of sources of support

(continued)

RUBRIC FOR ORAL PRESENTATIONS (Continued)

Ref #	Dimension	Poor (1 point)	Average (2 points)	Excellent (3 points)	Score
10	**Presentation Style and Delivery**	• Listeners are so distracted by the presenter's apparent difficulty with presentation that they cannot focus on the ideas presented • Read notes or slides and did not look away from notes or slides • Body language shows obvious nervous tension • No effort to make eye contact • Monotone voice	• Listeners can follow the presentation, but some difficulty in presentation is distracting from ideas presented • Read some notes or slides but also looked away from notes and slides • Body language shows some nervous tension • Occasional unsustained eye contact • Voice with some inflection	• Listeners are captivated by the presentation and are very focused on ideas presented • Referred to notes or slides but did not read notes or slides • Body language is relaxed • Consistent eye contact • Voice is clear with interesting modulation	
11	Continuity	• Transition between speakers was awkward and unprofessional	• There was some awkwardness when transitioning between speakers but some was smooth and professional	• Transition between speakers was smooth and professional	
12	Timeliness	• Entire presentation was 5 minutes or more over or under allotted time	• Entire presentation was within 2–5 minutes of allotted time	• Entire presentation was within 2 minutes of allotted time	

Adapted from Spurlin, Robbins, Lavelle, NCSU, College of Engineering; Fall 2002.

Developed by Spurlin, Fahmy, Alderman, NCSU, College of Engineering; Fall 2004. Reprinted with permission.

APPENDIX 3.F

RUBRIC FOR PAPER RELATED TO CONTEMPORARY ISSUES

Dimension	Poor (1 point)	Average (2 points)	Excellent (3 points)	Score
Relevance of Topic	Topic is not relevant to CI.	Topic is somewhat relevant to CI	Topic is highly relevant to a CI	
Writing	Text is inadequate.	Text is fairly choppy, or poor transitions between sections. Some concepts are not explained in layman's terms.	Transitions between paragraphs and sections are smooth. Ideas are presented in language appropriate to a layman.	
References	All reference materials are poorly chosen, or no references used.	Text is partially synthesized from resources, but much material appears to be from a single source. Many of the cited references are inappropriate, e.g., websites, etc.	Text is a synthesis of information from a number of appropriate reference sources, including books and journal articles.	
Global Context	Topic is not discussed in a global context.	Topic is discussed in a global context to some degree, but could be better.	Topic is discussed fully in a global context.	
Societal Context	Topic is not discussed in a societal context.	Topic is discussed in a societal context to some degree, but could be better.	Topic is discussed fully in a societal context.	
Ethical Context	Topic is not discussed in an ethical context.	Topic is discussed in an ethical context to some degree, but could be better.	Topic is discussed fully in an ethical context.	
Lifelong Learning Skills	Independent learning skills are poor.	Some evidence of independent learning skills, but they could be improved.	Shows strong independent learning skills.	

Adapted from Biomedical Engineering assessment, NCSU

Developed by Spurlin, Fahmy, Alderman, NCSU, Mechatronics Program, College of Engineering. Reprinted with permission.

APPENDIX 3.G

ANALYZING FUNDAMENTALS OF ENGINEERING EXAMINATION

To calculate overall pass rates, it is straightforward to calculate the average number of students who take the exam over each administration. However, the average of each subscore needs to be calculated carefully. One exam subscore's calculations are given here: It is necessary to calculate the number of possible correct questions based on the number of students who took the exam. Then add up this number, and derive an average for either each academic year or for the four years. An example of the calculation is shown below:

Step 1: In a spreadsheet, record data from each administration:

Test Date	Number of Students Who Take Exam From Institution's Engineering Program	National Number of Students Who Take Exam
Oct-05	35	1075
Apr-05	36	890
Oct-04	45	864
Apr-04	42	1544
Oct-03	36	902
Apr-03	40	1560

AM Subject for ETHICS			
Test Date	Number of Exam Questions	Institution's Engr Program's Average Percent Correct	National Average Percent Correct
Oct-05	5	52	63
Apr-05	5	56	62
Oct-04	5	66	70
Apr-04	5	77	80
Oct-03	5	57	78
Apr-03	5	77	76

Step 2: Calculate the total of all possible correct items. Multiply the number of items on the subtest by the number of students who take the test. For example, for October 2005: $5 \times 35 = 175$ possible correct items for the institution's program.

Step 3: Calculate the total number of items that were answered correctly for the test date. Multiply the number of items on the subtest by the number of students who take the test by percentage of correct responses. For example, for October 2005: $5 \times 35 \times 52\% = 91$ items correctly answered for the institution's program.

(*continued*)

ANALYZING FUNDAMENTALS OF ENGINEERING EXAMINATION (Continued)

Step 4: Add numbers calculated for steps 2 and 3 for a total number for the six administrations.

Step 5: Calculate the average correct percentage for the six administrations. Divide the total number of correctly answered questions by the total possible correct items.

Test Date	Number of All Possibly Correct Items for Institution's Program	Number of Correctly Answered Questions for Institution's Program	Average of All Administrations for Institution's Program	Number of All Possibly Correct Items Nationally	Number of Correctly Answered Questions Nationally	Average of All Administrations Nationally
Oct-05	175	91		5375	3386.25	
Apr-05	180	100.8		4450	2759	
Oct-04	225	148.5		4320	3024	
Apr-04	210	161.7		7720	6176	
Oct-03	180	102.6		4510	3517.8	
Apr-03	200	154		7800	5928	
Totals	1170	758.6	64.8%	34475	24791.05	72.5%

These data are fictitious but similar to the date available to any institution. The method for analysis was developed by Jim Nau and Joni Spurlin, North Carolina State University.

APPENDIX 3.H

SURVEY QUESTIONS USED BY NORTH CAROLINA STATE UNIVERSITY ENGINEERING PROGRAMS FOR ASSESSMENT OF ABET CRITERIA 3.a–k OUTCOMES

Survey Question Items Related to ABET Criteria	a	b	c	d	e	f	g	h	i	j	k
Please rate the preparation you received in your program for the ability to apply knowledge of mathematics and science.	x										
To what extent do you think your college education contributed to your knowledge in applying scientific methods of inquiry?	x	x									
To what extent do you think your college education contributed to your knowledge in using mathematics skills?	x										
Engineering lab courses provided me with a good foundation for practical application of the knowledge I gained in my program.	x		x								
Please rate the preparation you received in your program for the ability to apply knowledge from your major in engineering or computer science.	x										
To what extent do you think your college education contributed to your ability to critically analyze ideas and information?		x									
To what extent do you think your college education contributed to your ability to plan and carry out projects independently?		x									

(continued)

Survey Questions Used by North Carolina State University Engineering Programs (Continued)

Survey Question Items Related to ABET Criteria	a	b	c	d	e	f	g	h	i	j	k
My senior design projects(s) provided a good opportunity to integrate my learning in major and nonmajor courses.		x	x								
Please rate the preparation you received in your program for the ability to analyze and interpret data.		x									
Please rate the preparation you received in your program for the ability to design and conduct experiments.		x									
Design activities were integrated throughout my program.			x								
Please rate the preparation you received in your program for the ability to design a system, component, or process to meet desired needs.			x								
Please rate the preparation you received in your program for the ability to function on multidisciplinary teams.				x							
To what extent do you think your college education contributed to your ability to function as part of a team?				x							
To what extent do you think your college education contributed to your ability to lead or guide others?				x							
To what extent do you think your college education contributed to your ability to work with people from diverse backgrounds?				x							
To what extent do you think your college education contributed to your knowledge in enhancing analytic skills?					x						
Please rate the preparation you received in your program for the ability to identify, formulate, and solve engineering problems.					x						

Statement					
The course work activities in my program as a whole required synthesis, creativity, and open-ended thinking.				x	
Please rate the preparation you received in your program for an understanding of professional and ethical responsibility.			x		
To what extent do you think your college education contributed to your knowledge in recognizing and acting upon ethical principles?			x		
To what extent do you think your college education contributed to your comprehension skills (understanding written information)?		x			
To what extent do you think your college education contributed to your listening skills?		x			
To what extent do you think your college education contributed to your speaking skills?		x			
To what extent do you think your college education contributed to your writing skills?		x			
My program included enough classroom presentations for me to gain good oral presentation skills.		x			
My program included enough written reports for me to gain good report-writing skills.		x			
Please rate the preparation you received in your program for a broad education necessary to understand the impact of engineering solutions in a global and societal context.	x				
To what extent do you think your college education contributed to your ability to work with people from diverse backgrounds?	x				
To what extent do you think your college education contributed to your understanding of how science and technology influence everyday life?	x				
To what extent do you think your college education contributed to your understanding of issues and problems facing the world?	x	x			

(continued)

Survey Questions Used by North Carolina State University Engineering Programs (Continued)

Survey Question Items Related to ABET Criteria	a	b	c	d	e	f	g	h	i	j	k
To what extent do you think your college education contributed to your understanding of diverse culture and values?								x			
To what extent do you think your college education contributed to your understanding of the present as it relates to historical events?								x			
Please rate the preparation you received in your program for a recognition of the need for, and the ability to, engage in lifelong learning.									x		
To what extent do you think your college education contributed to your valuing learning as a lifelong process?									x		
My program provided an adequate knowledge of contemporary issues.										x	
My program included enough computing exercises for me to gain a good foundation in computing skills.											x
Please rate the preparation you received in your program for the ability to use modern engineering tools necessary for engineering practice.											x
Please rate the preparation you received in your program for the ability to use the techniques and skills necessary for engineering practice.											x
To what extent do you think your college education contributed to your developing computer skills?											x

Survey developed under leadership of Nancy Whelchel, Assistant Director for Survey Research, University Planning and Analysis, North Carolina State University

FACULTY OPINION SURVEY ON STUDENT'S PERFORMANCE

For each outcome that has a course YOU teach in column 2, please rate the percentage of students in that course who you feel have achieved that outcome.

INSTRUCTIONS:

For each outcome:

Step 1: Circle the course(s) that you are teaching this semester.

Step 2: Think about the ability students should have by the time they graduate and are ready for employment. Based on that level of ability, what percentage of students in your course would you consider to have each level of ability on each of the outcomes listed below?

- Excellent ability in this area
- Very Good, has just a little more to learn
- Average, has more to learn
- Below Average, has a lot more to learn
- Poor, has almost no ability in this area
- Not applicable or not observed

(continued)

FACULTY OPINION SURVEY (Continued)

Step 3: In the comments sections below each table, write specific areas of weakness you have noted in these students.

(The table below is an EXAMPLE: listed below are some examples of learning outcomes/specific skills that could be asked; add others as relevant to your program.)

Specific Learning Outcome	Course No. (Circle your course no.)	Put percentage of students in your course that fall under each category below on each outcome to the left.					
		Excellent ability in this area	Very Good, has just a little more to learn	Average, has more to learn	Below Average, has a lot more to learn	Poor, has almost no ability in this area	Not applicable or not observed
Demonstrate competency in applying mathematical skills to engineering problem solving	201 210 302 303 415 425 495						
Demonstrate competency in applying principles of chemistry and physics to engineering problem solving	201 210 302 303 415 425						

Assimilate knowledge of contemporary social and economic issues into the approach to and solution of engineering problems	303 401 402 404			
Show understanding of the mechanisms by which machines, devices, and systems operate	201 210 302 303 415 425 495			
Demonstrate understanding of society and design systems	201 301 350			
Possess an ability to find and use information, and to discriminate between fact and opinion	201 210 302 303 415 425 495			

Specific Learning Outcome	Course No. (Circle your course no.)	Put percentage of students in your course that fall under each category below on each outcome to the left.					
		Excellent ability in this area	Very Good, has just a little more to learn	Average, has more to learn	Below Average, has a lot more to learn	Poor, has almost no ability in this area	Not applicable or not observed
Draw on understanding of historical and contemporary issues in approach to engineering problem solving	302 303 401 402 495						
(Add other questions as relevant)							

Considering the outcomes above, were there any specific skills, knowledge, or abilities that the students lacked, or had a weakness in, that need to be addressed? If so, please describe below:

Survey used at College of Engineering, North Carolina State University

APPENDIX 3.J

EXERCISE FOR FACULTY TO USE TO INTERPRET ASSESSMENT DATA

Use this exercise with the program's Assessment Committee. This example is for one outcome, but can be used for any and all outcomes.

Step 1: Review the standard, performance criteria, or metric for the outcome. What level of achievement is to be attained by your graduates? Review previous assessment cycle's evidence, findings, and recommended changes. What changes were made, when?

Step 2: Only analyze the data that relates to the outcome. Collect together all the evidence that relates to that outcome. Determine the quantity of data that is best reflective of your program. For example, if the response rate on a survey is less than 25%, should this data be considered? What is an appropriate sample size for using a sample of student work?

Step 3: Interpret and summarize the data. Below are some questions to consider:

- Does the students' performance show that they meet your metric for this outcome?
- Is the data consistent? (typically within 3–5%)
- Does the percentage of the data increase or decrease over time? (typically an increase or decrease of more than 3–5% is considered "change")
- How does this evidence compare to all engineering programs at your institution, if available? (typically more than 5–8% difference is considered "different")
- How do the modifications or changes to the program or curriculum since the last assessment cycle impact the interpretation of this data?
- Is part or all of the outcome met? Is one dimension of the outcome an area of strength or concern?
- Is there a positive or negative trend over the past few years?
- Does one assessment method provide better quality data? How would

you compare the results from the senior design course with assessment within a junior-level course?

- Are there areas where their performance is adequate but where you would like to see a higher level of performance?

Step 4: Recommend modifications that the program needs to make based on the findings from step 3. The following types of modifications can be recommended:

- Modify learning outcome
- Modify assessment method
- Change performance metric
- Change order of material within a course
- Change order of courses or add more courses into curriculum
- Increase the number of lab sessions or problem sessions within a course
- Conduct more in-depth assessment of the cause of the issue during the next academic year
- Modify content within a course

Step 5: Document the summary of the evidence and the recommendations and discuss with entire program faculty.

Step 6: Document the final decisions about the findings and modifications the department wants to make. Be sure to note any procedures that need to be followed for this modification to take place. For example, to add or modify a course, approval may be needed from the department curriculum committee and others. Ensure that procedures are followed.

Step 7: Next assessment cycle, review the above results; follow modifications, if any; and consider new data.

4

USING ASSESSMENT RESULTS
FOR IMPROVING
STUDENT LEARNING

Barbara M. Moskal

The primary focus of this chapter is on the use of assessment results for the improvement of undergraduate student learning at the program level. The reason for concentrating on programs rather than courses or institutions is that the Accreditation Board for Engineering and Technology (ABET) accredits programs. Although ABET accredits both undergraduate and graduate programs in engineering, the majority of participating institutions select to have their undergraduate programs accredited rather than their graduate programs, because graduation from an accredited undergraduate program is considered to be appropriate preparation for an entry-level engineer. Many of the techniques discussed in this chapter, however, may be transferred to the graduate level. (For more information on the use of assessment in graduate education, see chapter 5.)

In order to collect useful data, the program-level assessment process needs to be planned before it is implemented. Collecting and analyzing data that cannot eventually be used for a purpose, whether that purpose be evaluating students' knowledge or informing the instructional process, wastes the researchers', instructors', and students' time. From the beginning of the assessment process, a plan should be established that addresses how the collected information will be used. This plan informs the methods for data collection, analysis, interpretation, and use. In order to develop such a plan, it is necessary to understand the phases of the assessment process as well as the levels at which assessment may occur.

There are a number of different models in the engineering education literature that describe the assessment process. These models vary based on discipline and academic level. Across most of these models, there are four common phases: (1) planning the assessment process based on desired student learning, (2) implementing the assessment plan, (3) analyzing and interpreting the collected data, and (4) using data to improve student learning and the assessment process itself (McGourty, Sabastian, & Swart, 1998; Rogers, 2006b). These phases can be conceptualized as forming a loop, as illustrated in Figure 4.1. As this figure suggests, at the conclusion of the fourth phase, the process begins again with a new or revised assessment plan and with a new or revised instructional program. Assessment information not only informs the process of instruction; it also informs future assessment activities. Positive changes to either of these can help to improve student learning. Instruction can be redesigned in a manner that better supports student learning; assessment can be redesigned in a manner that provides more complete or accurate information that may then be used to improve student learning.

Another model of the assessment process that is prevalent throughout

FIGURE 4.1
Model of the Assessment Process

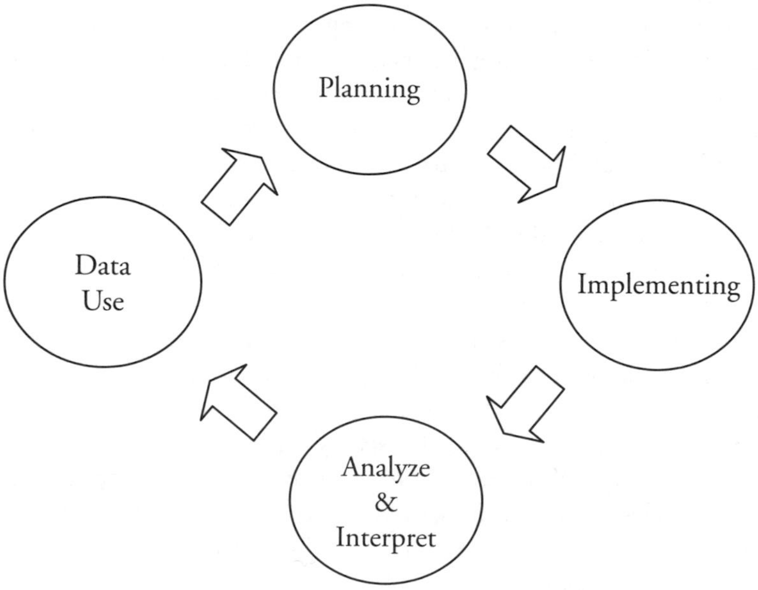

the engineering education literature is the double or multiple loop model (Bailey, Floersheim, & Ressler, 2002; Shaeiwitz, 1998). This model recognizes that there are typically at least two levels at which information is collected and used to support program assessment and improvement: course level and program level. In the double or multiple loop models, information is collected and used at the course level by the instructor. This may be conceived as a single loop at the course level or as multiple loops for each course represented. Some of this information as well as additional information is collected and used to improve the program, resulting in another loop. Information may also be shared across programs within a given institution. In this model, a series of nested loops is embedded throughout the assessment system, allowing for the examination of progress toward the desired outcomes throughout the assessment process (see Figure 2.1 in chapter 2 for an example of this type of model). This is conceptualized as a double or multiple loop, where information is continually being used, either by the instructor, by the program, or between programs, with the purpose of improving student learning. As described by Shaeiwitz (1998), the multiple loop structure supports ongoing assessment as a methodology for validating the instructional process itself. Each loop provides further verification as to whether students are achieving the desired level of learning.

The primary emphasis of this chapter is on two phases of the assessment process: analyzing and interpreting data and using data to improve student learning. As suggested by the double or multiple loop model, this data may be collected at either the course or the program level. Examples from each level and how information acquired through assessment is used to make decisions for the improvement of the larger program will be discussed.

Basic Definitions

Before beginning the discussion of using assessment information to improve student learning, it is important to develop shared definitions for several assessment terms. A summary of the terms and definitions used in this book is provided in the Glossary. Each definition is consistent with those used by ABET as part of its Engineering Criteria (ABET, 2005). There are several of these concepts that are especially important to this chapter: performance criteria, "faculty evaluator," and "ABET evaluator."

Performance Criteria

Once program educational objectives and program outcomes have been identified, efforts are needed to define how the faculty evaluator will know whether or not the program outcome has been reached. Performance criteria are statements that clearly define how a performance will be measured and the criteria that suggest success or lack of success in reaching the desired outcome. For example, a statement of success may be that 80 percent of senior-level students will correctly respond to a given problem that is designed to measure the application of mathematical models to engineering. The faculty evaluator will know that this outcome has been reached if 80 percent of the senior-level students respond correctly; they will know that the outcome has not been reached if the 80 percent cutoff is not reached. In other words, performance criteria define the cutoff values for the minimal acceptable level of performance.

Evaluators

In the accreditation process the "faculty evaluator" is the individual or set of individuals within a given program who are responsible for the collection, analysis, and interpretation of student data with the purpose of improving student learning. There is also the "ABET evaluator," or the individual or set of individuals who review a given program for ABET accreditation purposes.

Planning Ahead

An essential component of a successful assessment and evaluation plan is planning in advance. All too often, assessment is treated as something that can be added to the end of an educational process. Data or other artifacts that are available at that time are analyzed without a clear definition of purpose. These archived records are often the result of university requirements and do not necessarily fit with the program educational objectives and outcomes. Sometimes this method is successful in providing information that can be used for educational improvement purposes; more often, this data is inadequate or inappropriate for answering the pertinent questions.

As is the case in quality research, an assessment plan needs to be developed early so that it can guide and inform the data collection process. A researcher typically would not consider beginning a scientific study without a clearly defined set of research questions. These questions drive the methods of data collection and the analysis. Similarly, a faculty evaluator should not begin the assessment process without a clear definition of what is to be learned. Statements of program educational objectives and program outcomes are the faculty evaluator's equivalent to research questions. By understanding what is to be learned, data can be collected and analyzed that provides the appropriate information. Performance criteria are similar to the establishment of a null and alternative hypothesis in statistical applications. Meeting the criteria indicates that the program educational objectives and program outcomes have been reached; failing to meet the criteria indicates that the program educational objectives and program outcomes have not been reached.

Although the concept of planning in advance seems simple, its implementation often is not. For many, the purpose of instruction is obvious: to improve student learning. This outcome, however, is far too vague to guide the development and implementation of valid assessment instruments. Improving student learning has different meanings in different contexts. What students are expected to learn and be able to do in engineering calculus is different from what students should learn and be able to do in an electrical engineering course. These expectations differ even further from those set forth in a capstone senior design course. In summary, the outcome of improving student learning is too vague to guide the development of an appropriate assessment plan.

A starting point for creating student program educational objectives and program outcomes is ABET's Criterion 3. These statements, however, are too vague to guide the development of an assessment plan. ABET created these statements with the purpose of permitting individual programs the opportunity to fine-tune them in a manner that matches individual program needs. Therefore, an institution should not simply adopt this list as its program educational objectives. Rather, faculty within a given program should collaborate on refining these recommendations in a manner that fits their program and students. ABET created this flexibility on purpose. An important component of the development of the revised list of program educational objectives and program outcomes is the creation of a list that is specific enough that the components can be measured. For example, a program outcome may be "Students will understand and appreciate the relationship between mathematics and engineering within the engineering profession." A question that emerges from this statement is, What observable student behaviors will demonstrate that this objective has been reached? To answer this question, a refined statement or set of statements that describe the desired student outcomes is necessary. For example, "Students will demonstrate their understanding of the use of mathematical models in engineering by selecting and using appropriate models when solving engineering problems."

A word of caution is necessary here. Individual programs should not adopt program outcomes created by others, but rather these resources can be used to guide the development of program educational objectives and program outcomes that fit their programs. Ownership is a key component to implementing a successful assessment plan. If faculty do not believe that the identified program objectives and outcomes are important, they are unlikely to work with students to reach these objectives and outcomes. Chapter 2 of this book describes in detail the process of defining desired student learning outcomes and provides some examples. Other examples of measurable program outcomes can be found in the work of Besterfield-Sacre et al. (2000). These authors used Bloom's taxonomy to create a list of measurable outcomes that are consistent with Criterion 3.

Once program educational objectives and program outcomes have been defined, it is time to begin to develop the broader assessment plan. See chapter 3 and the work of Olds and Miller (1998a, 1998b, 1999) for further information on this process. Olds and Miller proposed a matrix to guide the development of an assessment plan, and this matrix jointly considers the processes of assessment and evaluation (the current version of this matrix may be viewed at www.mines.edu/fs_home/rlmiller/matrix.htm). The proposed framework includes reflection on when and how students progressing through a given program will acquire the knowledge required to reach the proposed outcomes. In summary, this matrix provides a systematic methodology for defining the assessment process with respect to the proposed program outcomes and objectives.

An example of a departmental assessment plan that was developed based on the original Olds and Miller assessment matrix can be found in Moskal (2006). In their chapter, the assessment plan for the Department of Mathematical and Computer Sciences (MCS) at the Colorado School of Mines, a support department to eight accredited engineering programs, is presented. A portion of this plan is reproduced here in Table 4.1. The terminology used in this plan has been altered from that used by Olds and Miller (1998a, 1998b) to be consistent with the current definitions of program educational objectives and program outcomes as defined by ABET. The first row of this plan includes a statement of the program educational objective, and the first column indicates the desired program outcome. This is followed by each of the categories discussed in the original Olds and Miller assessment matrix (1998a, 1998b). Performance criteria are clearly established, along with the method of evaluating the given criteria. Greater details concerning the assessment plan of the mathematical and computer sciences department at the Colorado School of Mines can be found in Moskal (2006) or at www .mines.edu/Academic/assess/.

TABLE 4.1

Portion of the Mathematical and Computer Sciences Department's Student Assessment Plan

Objective: Students will demonstrate technical expertise within mathematics/computer science by:

Outcomes	(1) Performance Criteria (PC)	(2) Implementation Strategy	(3) Evaluation Method (EM)	(4) Timeline (TL)	(5) Feedback (FB)
O1: Designing and implementing solutions to practical problems in science and engineering	PC1: Students in Calculus for Scientists and Engineers (CSE) I, II, and III will complete common exams that assess this objective. All students will pass the calculus sequence prior to graduation. PC2: Students in Programming Concepts and Data Structures will learn to use computer programs to solve problems. All majors in MCS will pass these courses prior to graduation. PC3: All MCS majors will pass field session prior to graduation. Field session requires that the student apply mathematics/computer science to the solution of original complex problems in the field. PC4: At least 80% of graduating seniors will agree with the statement, "My MCS degree prepared me well to solve problems that I am likely to encounter at work."	Core Coursework Major Coursework Field Session	EM1: PC1 will be evaluated by instructors of the calculus sequence. EM2: PC2 will be evaluated by instructors of Programming Concepts and Data Structures. EM3: PC3 will be evaluated by the field session instructors. EM4: PC4 will be evaluated through the senior survey.	TL1: EM1 implemented in F'97. TL2: EM2 implemented in F'97 TL3: EM3 implemented in F'97 TL4: EM4 implemented in S'99	FB1: Verbal reports will be given to the undergraduate committee and the department head concerning student achievements within the respective courses at the end of each semester. FB2: Degree audit will be completed prior to graduation to ensure that all students completed requirements of degree. FB3: A written summary of the results of the senior survey will be given to the department head.

Complete plan available at www.mines.edu/Academic/assess/Plan.html

Using Data to Improve Student Learning

Examining the assessment plan presented in Table 4.1, the reader may wonder when and how information is used to improve student learning. The Olds and Miller assessment matrix assumes that, once feedback is acquired, programs will use the information to improve student learning. If this assumption is correct, then this use of information completes the assessment loop as illustrated in Figure 4.1. However, programs may become so consumed with the process of data collection and analyses that the use of assessment information for program improvement is forgotten.

According to Prados, Peterson, and Lattuca (2005), ABET does not desire a voluptuous collection of data that has not been interpreted but rather a concise summary of data with descriptions of how the information was used for program improvement. This emphasis on information use reduces the data collection demand while simultaneously increasing the data interpretation and use demand. In the ABET context, less data with greater meaning is better than more data with little meaning. This provides a clear direction for faculty evaluators. Faculty evaluators should not seek to collect more and more data with little meaning but rather less data with a well-defined purpose. A faculty evaluator's time should primarily be dedicated to the process of analyzing and interpreting results.

One manner in which to discuss the assessment process is based on purpose. Formative assessment is the process of periodically checking whether progress has been made toward the attainment of the desired program outcomes. The purpose of formative assessment is to provide feedback with respect to the process so that the process can be improved to better reach the defined program objectives and outcomes. Summative assessment refers to the examination of whether or not the desired program educational objectives and program outcomes have been reached by the conclusion of the process. Summative assessment occurs when the faculty evaluator examines whether the performance criteria have been reached.

Assessments of academic programs serve both formative and summative purposes. By the end of an academic program, information is needed to determine whether students have reached the performance criteria. This information serves a summative purpose. If this information suggests that the established performance criteria have not been met by the given cohort of students, then revisions to the educational process are necessary to improve the learning of the next cohort of students. This is a formative use. ABET supports this notion of dual assessment purposes through its emphasis on a cyclical assessment structure. In this structure, the assumption is made that information acquired through the assessment process should be used for evaluating program educational objectives and program outcomes and for improving future student learning.

This section examines the different methods that have been used by various programs to summarize, interpret, and utilize data for the improvement of student learning. The discussion is divided according to whether the collected data was primarily quantitative (numerical), qualitative (descriptive), or mixed (combination of numerical and descriptive). As will be illustrated in the sections that follow, quantitative data is most often used to serve summative purposes. The numerical summaries offered through quantitative analyses support the evaluation of whether a set of outcomes has been reached across the student population. Qualitative data provides a detailed "snapshot" of an individual or subset of individuals within the target population. The details provided through this type of analysis are often used when making decisions concerning program improvement, serving a formative purpose. Given that the emphasis of ABET is on both formative and summative assessment, mixed methods or the use of a combination of qualitative and quantitative assessment techniques may offer the most powerful assessment option for the assessment of programs. For greater details concerning the techniques for data collection for summative assessment, see chapter 3, and for formative assessment, see chapter 10.

The reader should recognize that the discussion that follows presents only small components of a given program's assessment plan as reflected through the literature. Space limitations in this case resulted in the decision to restrict the discussion to critical components of assessment plans. Therefore, the information presented here should not be interpreted as a complete representation of a given program's assessment plan; no effort was made in this review to acquire complete assessment plans from any given program.

Quantitative

Quantitative data consists of numerical summaries of collected information. Often, this type of data is summarized using charts, tables, and statistical analyses. Quantitative data is frequently collected at the end of a course or instructional program with the purpose of summative assessment. However, quantitative data may be collected and analyzed at intervals throughout the instructional program in order to inform instruction itself, a formative purpose. Within the literature, quantitative data is reflected through summaries and analyses of categorical and numerical data. This section provides examples from the literature of the collection and use of quantitative data for the purpose of improving student learning at either the course or program level.

Categorical data. Categorical data is collected information that can be separated into specific groupings or categories. For example, responses to a survey can be divided into categories based on the respondents' ethnicity, gender, or stated opinions. Ordinal data, which is a subset of categorical data, has a natural order. For example, respondents may indicate that they strongly agree, agree, disagree, or strongly disagree with respect to a given statement on a survey. In this example, there is a natural order such that greater agreement can be assumed for a response of "strongly agree" as compared to "agree" for a given person. Nominal data, which is also a subset of categorical data, can be given a numerical code, but this code is used solely to distinguish data rather than to order data. An example of nominal data is assigning a zero to "male" and a one to "female." The increase from zero to one in this context has no meaning, but the separate categories do have meaning.

Categorical data is often summarized using descriptive statistics and is commonly presented in a table or a chart. An example of how categorical data may be used for the improvement of student learning can be found in the work of Sageev and Romanowski (2001). Their investigation surveyed alumni of the School of Engineering and Applied Science at the State University of New York at Buffalo, three to five years after graduation, as a method of evaluating the effectiveness of their technical communications curriculum. The questions contained on this survey were primarily categorical, asking respondents to select their responses from a predefined set of options.

Based on the survey results, Sageev and Romanowski (2001) were able to conclude that many of their graduates felt that they would have benefited from an increased emphasis on technical communication during their undergraduate education. On average, respondents indicated that 64 percent of their time at work was dedicated to some form of technical communication, oral or written, and that their skills in this area were vital to their career advancement. Based on these results, the School of Engineering and Applied Science proposed the expansion of its technical communications curriculum from a two-year sequence to a four-year sequence. This expansion would be achieved through the inclusion of communication modules throughout the required technical courses. They also established a steering committee to assist in the decision-making process during the curriculum revision process.

Another example of the use of categorical data to improve student learning is provided in the work of Pappas, Kampe, Hendricks, and Kander (2004). They set out to evaluate the Materials Science and Engineering Advanced Engineering Communications Program at Virginia Polytechnic Institute. This program integrates written and oral communication and design instruction into more than eight junior-, senior-, and sophomore-level engineering courses that are taught jointly by humanities and engineering faculty. Two additional one-credit required courses are designed to directly address communication skills. To evaluate the effectiveness of this communication sequence, similar to Sageev and Romanowski, Pappas et al. (2004) surveyed alumni. Their survey focused on alums' satisfaction with respect to the attainment of ABET Criteria 3.d, f, g, and i.

Based on the survey, Pappas et al. (2004) were able to determine the percentage of respondents who either agreed or strongly agreed that they had received the education appropriate to reach the specific ABET criterion. A separate analysis was completed to determine the number of course objectives across the department that were linked to a given ABET criterion, suggesting the level of emphasis that the given criterion received through the curriculum. Pappas et al. then generated what they referred to as a "quadrant chart." An example of a quadrant chart that originally appeared in Pappas et al. is reproduced here with permission in Figure 4.2. The x-axis of this chart indicates the extent of emphasis a given criterion was given in the curriculum, and the y-axis represents the percentage of respondents who agreed or strongly agreed that the given criterion had been met through the program. A horizontal line through the y-axis at 90 percent indicates the performance criteria for an acceptable level of agreement.

Examination of the quadrant chart in Figure 4.2 provides an immediate visual indication as to the extent to which a given criterion was covered through the curriculum and the level of respondents' satisfaction with respect to their education regarding that criterion. For example, using the quadrant chart displayed in Figure 4.2, it can be concluded that based on the industrial alumni responses, the program was not meeting the established performance criteria for Global & Societal Impacts and for System Design. This information may be immediately used in the program to reanalyze the instruction that students receive in these areas.

Using this method, Pappas et al. (2004) were able to demonstrate a dif-

FIGURE 4.2
Example Quadrant Chart

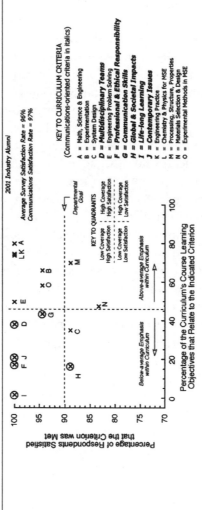

Reproduced with permission from Pappas et al. (2004)

ference in the satisfaction level of alumni who graduated in 1996 as compared to those who graduated in 2001. Students who graduated in 2001 were more satisfied with their education with regard to communication and design than were their 1996 counterparts. For summative assessment purposes, these results suggest that the changes made to the communication curriculum as experienced by the 1996 and 2001 graduating class had been effective for supporting the attainment of the desired student outcomes.

Pappas et al. (2004) also made comparisons between the responses collected in 2002 from alumni who graduated in 2001 and the responses of that same set of alumni to an exit survey that they had completed upon graduation a year earlier. This comparison suggested that the alumni had become more satisfied with their education after entering the workforce. They speculated that this outcome was attributable to the alumni's experiences at the workplace, which provided them with an appreciation of the importance of the courses that they had completed. From an assessment perspective, this suggests that the appropriate time to collect information concerning students' satisfaction with regard to their education may be after students enter the workforce. Using this information, the assessment process at Virginia Polytechnic Institute may be streamlined so that upon graduation students are asked only questions that they are equipped to answer. Other questions, such as the ones reflected through this survey, may be best responded to by alumni.

Pimmel (2003) provides yet another example, but at the course level, of the use of survey data to improve student learning. He used a combination of three survey instruments—student progress reports, peer performance evaluations, and end-of-project surveys—to evaluate team assignments in a senior-level electrical and computer engineering course in computer architecture and design. The progress report data was completed by students on a weekly basis throughout the semester and contained several selected response questions and two short response questions designed to evaluate the team's progress toward the desired outcomes. Students at the end of the course completed the remaining instruments, the peer performance evaluation, and the project survey. The peer performance evaluations required team members to evaluate the contributions that were made by each member of the team to the project, while the end-of-project survey collected feedback concerning the team experience. Based on summary statistics, Pimmel was able to evaluate the effectiveness of the team experience.

The survey information was also used to support several formative recommendations. Pimmel (2003) recommended that, in future offerings of the course, greater attention be given to cooperative learning exercises early in the course. This would help the students to establish collaborative behaviors before beginning the team process. He also recommended the inclusion of a journaling exercise designed to help students reflect on the team process, and the redesign of the peer performance evaluations to be a team activity rather than an individual activity. By having the teams discuss and complete the evaluations together, he theorized, students would have the opportunity for greater reflection on individual contributions. Peer evaluations were further used in this investigation as a summative evaluation that impacted student grades.

As these examples illustrate, summaries of collected data can be used to inform the process of improving student learning. In all of the examples, faculty evaluators used information provided through summaries of surveys to improve student learning. The next section examines the use of numerical data for the purpose of program improvement.

Numerical data. Often, categorical data is summarized by mapping categories to numbers. However, the numbers are only a method of distinguishing the categories—that is, nominal data—or of providing an indication of the natural order of the categories—that is, ordinal data—as was discussed in the previous section. This section examines data that is collected in numerical form and analyzed in numerical form.

Numerical data can be subdivided into two types: interval and continuous. Interval data has a consistent distance between any two values but lacks a true zero. A common example of interval data is years; the year "0" does not indicate the beginning of time nor does the year "2007" indicate the amount of time that the earth has existed. However, the length of each year is a consistent unit. Continuous data is data that may assume any value within a given interval. For example, length can be measured to any level of desired specificity. Theoretically, knowledge can also be measured to any level of specificity but is often limited by the sophistication of the available assessment instruments.

A benefit of numerical data is that it can often be analyzed using statistical techniques. A word of caution is necessary here. When using statistical techniques to analyze numerical data, an effort should be made to verify the underlying assumptions of the respective test before the analysis is completed. Analyses designed for continuous data should not be used on interval data, and vice versa. Furthermore, all statistical analyses have underlying assumptions. These assumptions should be examined before a statistical test is completed. Violation of an underlying assumption may lead to faulty conclusions. Articles have been written to assist faculty evaluators in avoiding common pitfalls in the statistical analysis of engineering education outcomes (Larpkiataworn, Muogboh, Besterfield-Sacre, Shuman, & Wolfe, 2003; Tebbs & Bower, 2003). (For more information on the use of statistical analyses in educational research and the underlying assumptions of statistical tests, see Gravetter & Wallnau, 2007.)

An example of the use of numerical data can be found in the work of Downey et al. (2006). They collected pre- and posttest scores from students who were completing either an online or a classroom version of Engineering Cultures using an instructor-developed test. Engineering Cultures is an elective course offered at Virginia Polytechnic Institute and the Colorado School of Mines that is designed to provide students with introductory knowledge that addresses ABET Criterion 3.h: Demonstrate that graduates have "the broad education necessary to understand the impact of engineering solutions in the global, economic, environmental, and societal context." The pre- and posttests were developed to be aligned with a stated set of expert-developed learning objectives. The summative purpose of the investigation was to determine whether the online course could support the same student outcomes as its classroom equivalent. The formative purpose of this investigation was to inform the investigators as to whether both versions of the course should be offered to students in the future.

Using a "paired t-test," Downey et al. (2006) were able to determine that the average student performance on the posttest was at least one grade level higher than the average performance on the pretest, regardless of whether the students completed the online or classroom version of the course. This was an important outcome, because it addressed whether the online course could be designed in a manner that supports the same outcomes as the classroom version of the course. For this particular course and this particular curriculum, the answer to this question appears to be "yes": The online and classroom versions of the course are supporting the attainment of the same outcomes. Recognizing that the knowledge acquired in both versions of the course is comparable provides support for the continued offerings of the course in both versions.

Another example of the use of numerical data in program assessment is provided through the Department of Civil and Geological Engineering at New Mexico State University. It used the Fundamentals in Engineering (FE) Exam, which all seniors in the department are required to complete, as part of their program-level assessment (Nirmalakhandan, Daniel, & White,

2004). In 1996, revisions were made to the hydraulic engineering course based on feedback from a variety of assessment sources. In order to examine the effectiveness of these revisions for improving student learning, statistical comparisons were made between students' performances on the fluid mechanics section of the FE Exam before and after the 1997 curricular revisions. Based on this analysis, the researchers were able to conclude that the revisions had resulted in improved student performance on the fluid mechanics section of the FE Exam. Furthermore, students in the Department of Civil and Geological Engineering at New Mexico State University were performing at the same level as their peer groups across the nation. From a summative perspective, this information supports the effectiveness of the current curriculum for the attainment of the desired student outcomes. From a formative perspective, these outcomes suggest that no further revisions are currently necessary in the given course, freeing a portion of the faculty evaluator's efforts to examine other areas of the curriculum in greater depth. This course, however, should continue to be monitored through the regular program assessment, as should all courses in a given program.

The example at New Mexico State University also illustrates the interplay between course and program assessment. Program assessment information identified hydraulic engineering as a course that was not supporting the attainment of the desired program outcomes. Revisions were made to this course and its curriculum based on assessment feedback. The revised course was then reexamined as part of the program assessment, using the fluid mechanics section of the FE Exam. In summary, program-level assessment was used to identify concerns at the course level. This concern was addressed at the course level, and the effectiveness of the changes was then evaluated at the program level.

A different type of statistical analysis, regression analysis, was used in the work of French, Immekus, and Oakes (2005). These authors completed three regression analyses on two cohorts of engineering students with the purpose of examining the relationship that a selection of variables had on the student outcomes of grade point average (GPA), university persistency, and engineering persistency. The purpose of their investigation was to identify the variables that had the strongest relationship to these student outcomes so that the university could make informed decisions concerning resource allocation. These authors found that students' prior academic performances in high school and on the SAT were the strongest predictors of students' college GPAs. Noncognitive indicators, such as participation in an orientation class, had little relationship to GPAs. Persistency within the university was related to GPA but did not appear to be influenced by participation in a first-year engineering seminar, students' level of academic motivation, or level of institutional integration. Persistency within engineering appeared to be related to prior academic achievement, GPA, and motivation. These findings suggest that, in order to increase persistency rates at this university within engineering, resources may need to be invested in improving students' academic achievements and motivation.

As these examples illustrate, statistical analyses have been used to inform the engineering education process. Test statistics provide a method for examining students' progression toward and attainment of desired program outcomes. They also provide a technique for comparing the outcomes of alternative offerings of a given course or program. Regression analysis offers a useful technique for identifying factors that are related to the attainment of program outcomes.

Qualitative

A common criticism of quantitative data is that through numerical summaries the details of a given data point are lost. Qualitative data is characterized by providing detailed descriptions of the phenomena under investigation (Leydens, Moskal, & Pavelich, 2004). Depending on the assessment purpose, these rich, detailed examinations can be valuable. Examples of qualitative data commonly collected with the purpose of evaluating engineering programs include open-ended interviews or surveys, student focus groups, student portfolios, and ethnographies.

An example of the use of qualitative data to improve student learning can be found in the work of Friesen, Taylor, and Britton (2005). They completed a study of an undergraduate biosystems engineering program in Canada utilizing instructor interviews, industrial interviews, and student focus groups. The purpose of their efforts was to better understand the teaching and learning experiences and perceptions of students as they completed a three-course sequence in design. Transcripts of the interviews were analyzed using a constant comparative analysis that requires identification of common themes across respondents.

Based on this methodology, the investigators were able to identify disconnects between the intentions of the instructors and the students' perceptions. For example, the students perceived that there was greater value in the process of design than there was in the final resultant product. This was inconsistent with the instructors' intentions. The investigators also found differences in the manner in which students understood the design process as they progressed through their academic studies. Students who were just beginning their academic careers had difficulty understanding the open-ended nature of design, and this difficulty decreased with academic progression. Based on this observation, the researchers recommended that greater attention be given to the open-ended nature of design problems during introductory courses, followed by a gradual decrease in this emphasis over the progression of the curriculum.

Portfolios offer another form of qualitative data that may be used for the purpose of improving student learning. Heinricher et al. (2002) at Worcester Polytechnic Institute examined the benefits and drawbacks of three different models of portfolio assessment in the examination of student learning outcomes. In the first model, the investigators paid a subset of undergraduate students to maintain portfolio entries throughout an academic year and submit these entries via e-mail. In the second model, portfolio entries were included as assignments in selected courses. The third and final model embedded portfolio entries into key courses throughout the academic sequence. As part of the third model's design, academic advisors were to discuss the entries as they related to designated program outcomes during advising meetings. Qualitative comparisons were then made among these models.

Through this comparison, the investigators found that the most effective model for improving student learning was the course-based model, or model two. Since the portfolio entries replaced other course assignments, course instructors were willing to provide feedback to their students concerning their entries. Students in the second model were more likely to complete the portfolio assignments because they impacted their grades. Even when students were paid, as was the case with the first model, fewer than a third of the students completed all of the portfolio entries. A flaw with the third model was that academic advisors did not complete the final step of discussing portfolio entries with students, eliminating the critical component of providing students with feedback. This study illustrates the formative purpose of using assessment information to inform the assessment system itself. By identifying the most effective model, the faculty evaluators may now focus their attention on fine-tuning this model to better inform the instructional process.

In a study completed by Loui (2005) as part of an elective course on engineering ethics at the Department of Electrical and Computer Engineering and Coordinated Science Laboratory at the University of Illinois at Urbana-Champaign, student essays were used to examine students' understanding of their professional and ethical responsibilities as professional engineers. At the start of the semester, students completed a one-hour essay in which they addressed the characteristics and responsibilities of a professional engineer, the factors that have shaped their understanding of what it is to be an engineer, and whether they felt prepared to undertake the responsibilities of a professional engineer. At the end of the semester, students were asked to reflect on their original essays and explain how they would revise these essays. They were also asked to reflect on the course activities that had influenced their ethical development as professional engineers. These essays were examined to identify changes in students' understanding of the characteristics and responsibilities of a professional engineer and changes in their personal professional identities. The two course factors that were repeatedly identified by students as having had the strongest influence on their ethical development were (1) participating in the analysis of case studies and (2) participating in the analysis of diverse perspectives. From a formative perspective, this information provides support for an increased emphasis on case studies and on the analysis of diverse perspectives. From a summative perspective, this study offers evidence that the desired student outcomes were being reached.

Courter, Millar, and Lyons (1998) provide an example of the use of ethnographic techniques for the purpose of better understanding first-year engineering students' educational experiences. Courter et al. (1998) collected data through student interviews, focus groups, observations, open-ended surveys, and document analysis of a freshman design course, and examined this information using an ethnographic approach. Based on this work, the authors were able to identify six central experiences of students in the course, and these were used to identify the components of the course that were effective for promoting student learning. Positive components of the course as identified by students were the opportunity to work in autonomous groups and the realistic nature of the design project. Aspects of the course that were viewed with less enthusiasm were homework assignments, lectures, and laboratory work. Feedback acquired from the students was continuously shared with the instructors throughout the semester with the purpose of improving student learning.

As these examples illustrate, qualitative methods have been used in the engineering education literature with the purpose of improving student learning. The primary emphasis as reflected in the literature of these techniques has been on formative assessment purposes. The use of qualitative methods provides the advantage of detailed information with respect to a given data point. Quantitative methods result in summaries across populations that can be used to make broader generalizations. As will be discussed in the next section, program assessment often requires both of these benefits, and this can be supported through the use of mixed methods.

Mixed Methods

According to ABET, program outcomes should be achieved by all students when they complete an engineering program. In other words, program outcomes should reflect what is considered to be the minimal level of competency required in the given field (Prados et al., 2005). Demonstration of the attainment of program outcomes, however, may be based on a compelling sampling of student work. One manner in which to construct a convincing argument that all students have achieved the desired outcomes is to collect detailed qualitative data from randomly selected students, accompanied by quantitative summaries across student populations (Rogers, 2006a). By using mixed methods or a combination of qualitative and quantitative data, faculty evaluators have the opportunity to provide a detailed description of some members of the population while also providing information that can be generalized across the larger population. This combination of information can be very powerful when making decisions regarding program changes with the purpose of improving student learning, and is referred to as "mixed methods."

Mixed methods studies take several forms. Some assessment programs collect a combination of quantitative and qualitative data, analyze that data, and use the convergence of the results of that data to inform the learning process. Others collect qualitative data and then quantify that data through a coding process and analyze that data using quantitative techniques. Examples of each are provided in this section.

In a study completed in the mathematical and computer sciences department at the Colorado School of Mines (Moskal, Strong, & Fairweather, 2006), quantitative data was used to identify differences in student performances and attitudes across core, required engineering mathematics courses. A sequence of five courses, all of which were coordinated, was examined for grade distributions and summaries of student satisfaction. In these courses, a faculty member was assigned as a course coordinator. The course coordinator was responsible for ensuring that course outcomes were addressed through common exams and that student responses to common exams were scored in a reliable manner regardless of section and instructor. Comparisons were made (1) between sections taught by the course coordinator and sections taught by noncoordinators and (2) across the different course sections. A summary of the results of this analysis is displayed in Figure 4.3.

Based on the analysis, specific courses were identified in which students in the noncoordinators' sections displayed lower grades and reduced satisfaction as compared to the coordinators' sections. A qualitative analysis, which included open-ended surveys of students and faculty, revealed that in these sections little collaboration was occurring between the coordinators and the noncoordinators. The coordinators in charge of these sections were using a top-down design in which the coordinator made all of the decisions with regard to the course, including test development and scoring. In the courses that displayed comparable student satisfaction, the course coordinators employed a collaborative approach among instructors, in which all instructors contributed to the course decision-making process. Based on this, changes have been made with the purpose of improving student learning and fairness across sections. Using this study as a stimulus, the head of the department has discussed with course coordinators the importance of using a collaborative approach rather than a top-down design. The importance of the collaborative approach was further illustrated to the coordinators using anonymous comments provided by students and faculty.

Another example of a mixed method approach to assessment is provided through the work of Besterfield-Sacre, Gerchak, Lyons, Shuman, and Wolfe (2004) at the University of Pittsburgh. These investigators used a combination of qualitative and quantitative methods to better understand the

FIGURE 4.3
Summary of Results Reported in Moskal, Strong, & Fairweather (2006)

- Course coordinators assigned significantly more *A*s than noncoordinators.
- Noncoordinators had significantly more students withdraw from the course.
- Course coordinators received significantly higher ratings than noncoordinators.
- Students in noncoordinators' courses in which the coordinator made all of the decisions concerning testing and grading rated the fairness of the common exams to be low.
- Noncoordinators who taught courses in which the coordinator made all of the decisions concerning testing and grading displayed weak support for the coordination process.
- Noncoordinators who taught courses in which the coordinator used a collaborative approach to course decision making displayed strong support for the coordination process.

perceptions of industrial engineering students with respect to their field. Sophomore, junior, and senior students were asked to create concept maps—a qualitative technique—based on their perceptions of industrial engineering. The researchers were seeking to examine the effectiveness of the concept maps for capturing conceptual change in students' knowledge during the final three years of their undergraduate education. Two analysis methods were used: The first approach was to quantify the analysis by counting nodes and lines. The second was based on the qualitative analysis of experts in the field. The expert evaluations were also quantified through an overall evaluation of the student concept maps.

Statistical and graphical methods were then used on the resultant numerical values to evaluate changes in the concept maps that occurred because of instruction. Based on the first technique, only one statistically significant difference was identified: Women included more concepts on their maps than did men. Using the method of expert review (second method), a number of observations were made, some of which were used to improve student learning. For example, only a few maps included statistics as a concept within industrial engineering. This suggested to the faculty evaluators that students did not recognize the significance of their statistical knowledge with respect to their future careers. This resulted in a reevaluation of and changes to the two required statistics courses. Recognizing the value of the second methodology for assessment purposes, the researchers further developed a scoring rubric that could be used by others and that was designed to reflect the expert evaluation.

The Department of Civil and Mechanical Engineering at the United States Military Academy provides yet another example of combining quantitative and qualitative data for the purpose of improving student learning. Bailey and associates (2002) describe a process that directly links course-level assessment with program-level assessment. In courses that are offered in multiple sections at the academy, a course director is assigned to ensure consistency in instruction across sections. The course director is also responsible for preparing a "Course Assessment Package" each spring, which includes general course information (syllabi with course objectives, lessons, and assignments) and summaries of analyzed quantitative and qualitative data collected across the academic year. Quantitative data includes summaries of course evaluations, student self-assessment instruments, and grade summaries. Qualitative data includes reflections based on student feedback.

As part of the assessment process, the course director is asked to make recommendations for the improvement of future implementations of the courses, and these recommendations are reviewed and discussed with the department head. Each recommended course change is required to be directly supported by the information provided in the assessment package. This methodology ensures that each course is reviewed for instructional change on a yearly basis. Furthermore, these assessment packages are maintained for a period of five years, allowing the ongoing review of proposed and implemented changes. The authors report that three to four proposed changes are made with respect to each course every year, supporting a continuous assessment and improvement cycle.

This methodology for program assessment further illustrates the interplay between course- and program-level assessment. The assessment packages are completed at the course level. The information that is acquired is reviewed to support improvements at both the course and program levels. By presenting all of the recommendations to one common source, the department head, decisions can be made based on the collection of data concerning the larger program.

All of these examples illustrate a mixed methods approach to program assessment. As was discussed, mixed methods provide the opportunity to acquire detailed information on a subset of data points and a summary across the entire set of data points. When implemented correctly, this methodology can provide compelling evidence to support the decisions that are made with the purpose of improving student learning.

Validation, Triangulation, and Documentation

In quantitative research, concerns are often raised with respect to the validity and reliability of the interpretations that are made of the resultant data (Moskal, Leydens, & Pavelich, 2002). *Validity* refers to the extent to which the interpretations of data accurately reflect the true state of what is being studied. *Reliability* refers to the dependability of the evaluation process over time and situations. The establishment of reliability with respect to a given instrument is necessary but insufficient for the establishment of validity. A given instrument may provide consistent results (highly reliable) that do not accurately reflect the true state of what is being studied (invalid). A term that is similar to validity in qualitative research is trustworthiness (Leydens et al., 2004). *Trustworthiness* refers to the extent to which the interpretations of the data accurately reflect the true state of the phenomena under investigation. Within research investigations, there is a broad range of methodologies that may be used to establish validity, reliability, or trustworthiness of research interpretations. Although these methods may also be used for program assessments, the process of learning these techniques is likely to overwhelm most faculty evaluators.

A common approach for supporting the validity or trustworthiness of a program assessment is triangulation. *Triangulation* refers to the concept of collecting and analyzing data that has been acquired through multiple sources with respect to a given outcome. Two, three, or even more methods may be used when examining a single desired outcome. Each method employed may have a different set of performance criteria. If multiple methods are used and the results all support the same conclusion, then the argument that the given conclusion is appropriate is more compelling. Triangulation may include more than one quantitative method, more than one qualitative method, or a combination of both qualitative and quantitative methods (mixed methods). In order to triangulate assessment results, programs may also opt to collect data on both the course and the program level and compare the interpretations.

As the preceding discussion suggests, an assessment plan may consist of multiple methods for measuring a given outcome and multiple levels on which assessment information is collected, analyzed, and interpreted. Furthermore, if an assessment plan is implemented correctly, then a given program will move through the assessment cycle multiple times between each ABET visit, each time collecting data and implementing changes. This process of data collection, analysis, and use needs to be documented at the course and program level for accreditation purposes. Moskal, Olds, and Miller (2002) provide a process for documenting how information is used for the improvement of student learning and the improvement of the assessment process itself. In this chapter, a feedback matrix is proposed that consists of identifying the semester in which information was collected, the source of that information, concerns the information raised, the department's response to the information, and how the information was used for improvement purposes. This matrix for documenting the feedback process is used by the Department of Mathematical and Computer Sciences at the Colorado School of Mines, and an updated version can be found at www.mines.edu/Academic/assess/Feedback.htm. A portion of the completed matrix is displayed in Table 4.2.

Summary

The purpose of this chapter is to illustrate how information acquired through the assessment process may be used to improve student learning.

TABLE 4.2
Feedback Matrix

Semester	Source	Concern	Response	Follow-up
Spring '02	General Review of Assessment System	Revised goals and objectives resulted in the need to implement a revised assessment plan.	New assessment plan that was consistent with revisions was implemented.	Plan currently in use.
Fall '02	Feedback From Head of Department	Additional courses were designated as coordinated courses. The purpose was to improve assessment methods and increase consistency in quality of student learning.	Differential Equations, Programming Concepts, and Data Structures became coordinated courses.	Courses continue to be coordinated.
Spring '03	Student Feedback	Students who were majoring in mathematics or computer science expressed an interest in acquiring a minor in education.	Efforts began to explore the potential of establishing such a minor with partner institutions.	Two grants were acquired to support this effort. Minor approved by Undergraduate Curriculum Committee in Spring 2005.
Fall '03	Accreditation Feedback	State listed requirements for K-12 teachers.	Mapping of MCS course objectives and outcomes to the state requirements.	Review and revision of this mapping completed. Holes in this mapping were used to identify courses to be completed as part of the education minor.
Spring '04	Feedback From Head of Department	Desire to acquire external feedback concerning assessment efforts.	Two faculty attended the Supporting Assessment in Undergraduate Mathematics (SAUM) workshop.	Ongoing activities with SAUM.
Spring '05	Feedback From Faculty	Desire to acquire feedback from students concerning fairness, appropriateness, and effectiveness of assessment system.	Extensive data was collected through student surveys and grade analyses to evaluate the effectiveness of core courses.	Inconsistencies identified in the implementation of core courses. Discussions under way with coordinators of these courses for improvement purposes.
Fall '05	Mapping of Student Outcomes to Questions on Student Finals	Technology was not consistently being used in the classroom, which was contrary to objectives and outcomes.	Concerns were raised to the Undergraduate Curriculum Committee concerning inconsistency between objectives and outcomes and implementation.	Ongoing discussions in Undergraduate Council.

The assessment process begins by defining program educational objectives and program outcomes. These are then used to identify appropriate performance criteria at both the program and course level. Attainment of the performance criteria suggests that the desired student outcomes have been reached, while failure to reach the criteria indicates that revision to a course or program is necessary. An important component of the assessment process is the exchange of information between program- and course-level assessments. Both levels of information can be used to improve student learning.

The concept of collecting, analyzing, interpreting, and using data to improve student learning appears to be simple. However, its implementation is often difficult. The assessment process is complex and requires reflection on a number of different components. Failure to consider any of these components can lead to the collection of information that cannot be used. Olds and Miller (1998a, 1998b, 1999) proposed an assessment matrix (see Table 4.1) as a framework for planning and implementing program assessments. This framework requires the reflection and identification of key assessment activities such as defining the objectives, outcomes, and performance criteria; identifying when and how students will develop the desired knowledge; selecting assessment instruments; establishing a timeline; and defining who will receive feedback. This framework in combination with the feedback matrix proposed in Table 4.2 provides a fairly complete overview of a program's assessment process and information use, as shown in this chapter, for the Department of Mathematical and Computer Sciences at the Colorado School of Mines.

The reader should note that, even with these sources of documentation, a complete picture of the assessment process within a given program is difficult to acquire. Based on the assessment plan displayed in Table 4.1 and information acquired through the implementation of that plan, the Department of Mathematical and Computer Sciences at the Colorado School of Mines decided to complete a detailed study of the core coordinated courses. This analysis was not part of the original assessment plan but, rather, was an outcome of the implementation of that plan. Results of the analysis of the core coordinated courses are displayed in Figure 4.3, and details of that investigation can be found in Moskal et al. (2006). This investigation, which resulted in a research article (Moskal et al., 2006), and the actions in response to the investigation are summarized in a single row of the feedback matrix displayed in Table 4.2, for the spring of 2005. In summary, a single row of this matrix reflects a great deal of effort, including multiple forms of data collection, analysis, interpretation, and use.

Given the complexity of the assessment process, a faculty evaluator can easily find the task of planning to use assessment information for the improvement of student learning overwhelming. There are many options available for the collection and analysis of assessment data; these include quantitative, qualitative, and mixed method approaches. The selection of a method for collecting and analyzing data should be guided by the purpose of the assessment. Assessment information may be used to serve formative or summative purposes. Formative assessment refers to the use of assessment information for the improvement of the learning process or for the improvement of the assessment process in a manner that supports the attainment of the desired student outcomes. Summative assessment refers to the use of the information to evaluate the attainment of student outcomes. As is suggested by the feedback loop displayed in Figure 4.1, program assessment is typically designed to serve both of these purposes. Examination of the engineering education literature, as was done in this chapter, provides a wealth of examples of how programs have used assessment information to serve formative and summative purposes at the undergraduate level. A summary of the reviewed articles is provided in Table 4.3.

Depending on the type of data that is being collected, quantitative or qualitative, and the method of analysis, faculty evaluators must also consider the validity or trustworthiness of the interpretations that are made. Rigorous methods for establishing the validity or trustworthiness of instruments used in the assessment of research projects are available in the educational literature. However, most faculty evaluators are not equipped with the background knowledge or the necessary time to learn and implement these techniques. A common and accepted approach for supporting the validity or trustworthiness of assessment interpretations in engineering education is triangulation, the use of multiple methods in the evaluation of a given program outcome. If the preponderance of evidence supports that attainment of the outcome, then the outcome is assumed to have been reached.

Given the complexity of the assessment process, it is difficult for faculty evaluators not to become overwhelmed by data collection, analysis, interpretation, and use. The final goal of the assessment process is to use information to improve student learning. As argued by Prados et al. (2005), collecting less data that is analyzed and used is better than collecting more data that is never interpreted. Initial efforts into the assessment process may begin with the collection and analysis of a small but useful data set. After an initial assessment process has been implemented, greater attention can be given to the

TABLE 4.3
Prior Research Summaries

Study	Method	Summative Results	Formative Results
Bailey et al. (2002)	Mixed	• Evaluation of student performances within courses	• Identification of necessary revisions to departmental courses
Besterfield-Sacre et al. (2004)	Mixed	• Evaluation of student perceptions of industrial engineering • Development of a scoring rubric for the analysis of industrial engineering perceptions	• Identification of an effective methodology for examining student concept maps • Revisions to statistics sequence
Courter et al. (1998)	Qualitative	• Evaluation of student retention rates	• Identification of positive and negative aspects of the course based on student feedback
Downey et al. (2006)	Quantitative/Numerical	• Evaluation of outcome attainment in two versions of a course	• Supports the continued offering of online and classroom versions of Engineering Cultures
French et al. (2005)	Quantitative	• Identification of a list of factors that influenced student grade point averages and persistency	• Identification of areas within the curriculum that could benefit student persistency and therefore may warrant further resource allocation • Identification of components of the curriculum that did not appear to be contributing to persistency in the manner expected
Friesen et al. (2005)	Qualitative	• Identification of students' current understanding of the design process	• Identification of disconnects between the intentions of instruction and student outcomes • Increased emphasis needed on the open-ended nature of the design process early in students' studies

Heinricher et al. (2002)	Qualitative	• Evaluation of students' knowledge of engineering	• Identification of an appropriate model to be used in future courses for portfolio assessment • Grades provided a greater motivator to undergraduate students than money
Loui (2005)	Qualitative	• Evaluation of effectiveness of Engineering Ethics course	• Increased course emphasis on case studies • Increased course emphasis on diverse perspectives
Moskal et al. (2006)	Mixed	• Different student outcomes based on method of coordination across courses	• Greater emphasis on collaboration among course instructors
Nirmalakhandan et al. (2004)	Quantitative/ Numerical	• Evaluation of students' attainment on fluid mechanics section of the FE Exam • Evaluation of the current version of the hydraulic engineering course	• Supports the continued offering of the revised hydraulic engineering course
Pappas et al. (2004)	Quantitative/ Categorical	• Measurement of graduate students' communication skills • Demonstration of improved perception of communication skills from graduates in 1996 to 2001	• Identification of ABET outcomes that require further curricular attention • More focused assessment process
Pimmel (2003)	Quantitative	• Feedback used to assign student grades • Evaluation of the effectiveness of the team experience	• Weekly progress report data used to examine project progression over time • Greater attention needed with regard to cooperative learning early in course • Inclusion of a journaling exercise throughout the semester • Redesign of performance evaluations to be a team activity
Sageev & Romanowski (2001)	Quantitative/ Categorical	• Graduates did not express confidence in their technical communication skills	• Expansion of technical communications curriculum from a two-year sequence to a four-year sequence • Establishment of steering committee

concerns of validity, trustworthiness, triangulation, and the completeness of the plan itself.

References

Accreditation Board for Engineering and Technology. (2005). Criteria for accrediting engineering programs. Retrieved January 22, 2007, from http://www.abet .org/Linked%20Documents-UPDATE/Criteria%20and%20PP/E001%2006-0 7%20EAC%20Criteria%202-9-06.pdf

Bailey, M., Floersheim, R. B., & Ressler, S. J. (2002). Course assessment plan: A tool for integrated curriculum management. *Journal of Engineering Education, 91*(4), 425–434.

Besterfield-Sacre, M., Gerchak, J., Lyons, M., Shuman, L., & Wolfe, H. (2004). Scoring concept maps: An integrated rubric for assessing engineering education. *Journal of Engineering Education, 9*(2), 105–115.

Besterfield-Sacre, M., Shuman, L. J., Wolfe, H., Atman, C. J., McGourty, J., Miller, R., Olds, B., & Rogers, G. (2000, April). Defining the outcomes—A framework for EC 2000. *IEEE Transactions on Engineering Education, 43*(2), 100–110.

Courter, S. S., Millar, S., & Lyons, L. (1998). From the students' point of view: Experiences in a freshman engineering design course. *Journal of Engineering Education, 87*(3), 283–287.

Downey, G. L., Lucena, J., Moskal, B., Parkhurst, R., Bigley, T., Hays, C., Jesiek, B., Kelly, L., Miller, J., & Ruff, S. (2006). The globally competent engineer: Working effectively with people who define problems differently. *Journal of Engineering Education, 95*(2), 107–122.

French, B., Immekus, J., & Oakes, W. (2005). An examination of indicators of engineering students success and persistence. *Journal of Engineering Education, 94*(4), 419–425.

Friesen, M., Taylor, K. L., & Britton, M. G. (2005). A qualitative study of a course trilogy in biosystems engineering design. *Journal of Engineering Education, 94*(3), 287–296.

Gravetter, F. J., & Wallnau, L. B. (2007). *Statistics for the behavioral sciences* (7th ed.). Belmont, CA: Wadsworth/Thompson.

Heinricher, A. C., Miller, J., Schachterie, L., Kildahl, N., Bluemel, V., & Crawford, V. (2002). Undergraduate learning portfolios for institutional assessment. *Journal of Engineering Education, 92*(2), 249–253.

Larpkiataworn, S., Muogboh, O., Besterfield-Sacre, M., Shuman, L., & Wolfe, H. (2003). Special considerations when using statistical analysis in engineering education assessment and evaluation. *Journal of Engineering Education, 92*(3), 207–215.

Leydens, J., Moskal, B., & Pavelich, M. (2004). Qualitative methods used in the assessment of engineering education. *Journal of Engineering Education, 93*(1), 65–72.

Loui, M. (2005). Ethics and the development of professional identities of engineering students. *Journal of Engineering Education, 94*(4), 383–390.

McGourty, J., Sabastian, C., & Swart, W. (1998). Developing a comprehensive assessment program for engineering education. *Journal of Engineering Education, 87*(4), 355–361.

Moskal, B. (2006). The development, implementation and revision of a departmental assessment plan. In A. L. Steen (Ed.), *Supporting assessment in undergraduate mathematics* (pp. 149–155). Washington, DC: Mathematical Association of America.

Moskal, B., Leydens, J., & Pavelich, M. (2002). Validity, reliability and the assessment of engineering education. *Journal of Engineering Education, 91*(3), 351–354.

Moskal, B., Olds, B., & Miller, R. (2002). Scholarship in a university assessment system. *Academic Exchange Quarterly, 6*(1), 32–37.

Moskal, B., Strong, S., & Fairweather, G. (2006). Assessing core courses in mathematics: A case study at the Colorado School of Mines. In B. L. Madison (Ed.), *Assessment of student learning in college mathematics: Towards improved programs and courses* (pp. 131–143). Tallahassee, FL: Association for Institutional Research.

Nirmalakhandan, N., Daniel, D., & White, K. (2004). Use of subject-specific FE exam results in outcomes assessment. *Journal of Engineering Education, 93*(1), 73–77.

Olds, B. M., & Miller, R. (1998a). Assessing a course or project. In *How do you measure success? (Designing effective processes for assessing engineering education)* (pp. 35–43). Washington, DC: American Society for Engineering Education.

Olds, B. M., & Miller, R. (1998b). An assessment matrix for evaluating engineering programs. *Journal of Engineering Education, 87*(2), 173–178.

Olds, B. M., & Miller, R. (1999). Olds and Miller assessment matrix. Retrieved January 22, 2007, from http://www.mines.edu/fs_home/rlmiller/matrix.htm

Pappas, E., Kampe, S., Hendricks, R., & Kander, R. (2004). An assessment analysis methodology and its application to an advanced engineering communication program. *Journal of Engineering Education, 93*(3), 233–246.

Pimmel, R. L. (2003). A practical approach for converting group assignments into team projects. *IEEE Transactions on Education, 46*(2), 273–282.

Prados, J., Peterson, G., & Lattuca, L. (2005). Quality assurance of engineering education through accreditation: The impact of engineering criteria 2000 and its global influence. *Journal of Engineering Education, 94*(1), 165–184.

Rogers, G. (2006a). Death by assessment. *Communications Link.* Retrieved January 22, 2007, from http://www.abet.org/Linked%20Documents-UPDATE/Assessment/Assessment%20Tips2.pdf

Rogers, G. (2006b). Flowchart. Retrieved January 22, 2007, from http://www

.abet.org/Linked%20Documents-UPDATE/Assessment/mainflowchart_full_co lor.jpg

Sageev, P., & Romanowski, C. (2001). A message from recent engineering graduates in the workplace: Results of a survey on technical communication. *Journal of Engineering Education, 91*(4), 685–692.

Shaeiwitz, J. (1998). Classroom assessment. *Journal of Engineering Education, 87*(2), 179–183.

Tebbs, J., & Bower, K. (2003). Some comments on the robustness of Student t Procedures. *Journal of Engineering Education, 92*(1), 91–94.

5

TOOLS AND ASSESSMENT METHODS SPECIFIC TO GRADUATE EDUCATION

J. Joseph Hoey, IV

T he progressively more individualized nature of graduate programs in engineering poses a number of challenges concerning assessment. While many assessment methods related to graduate programs are similar to those of undergraduate programs, graduate education also affords unique opportunities to assess student competencies. Even though graduate programs tend to be taught in smaller courses, with much more individualized instruction, the purpose of assessment is still the same: to improve student learning. Assessment methods include formative as well as summative assessment strategies/approaches to enhance best practices within graduate education—not just at the end. How does assessing students' incoming ability affect their education? At what points during their graduate education is measuring their abilities most useful? Conducting formative assessment is more thoroughly discussed in chapter 10. This chapter focuses on the following objectives: differentiating the assessment of graduate programs from undergraduate assessment and the attendant challenges; defining faculty expectations for graduate students and distinguishing them from operational objectives; articulating the concept of and importance of a well-developed assessment plan for graduate programs; elucidating principles of practice for graduate assessment; articulating a taxonomy of graduate assessment approaches and specific methods for graduate assessment; and locating the assessment of graduate programs in engineering within the larger context of institutional effectiveness.

Background

The development of assessment of undergraduate programs in engineering received a huge boost from the Engineering Criteria 2000 and subsequent ABET criteria (ABET, 2007). Accreditation standards promulgated by regional accreditation bodies (e.g., Commission on Colleges, Southern Association of Colleges and Schools) have prompted many institutions to encourage the development of viable approaches to assessment in their graduate programs as part of an overall process of institutional effectiveness, yet the actual assessment of graduate engineering programs remains an area that is neither well explicated nor well understood. Nevertheless, the underlying rationale for assessment of both undergraduate and graduate programs remains the same: to improve student learning. As Maki (2006) points out, "We are educating the next generation of experts in our disciplines. We should be curious about how we are educating those future experts and the pedagogy that underlies that education."

The notion of assessing graduate programs on a periodic basis dates back to at least the latter part of the nineteenth century, in the form of academic program review (Harcleroad, 1980). Traditionally, the evaluation of graduate programs has relied on measures of incoming student quality, inputs such as resources available to the program, library holdings, faculty qualifications and research productivity, and reputational measures such as the periodic National Research Council (NRC) surveys of research-doctoral programs (e.g., Kuh, 2005). Yet with domestic enrollment in graduate programs in engineering declining and the need for master's- and doctoral-prepared engineers rapidly increasing, the pressure to reexamine and perhaps rethink assessment in the context of graduate engineering programs is undeniable.

Challenges

While pressures for graduate assessment are on the rise, a number of factors complicate graduate program assessment (Hoey, 2005). To begin with, the literature base is sparse, and solid definitions of what constitutes graduate program assessment are not readily available. Student learning objectives in graduate programs tend to be at a high level of cognitive complexity and require more effort to measure. Many graduate programs are smaller than their undergraduate counterparts, and feature more individualized instruction—especially at the doctoral level. One-on-one mentoring is the norm for thesis and dissertation work at the graduate level, thus raising questions concerning the unit of analysis and, because of sample size restrictions, how trustworthy assessment data obtained through group-level methods (so frequently used at the undergraduate level) can be (Banta, Black, & Ward, 1999; Green & Rittman, 2001). The interdisciplinary nature of many graduate programs means that the notion of siloed, department-based assessment will need to be expanded to encompass the interdisciplinary connections that are characteristic of, for example, biomedical engineering graduate programs.

Program Structure and Perspective Shift

The substantial difference in program structure between graduate and undergraduate education is another one of the factors that forms an impediment to the assessment of graduate programs. Doctoral engineering programs and, to a lesser extent, master's programs tend to be far less lockstep in structure than undergraduate engineering programs and to focus more on the one-on-one mentoring relationship between individual students and their research directors. Traditionally, our view of graduate education is one of the development of individual scholars along a unique path dictated by student research interests. Tempered by this traditional view, graduate education in engineering appears to be less visible structurally than undergraduate education. Undertaking assessment of graduate programs, however, involves a shift in perspective. A prerequisite to gaining systematic feedback about graduate programs is an understanding of their programmatic structure and the logical points at which to conduct assessment of multiple students. Graduate education is both a process and a system; thus, necessary precursors to designing interventions to optimize that system include making it visible as a process and defining the boundary parameters of it as a system. As Schilling and Schilling (1998) point out, "To change or improve an invisible system, one must first make it visible" (p. 172).

Mentoring is a key element of the "invisible system" of graduate education, but has hitherto been a poorly understood process that has long been practiced in a craft-based fashion. A limited body of research on mentoring in graduate higher education has recently begun to emerge. Tsang et al. (2006) address the dual role of graduate mentoring in not only monitoring student advisee progress but also directing the advisee toward activities intended to reinforce professional socialization. Given the developmental and eventually transformative nature of the graduate mentoring relationship, Bagayoko (1998) recommends addressing both processes and outcomes in developing standards for assessing mentoring activities. Following that logic,

Fentiman (2006) notes that a set of parallel assessments is needed to ascertain the individual and collective impact of the diverse elements of a defined graduate mentoring program such as Purdue's graduate mentoring program in the College of Engineering. Thus, understanding and steadily improving the knowledge and practice base around mentoring practices is a key task in graduate assessment.

Once the notion of graduate education as both a process and a system has been adopted, the next task is to design a closed-loop feedback process that generates valid and reliable information on student learning. Typically, this task begins with the development of an assessment plan.

Assessment Plan Development

In designing assessment plans for graduate programs, several questions are appropriate to ask (Kuffel & Hoey, 2006):

- Do our degree programs have clearly defined faculty expectations for students?
- Are they published, and are they measurable or observable?
- Do we obtain data to assess the achievement of faculty expectations (learning outcomes) for students?
- Do we document that assessment results are used to change or sustain the excellence of program activities as well as further student gains in professional and attitudinal skills and experiences?
- Based on assessment results, do we reevaluate the appropriateness of departmental purpose as well as expectations for students?

Experience demonstrates that the amount of work needed to develop a successful graduate assessment plan and process is proportional to the number of "no" responses to these preceding questions. In fact, several key considerations exist in the development of graduate assessment plans. Perhaps the foremost consists of defining what knowledge, skills, abilities, and professional attitudes faculty expect to see demonstrated by graduate degree recipients in engineering.

Many institutions have begun to develop assessment of their engineering programs. Table 5.1 lists some of the institutions that have plans accessible via the Web. This is not intended to be an exhaustive list but to give the reader some examples of the state of graduate program assessment at this point.

TABLE 5.1
Examples of Engineering Graduate Program Assessment Plans

Institution	Engineering Program	Website of Plan
Georgia Institute of Technology	Aerospace Engineering	www.ae.gatech.edu/academics/graduate/aero_assessment_plan.html
North Carolina State University	Mechanical and Aerospace Engineering	www.fis.ncsu.edu/grad_publicns/program_review/assessment_pilot.htm
University of Alabama	All Schools in the College of Engineering	http://uaops.ua.edu/right_arm.cfm?col=1
Southern Illinois University–Edwardsville	Mechanical Engineering	www.siue.edu/ENGINEER/ME/graduate_program/assessment.htm
University of Arizona	Biomedical Engineering	http://outcomes.web.arizona.edu/data.php?uid=554
University of North Dakota	Electrical Engineering	www.und.nodak.edu/dept/datacol/assessment/unsecure/0405/EE_gr.pdf
University of South Carolina	Civil and Environmental Engineering	www.cc.sc.edu/DeptInfo/GradAssessPlan.htm

Defining the Nature of Expected Competencies at the Graduate Level

At the undergraduate level, the EC2000 criteria provide a series of competency-based program outcomes for engineering programs. Many of these same competencies remain relevant at the graduate level, yet at a more advanced stage (Sluss, Crain, & Tull, 2005). The individualized nature of learning at the advanced stages of graduate engineering programs may cause us to think that student learning in these programs is essentially noncomparable across students. However, a number of commonalties may apply to graduate programs in engineering. This revolves around the notion that at the graduate level we can expect to see students demonstrate increased breadth and depth of *professional* and *attitudinal* skills, including the following:

- Advanced oral, written, and mathematical communication skills;
- Knowledge of concepts in the discipline;
- Critical and reflective thinking skills;
- Knowledge of the social, cultural, and economic contexts of the discipline;
- Ability to apply theory to professional practice;
- Ability to conduct independent research;
- Ability to use appropriate technologies;
- Ability to work with others, especially in teams;
- Ability to teach others; and
- Demonstration of professional attitudes and values such as workplace ethics and lifelong learning (Banta et al., 1999).

Differentiating operational objectives from learning outcomes. A common pitfall when beginning the assessment of graduate programs in engineering is the conflation of managerial objectives for the program with student learning outcomes. Managerial objectives for a graduate program might include things like increasing the number of quality applicants to the program, increasing yield rates, decreasing program time-to-degree, increasing the number of research proposals, or increasing faculty salaries relative to peers. While these operational objectives are all of clear importance to the vitality of a graduate engineering program, they are not concerned with learning outcomes: the competencies, skills, and attitudes we expect graduate students to acquire through their programs of study. Thus, making a clear distinction in practice between the two important types of measurement is important for assessment planning purposes.

Principles of Graduate Program Assessment

When beginning to plan for graduate program assessment in engineering, experience has shown that a number of principles are involved, the observance of which may make the task much easier:

1. *Decide what is important to measure.* The task of where to begin measurement is difficult, and the tendency is to attempt to measure everything. This frequently results in plans that are completely unwieldy and unsustainable. A better approach is to start with a consensus to assess only a few learning outcomes at the graduate level, and to expand the areas assessed as experience is gained.

2. *Clearly differentiate levels of expectations among degree types (i.e., master's, doctoral level).* There exists a clear difference in the expectations faculty hold for student accomplishment at the master's and doctoral levels, and it follows that assessment plans should reflect this notion. For example, the ability to conduct independent research and the ability to teach others are basic expectations for competence at the doctoral level.

3. *Make assessment responsive to the more individualized nature of programs.* Since graduate (especially doctoral) programs in engineering are smaller than their undergraduate counterparts, assessment plans should be adjusted accordingly. Assessment studies may entail a longer time span, say two or three years instead of one. They may be more qualitative in nature, relying on analysis of verbal protocols obtained through focus groups, interviews, and longitudinal follow-up on the career paths of graduate degree recipients.

4. *Assessment of real student works is preferable; students already create many of the products we can use for assessment.* At the graduate level, the production of individual creative works is generally expected. Think about how to use projects, seminar presentations, proposals, preliminary exam results, and similar opportunities to assess not only individual student progress and competence—according to the learning expectations that faculty have established—but the extent to which the program as a whole meets faculty expectations for student learning. The artifacts created by students are already in hand; they just need to be reanalyzed from the group level and used as a basis for discussion on overall program performance.

5. *Use natural points of contact with program processes for assessment.* This

principle, long espoused in the literature (e.g., Ewell, 1984), suggests that those transition points where graduate students come into contact with the administrative system are ideal for conducting assessment. Admission processes, application for prelims, annual advising appointments, and program exit are all viable opportunities. For example, few graduate students are likely to turn down the completion of an exit survey while a graduate thesis editor is reviewing their work!

6. *Use assessment as both an evaluative and a self-reflection tool.* Assessment at the graduate level enables faculty to evaluate student progress, but also provides a fertile opportunity for programs to provide formative feedback to students. Students need targets, checkpoints, and feedback to self-assess; when graduate students are asked to reflect, it aids cognitive restructuring of what has been learned and metacognition. Long understood as a basic tenet of performance improvement, the charting of graduate student progress toward specific standards of practice and the application of cogent suggestions by graduate mentors, when structured around consistent standards, is a basic motivational intervention that may significantly aid graduate retention, progress, and completion.

7. *Often the most useful comparisons are those made to the program itself over time.* The typically smaller size of graduate programs in engineering relative to undergraduate counterparts, the general lack of useful benchmark assessment data from true peer programs, and the attenuated nature of doctoral study are all factors that argue for the utility of program self-comparisons over time. Faculty may also find internal longitudinal comparison to be culturally more acceptable and trustworthy than external comparisons.

Framework for Graduate Assessment

In this section, a framework is advanced to clarify the relationship among faculty expectations or observation, the type of information and linkage points used in the program, and the assessment methods that may be useful.

Figure 5.1 is not intended to be an exhaustive list but rather to serve as a heuristic device for clarifying needed areas of coverage in designing a comprehensive approach to graduate engineering program assessment. The first column serves to articulate the general category of information being sought

FIGURE 5.1

Matrix for Assessing the Outcomes of Graduate and Professional Education

General Category of Faculty Expectations and Observations	Type of Information and Linkage Points to Use				
	Information obtained prior to matriculation	Basic facts from institutional records	Information on processes	Information on outcomes at completion	Information on long-range outcomes
Degree completion	Academic preparation Motivation Personality Learning style Student goals Previous mentoring relationships	Percentage of total group graduating, by gender, race, age Years to degree	Views of current students from surveys, studies of departmental climate, student advisory groups Views of faculty on factors in degree completion	Exit surveys or interviews	Alumni surveys or interviews
Content knowledge	Writing samples Interviews Presentations GRE and subject-matter exams Professional school entrance exams	Success on licensure exams Pass rates on qualifying exams External examination by reviewers	Views of current students from surveys, student advisory groups	Summarized information from evaluation forms of external evaluators Nondepartmental readers Rewriting of standard evaluation forms Exit surveys and interviews Panel of experts reads most recent dissertations	Alumni surveys or interviews

(continued)

FIGURE 5.1 (Continued)

Type of Information and Linkage Points to Use

General Category of Faculty Expectations and Observations	Information obtained prior to matriculation	Basic facts from institutional records	Information on processes	Information on outcomes at completion	Information on long-range outcomes
Preparation for professional practice	Participation in (student chapters of) professional societies Completion of a report Student critique of a report or research paper	Evaluations from supervisors of internships, graduate co-ops, and practica Evaluations of student success in their training roles	Current student surveys Climate surveys Student advisory groups Panels of working professionals	Exit surveys and interviews External evaluation of students	Alumni surveys or interviews Feedback from employers
Preparation for research and inquiry	Prospective research study plan	Assessment of student research skills as part of regular assistantship evaluation Number and quality of students' publications	Behavioral samples of literature reviews, research designs, etc.	Exit surveys and interviews External evaluation of students	Alumni surveys or interviews Feedback from employers Publication records of graduates
Preparation for teaching	Presentations Communication skills Motivation Personality Learning style Student goals	Student evaluations of instruction Comparison of student performance on common exams with experienced faculty	Classroom observation Portfolios Peer critiques	Teaching awards and recognition Exit surveys and interviews	Alumni surveys or interviews

Adapted from Baird (1996)

about the graduate program: information related to degree completion, content knowledge, preparation for professional practice, preparation for a research career, and preparation for teaching in a higher education context. The variety of options presented should serve to reinforce the necessity for triangulation of measurement in graduate program assessment, ideally using both multiple sources of information and multiple time periods during the graduate's career to collect assessment information.

The next five columns in the framework detail the type of information to be obtained and the linkage or transition points in the program that form appropriate data collection opportunities. Two broad points deserve mention in this connection. First, it may be useful to think about the various information sources as comprising actuarial information (basic facts from institutional records); attitudinal information from surveys, interviews, and focus groups; direct measures from rubric-based analysis of actual student works; and productivity measures including papers published, proposals generated (if appropriate), competitions entered, grants obtained, etc. Second, using multiple points during and after the program is a key to building a longitudinal, rigorous understanding of the program's effects. This includes information obtained prior to matriculation, information on program processes, information obtained at linkage/transition points during the program, outcomes on completion of the program, and long-term impact of the program following degree completion. While an in-depth discussion of each of these points in the program is beyond the scope of this chapter, explanations of the rationale around collecting information prior to matriculation and information about program processes may serve as an example of how to approach assessment of the other linkage or transition points.

The extent to which key competencies normally obtained through an undergraduate engineering program form a sufficient basis for acceptance into a program of graduate study deserves reconsideration. The academic basis for acceptance into graduate study needs to be examined and assessed, whether through diagnostic entrance examinations, performance on the FE Exam, or through some other mechanism. Reliance on grades as evidenced in an undergraduate transcript alone, albeit from an accredited program in an engineering field, fails to yield a composite picture of the extent to which incoming student competencies match the expectations of faculty in a graduate program. Furthermore, in an environment where only 50 percent of graduate students nationally complete their degrees (Nerad & Miller, 1996), indicators such as writing samples, interviews, presentations, and even a short research proposal may serve to round out the view of incoming graduates, as may assessment of attributes such as motivation, personality, learning style, career goals, and participation in previous mentoring relationships.

Like information obtained prior to matriculation, the inclusion of process assessment is an important component of assessment at the graduate level in engineering programs. Departmental climate is typically underassessed (perhaps through informal feedback from a graduate student committee), yet information on the efficacy of mentoring processes; the departmental climate for research, growth, and innovation; the mechanisms in place for professional socialization; the extent to which a "chilly climate" (Sandler & Hall, 1986) exists at the graduate level for women and underrepresented groups; and departmental progress toward the formation of reflective, interdisciplinary communities of research and practice can yield a composite picture of departmental health and, other things being equal, the likelihood of graduate student persistence to completion.

Methods Appropriate to Assessing Graduate Programs

When considering assessment methods, the temptation is to use whatever is currently available, yet it is vital to establish conceptual direction for graduate program assessment at the outset. To this purpose, faculty may find it valuable to utilize simple decision matrices of (1) appropriate selection criteria (e.g., development time, cost, likely quality of information) in relation to assessment methods being considered, and (2) coverage of the appropriate faculty expectations for student competence (i.e., graduate program outcomes and educational objectives) in relation to the assessment methods being used or considered for use.

The availability of a wide variety of student works at the graduate level means that conducting direct assessment of actual student works is feasible, affordable, and likely to result in the production of usable information for program assessment. Evaluation forms keyed to expectations for professional competence may be used for departmental research seminar presentations. For course work at the graduate level, rubric-based assessment of portfolios, presentations, project/paper evaluation by raters, and 360-degree cross-disciplinary teamwork evaluation forms may be used. Verbal feedback from design competitions, where appropriately recorded, may offer key insights on program strengths and needs for adjustment. Simple rubrics constructed to rate preliminary exams, thesis/dissertation proposals, and final defenses may result in some of the most valuable information. For example, faculty in the Department of Biomedical Engineering at Georgia Tech found it most useful to start with a simple three-point check sheet ("exceeded standards," "met standards," "did not meet standards") across each of the faculty expectations for student competence: While faculty at first expressed reservations about using rubrics to assess student proposals and defenses, the annual compilation of this assessment information revealed variance in student performance that has been useful for programmatic adjustment (T. Wick, personal communication, April 20, 2006). If the graduate program includes internships, then supervisor evaluations, behavioral assessments, and even focus groups of internship supervisors or mentors may be very useful sources of in-process information on a particular graduate program. Widely used indirect assessment methods at program exit include graduate exit surveys (see, for example, www.assessment.gatech.edu/surveys/GT_Graduate_Exit_Survey 061704_SAMPLE.pdf), one-on-one graduate exit interviews, and graduate exit focus groups. Long-term follow-up typically centers on the use of graduate alumni surveys, searches of citation indices, and in smaller programs may include simple techniques such as a periodic request for alumni vitae.

Integrating Graduate Assessment Into a Process of Institutional Effectiveness

In the long run, the purposeful inclusion of assessment of student learning in core academic processes is the only practical road to establishing a sustainable culture of evidence in graduate engineering programs. Thus, this portion of the chapter focuses on sustaining graduate program assessment through making assessment a key element of organizational infrastructure and recurring organizational processes. A number of key processes are addressed, and a brief discussion of how assessment may be successfully integrated into each process is advanced.

1. *Annual reporting:* Assuming that the graduate program in question has an annual assessment component, then in annual reporting at the unit level on the health, productivity, and viability of graduate programs via a unit-based graduate assessment update becomes part of the annual report at the school, college, and then institution level. Annual updates on broad institutional performance indicators and critical success factors at the graduate level should be included across the institution, thus guaranteeing a future demand for such information. In this context, it is important to examine the relationship of annual reports to metrics established in the strategic plan to help determine institutional progress.

2. *Budgeting:* The annual budget development cycle forms an ideal home for advancing graduate assessment results in the context of budget requests, since it may ground the request in the direct results of program impact on graduate student learning. Expectations for linkage to assessment results should be clearly established through inclusion in an annual budget letter to units, as part of a compact planning process, or through other direct communication channels. From the institutional level, a teachable moment in creating a culture of evidence can be created very quickly by the provost. With new initiatives, recommendations, or increases over base, simply ask for evidence of graduate student learning that establishes the budget need. "Show me the data before I show you the money" may be thought of as a workable mantra, one that will serve as a notable catalyst for furthering faculty engagement in graduate assessment.

3. *Socialization processes:* One consequence of the rapidly advancing generational turnover in engineering departments throughout the country is that institutional memory is being lost. A number of those engineering faculty and administrators who have become socialized to assessment programs, who can recite ABET EC2000 Criteria 3.a–k in their sleep, and who have become key players in sustaining assessment in their departments may have increasing designs on retirement rather than on designed experiments. To counteract this, it is vital to build into new faculty orientation an overview of institutional practices relative to graduate and undergraduate assessment, as well as presentations to new chairs and to the students themselves during new graduate student orientation, to reinforce the message that a culture of evidence-based feedback on student learning characterizes the graduate educational programs at the institution.

4. *Promotion/tenure/reward structure:* A problematic area for many engineering departments has been the rise of expectations related to the quality of teaching as the pressure for research funding has also steadily increased. From a previous era of Darwinistic thinking on teaching at the undergraduate level, general practice has moved to the recognition that good teaching is a crucial precursor to student persistence, graduation, and interest in graduate study in engineering. Yet, for department chairs in particular, striking a balance among the expectations for research productivity, the need for extramural funding, and ensuring the graduation of educationally engaged engineers who are interested in graduate studies—and thus the future of domestic graduate engineering programs—is a daunting task. In this regard,

a crucial administrative role is to act as catalyst for innovations in student learning at the graduate level by providing recognition and rewards for innovative teaching and learning projects that include assessment components, by providing competitive grants for such programs, by institutionalizing graduate mentor awards, and by facilitating the recognition of graduate educational research projects in the promotion and tenure process (see Boyer, 1990). Chairs will certainly encourage the pursuit of extramurally funded research projects related to educational improvement and interdisciplinary studies in engineering at the graduate level (e.g., National Science Foundation IGERT or Department of Education GAANN programs), but since most funding agencies (e.g., NSF, NIH, Sloan Foundation) require solid project evaluation as part of proposal funding, this is also an ideal opportunity to involve faculty in graduate assessment within their area of interest and demonstrate project results in terms of student learning.

5. *Professional development opportunities:* In higher education, success that is publicly recognized gets emulated. A key to furthering diffusion of innovations in graduate student learning is the widespread communication and recognition of best practices within all engineering departments, a practice that will reinforce the culture of reflection and action. This communication effort must feature numerous Web links to assessment efforts in appropriate pedagogical areas. It is vital to keep the information provided clear and understandable; for example, see Central Michigan University's assessment "toolkit" developed by faculty (including a section on graduate assessment), at www.provost.cmich.edu/assessment/toolkit/toolkit.htm, and links to the various engineering assessment tools developed under the auspices of the Foundation Coalition (see www.foundationcoalition.org/home/keycomponents/assessment_evaluation.html). The goal of these and other examples should be to provide faculty with the necessary tools to accomplish assessment as part of their responsibilities in graduate education. Forums and assessment seminars may also be beneficial, as may sponsorship of faculty attendance at assessment-related conferences such as Rose-Hulman's long-standing annual Best Assessment Processes conference.

6. *Integrating assessment and graduate program review:* As noted at the beginning of the chapter, graduate program review has a long history in American higher education. What was traditionally a process that focused on the inputs to graduate programs has shifted notably toward an emphasis on processes and outcomes (Baker, 2005). In this regard, it is of paramount

importance to incorporate evidence of student learning in the graduate review and to ensure that assessment stands as an equal partner with the research program at the heart of the program review self-study. Prior to development of a program review self-study, Wergin (2003) advises thorough preliminary work to identify those key issues that will focus the review and give it strategic relevance. If it is to be workable as a graduate assessment process, program review needs to be performed on a more frequent cycle (e.g., five years), one in which annual graduate assessment results already published may be used to lessen the data collection burden and support meaningful trend analysis by the program. A final feature of successful program review models in the current environment is the creation of a governance structure or institutional oversight committee for continued discussion of findings and recommendations produced through program review. This committee reviews the findings across reviews, discusses the implications, and makes recommendations, and these recommendations are fed into the planning process. At Georgia Tech, the Institute Graduate Committee has long played a key role in making recommendations from its examination of graduate program review studies, typically including a multidisciplinary perspective on how interconnections at the graduate level may be strengthened. Guidelines for incorporating assessment into program review processes at North Carolina State University can be found at its graduate school's website: www.fis.ncsu.edu/grad_publicns/program_review; also at its website can be found workshop materials on how to develop graduate program assessment plans.

7. *Linking graduate assessment and strategic planning:* At the institutional level, assessment information from graduate programs is used to inform the institution of the needs and expectations of internal and external clients and stakeholders, to bring forward externalities that may impact the institution, to chart progress toward campus planning goals and illuminate trends in institutional effectiveness, and thereby to inform the process of establishing/modifying strategic direction for the institution. Information derived from multiple graduate program reviews during a given time period and trends in assessment data on graduate programs both form an important basis for analysis of internal strengths and needs for improvement. Feedback from graduate alumni and employers is an important basis for considering external opportunities and threats. Finally, roll-up metrics that indicate department-level progress on usage of assessment data to drive and achieve improvements in, for example, graduate retention rates or semesters to completion can be

used as part of an institutional performance indicator system to inform the planning, budgeting, and resource allocation process and thus provide a link to overall institutional effectiveness efforts.

Summary

The structure of graduate programs in engineering sets them apart from undergraduate programs in terms of assessment. A necessary precursor to developing a viable plan for assessing graduate engineering programs is an understanding of that structure and, in particular, the role of mentoring processes. A focus on professional competence and disciplinary socialization is likely to characterize faculty expectations for student learning at the graduate level in engineering, but care must be given to appropriately defining those expectations and distinguishing them from operational objectives. Planning for graduate program assessment is further facilitated by careful attention to a number of principles, such as using contact or program transition points as opportunities for data collection and using assessment as both an evaluative and a self-reflection tool. A heuristic framework for graduate assessment was advanced in this chapter to clarify the relationship among the general category of faculty expectations or observations, the type of information and linkage points in the program to use, and the assessment methods that may be of greatest utility; it was pointed out that a solid graduate program assessment schema will include multiple methods as well as multiple program points. Assessment methods appropriate to graduate programs in engineering were discussed, and the notion was advanced of using rubric-based assessment of student works and transition points such as thesis proposals, preliminary exams, and final defense as a viable, direct assessment alternative to common survey research methods of indirect assessment. The chapter concluded with a discussion of ways in which sustainable assessment of graduate programs in engineering may be achieved through integration with known and accepted institutional processes and infrastructure, thus leading to advances in institutional effectiveness.

References

ABET. (2007). Criteria for accrediting programs. Retrieved February 10, 2007, from http://www.abet.org/

Bagayoko, D. (1998). *Towards an assessment and evaluation framework for mentoring processes and results.* Louisiana Alliance for Minority Participation, Southern University, and A&M College, Baton Rouge, LA. Retrieved January 15, 2007, from http://www.phys.subr.edu/homepage/academy/mentoring.htm

Baird, L. L. (1996). Documenting student outcomes in graduate and professional programs. In J. Haworth (Ed.), Assessing graduate and professional education: Current realities, future prospects. *New Directions for Institutional Research, 92,* 77–87. San Francisco: Jossey-Bass.

Baker, M. J. (2005). *Assessment and review of graduate programs: A policy statement* (Revised and updated by M. F. King, D. K. Larick, & M. P. Carter). Washington, DC: Council of Graduate Schools.

Banta, T., Black, K., & Ward, E. (1999). Using assessment to ensure the quality of post-baccalaureate programs. *Continuing Higher Education Review, 63,* 87–97.

Boyer, E. L. (1990). *Scholarship reconsidered: Priorities of the professoriate.* Princeton, NJ: Carnegie Foundation for the Advancement of Teaching.

Ewell, P. (1984). *The self-regarding institution: Information for excellence.* Boulder, CO: National Center for Higher Education Management Systems.

Fentiman, A. (2006). Inspiring leaders. In *In Focus.* Retrieved January 15, 2007, from Purdue University, College of Engineering website: https://engineering.purdue .edu/Engr/AboutUs/FactsFigures/InFocus/2006_2

Green, R., & Rittman, R. (2001, June). *Institutionalizing the assessment of graduate education.* Presentation at the American Association of Higher Education Assessment Forum, Denver, CO.

Harcleroad, F. F. (1980). *Accreditation: History, process and problem* (AAHE/ERIC Higher Education Research Report No. 6). Washington, DC: American Association of Higher Education.

Hoey, J. (2005, October 25). *Re-engineering assessment: Reconsidering our tools and practices.* Plenary address at the IUPUI Assessment Institute, Indianapolis.

Kuffel, L., & Hoey, J. (2006, December). *Assessing graduate programs in doctoral research universities.* Workshop presented at the 2006 meeting of the Commission on Colleges, Southern Association of Colleges and Schools, Orlando, FL.

Kuh, C. (2005). An assessment of research-doctorate programs. Retrieved January 15, 2007, from National Research Council website: http://www8.nationalacade mies.org/cp/projectview.aspx?key=202

Maki, P. (2006, July 31). *Sustaining assessment of student learning across the institution.* Plenary address at the SACS Summer Institute, Orlando, FL.

Nerad, M., & Miller, D. (1996). Increasing student retention in graduate and professional programs. In *New Directions for Institutional Research, 92,* pp. 61–76. San Francisco: Jossey-Bass.

Sandler, B. R., & Hall, R. (1986). *The campus climate revisited: Chilly for women faculty, administrators and graduate students.* Washington, DC: Association of American Colleges and Universities.

Schilling, K., & Schilling, K. (1998). *Proclaiming and sustaining excellence: Assessment as a faculty role* (ASHE-ERIC Higher Education Report 26: 3). Washington, DC:

The George Washington University, Graduate School of Education and Human Development.

Sluss, J. J., Crain, G., & Tull, M. (2005, October). *Work in progress—Assessment of graduate electrical and computer engineering degree programs at the University of Oklahoma.* Presented at the 35th ASEE/IEEE Frontiers in Education Conference, Indianapolis.

Tsang, E., Halderston, C., Abdel-Qader, I., Aller, B., Butt, S., Kline, A., Miller, D., Place, T., Yehia, S., & Kallen, K. (2006, October). *Assessment of faculty mentoring strategies of student learning communities at Western Michigan University College of Engineering and Applied Sciences.* Presented at the 36th ASEE/IEEE Frontiers in Education Conference, San Diego.

Wergin, J. F. (2003). *Departments that work.* Bolton, MA: Anker.

PART TWO

BARRIERS AND CHALLENGES

6

BARRIERS AND CHALLENGES TO ASSESSMENT IN ENGINEERING EDUCATION

J. Joseph Hoey, IV and Eleanor W. Nault

Over a decade of mandated assessment and state evaluation mandates and, more recently, the ABET Engineering Criteria 2000 (EC2000) have focused attention on the need to systematically assess student learning in engineering curricula, yet excellence in assessment still appears in pockets and not as the norm for most engineering programs. A crucial problem is that the methods and outlook of assessment have often been advanced without acknowledging the barriers that exist to implementing organizational change and curricular reform, without requisite faculty development, and without developing the indispensable basis of organizational trust upon which assessment relies. Assessment as a long-term strategy is intended to enable high-performance student learning systems through the continuous measurement of processes and outcomes, and through the use of results to further refine performance (Clark, n.d.). Systematic assessment of student learning is the first step in an ascending stairway of structured introspection that enables individual faculty members, programs, and institutions to build a learning organization. This chapter articulates the barriers that exist to implementing assessment and describes the contextual factors that contribute to the relative resistance of those impediments.

Characteristics of an Environment Promoting a Culture of Assessment

Shaw (1997) observed that trust is founded and kept alive within organizations in three primary ways: through culture, organizational structure, and leadership. Other things being equal, more successful organizations will feature cultures based on a shared vision and ground rules that are understood and shared by all members. Successful organizational cultures encourage risk taking and experimentation, continuous learning, and open communication. The organizational structure has to be simple enough to be understood by all, and needs to be marked by understood roles and responsibilities as well as clear communication lines in all directions. Resources and opportunities for professional development need to be available to support continued learning and fulfillment of organizational roles. These areas are all subject to influence by organization leadership. Most important, the role of leadership is to model attributes of trustworthiness, to demonstrate attitudes conducive to building trust, and to foster trust throughout the organization.

Desirable characteristics of an environment promoting a culture of assessment include many of the elements necessary for any successful organization. Leadership in promoting a culture of evidence-based decision making about academic programs, both at the highest administrative level and the closest unit level, is critical. An environment that does not support the practice of assessment may include a lack of incentives (perceived as a lack of value or interest in the practice), fear of change and valuing the status quo, reduced resources for the office and/or function of assessment at the institutional level, and burnout of those charged with the assessment process or those who could contribute. Being strapped with "long marchers" (those who have been in the institution for a long time, who have lost a vision of change, and who are not leaders but continue to participate—perhaps waiting for retirement) is a challenge to creating a change in the culture.

Faculty may perceive they are expected to do more assessment, but they may not perceive that their efforts will be supported unless public, demonstrated support from senior levels of the organization is apparent, and support resources are available in the form of professional development, consultation, easily available information resources, internal examples of good practice in assessment, and the like. The faculty must have support—both administrative within the institution and the professional support of the outside world—that substantiates the notion that assessment is valued and change toward active, quality assessment is embraced. This may be evidenced by the use of results in presentations; part of the department's annual review; postings of highlights on the program's Web page or other publicly accessed media; or best of all, through public leadership support of a culture of evidence: "It's how we manage our academic programs here." Also, support may be demonstrated with avowed assessment purposes linked to institutional priorities as expressed in program initiatives, budgeting, and resource allocation. Sharing of assessment results and participatory decision making bring to light the support of integrated efforts to collect and analyze data for program improvement. The practice and outcome of assessment efforts must be shared across the institution, and changes necessary to enhance or improve the outcomes need to be integrated into the assessment process. Consistency and reliability of practice, including recognition and rewards provided for initiative in assessment projects, are hallmarks of supportive leadership in a culture of assessment.

In addition to having institutional leadership that endorses the practice of assessment and the professional guidance and development to undertake the assessment process, the academic units must have the ability to implement essential enhancements to improve learning objectives and outcomes. If a department or division is unable to initiate or implement change, the critical purpose of practicing assessment in academic units ("closing the loop") is eliminated. Support in this context includes allocating fiscal resources, laboratories and classrooms, and personnel that may have been identified as lacking when the data collected in assessment processes were collectively reflected upon by departmental faculty, who arrived at a decision to implement change. Engaged leadership and dedicated resources generally emerge not from a static environment but from one where needs for the improvement of student learning are balanced with other factors in the political milieu that characterize decision making in academia.

Engaging in this change is by no means a task to be taken lightly or one that is certain of a successful outcome. The very stability of higher education institutions may mitigate the active adoption of a culture of assessment, as may the existence of strong disciplinary cultures, as is the case with engineering. Nardini (2001) notes that "one barrier to developing a culture of assessment is that culture, by its very nature, is stable and resistant to change." Tolan and Hurny (2004) address the underlying cultural barriers to the integration of assessment into engineering education in plain terms: "The 'elephant' on the table that no one wants to talk about is the decisions and systems change that must accompany implementation, and the deep cultural change that must occur in the organization to sustain outcomes assessment."

Moving to an active learning environment and a pedagogy of engagement, and the fundamental shift in perspective that such a shift presumes, may be perceived as outside of individual instructors' comfort zones, threatening, and against the prevailing norms of institutional or disciplinary culture.

Implementing Change

The degree to which implementing change in leadership and support, developing an environment of trust, and furthering knowledge and professional development concerning assessment is necessary in a given institutional context is directly related to the extent to which barriers in the organization must be overcome if assessment is to succeed and to have a realistic chance of achieving sustainability as an organizational process. Without these three manifestations of change, the likelihood of an environmental shift sufficient to bring about a position of success is limited. To further elucidate these barriers, Hoey and Nault (2001) described a taxonomy of barriers to assessment, based around aspects of trust. They see the level of trust as the most basic and fundamental factor involved in assessment design and implementation. Environments in which assessment practices are not viable are characterized by one or more of a set of identifiable barriers as detailed in Figure 6.1.

Trust or lack of trust in assessment is played out in at least four ways within institutions of higher education: The motives for collecting assessment data may be mistrusted by faculty; the methodological foundation and instrumentation used may be lacking and a source of low trust in assessment; the questions raised through assessment may not be relevant to issues of interest to faculty and not regarded as trustworthy; and fear concerning the misuse or inappropriate interpretation of the data generated through assessment may cause deep mistrust of assessment. As noted above, leadership support, fear orientation, and planned change orientation within the organization also play a major role in determining the success or failure of an assessment initiative.

A significant number of barriers are laden with fears such as punishment for asking difficult questions, discovering that the learning outcomes of a specific course are not meeting the benchmark, or finding out that one's teaching is ineffective. Fears beyond the classroom include that assessment results will affect individuals through the faculty reward system (remuneration, tenure, etc.). The behavioral response system as practiced in most institutions forms a key construct of institutional culture: The actions that are

FIGURE 6.1
Aspects of Trust as Characterized in Low- and High-Trust Environments for Assessment

Aspect of Trust in Assessment	Low-Trust Environment	High-Trust Environment
Trust in the motives	• Belief that data will be collected ostensibly for one purpose, but used somehow to punish faculty	• Linkage evident between university, college, and department plans • Culture of assessment instilled and routines set up that will keep everyone focused on enhancing what we do
Trust in the questions	• "Safe" questions asked whose outcome will not require change	• Meaningful questions asked in assessment to investigate aspects of teaching and curriculum effectiveness
Trust in the methods	• Inadequate methodological basis • Role of faculty in process unclear • Required short-term orientation for reporting results of assessment projects and activities	• Sound methodological frameworks • Faculty participate in developing approaches and selecting/developing instrumentation • Familiar format used for reporting • Sense of faculty ownership in process and knowledge of how individual efforts contribute to the whole • Longitudinal, multiyear projects undertaken that may take several years to report • Departmental timeline developed, and assessment incorporated throughout yearly activities

(continued)

FIGURE 6.1 (Continued)

Aspect of Trust in Assessment	Low-Trust Environment	High-Trust Environment
Trust in the data	• Low response or participation rates on surveys lead to unusable data • Grades are unstable and don't provide actionable data	• Clear linkage between data source and appropriate question being asked • Use of Primary Trait Analysis to disaggregate grading data into central components of the discipline
Leadership support	• Little or no public support • Avowed assessment purposes not linked to institutional priorities as expressed in initiatives or budgeting • Assessment results not shared with institution	• Strong, public support • Data shared and participatory decision making used • Consistency and reliability evident • Recognition and rewards provided for initiative in assessment projects
Fear orientation	• Fear of punishment for asking difficult questions • Fear of hearing bad news • Fear of finding out that one's teaching is ineffective	• Risk taking and engagement with questions of teaching and learning encouraged and rewarded • Disclosure and asking for help encouraged—asking and sharing
Planned change orientation	• Members unwilling to participate in introspective processes and unwilling to admit possibility of need for change • Vision of faculty role as solo contractor	• Results linked to mission • Needs, strengths, and philosophy identified and agreed upon • Vision of faculty role includes larger institutional responsibility and goal setting

Adapted from Hoey & Nault (2001)

most frequently rewarded are likely to be repeated; the actions most frequently sanctioned are those most likely to be avoided. Not only can this form a sizable barrier to progress on assessment, but the simple predominance of a behaviorist organizational model can itself be a detriment to developing a culture of assessment. If faculty are conditioned to accept change and to change behavior only through extrinsic rather than intrinsic stimuli, an avowedly introspective undertaking such as assessment will have little chance of success. The barriers of culture may further include generational differences in thinking about assessment, organizational development, or planned change. There may be a chasm between the talents and abilities of faculty who do their job very well in their field, their expertise, and their ability to examine the program as a whole. The perception of being a "solo contractor" rather than an engaged player in the curriculum may be pervasive or, at a minimum, a philosophy of faculty, rather than an orientation toward collective faculty ownership of the curriculum (Wergin, 2003). Members could be unwilling to participate in introspective processes and unwilling to admit the possibility of need for change, all of which can impede the assessment process at the program as well as institutional level.

Assessment practices within each institution and program vary in levels of success and may have equally varied limitations. Identifying and understanding the fears that faculty hold are steps toward creating a climate of success. Moving from an environment of distrust toward a culture of success in integrating assessment and quality enhancement into an academic culture requires that the academy take action and make commitments. The charge is to work within the span of control of those taking the action, have an effect where possible to advance professional development and understanding, and to further connections rather than misunderstandings and excuses.

Institutional Change

For a rollout of assessment to successfully take root and grow, an environmental shift is necessary—one that must be guided by an understanding of theories of organizational development and planned change. Leadership of both programs and the institution must implement change according to known successful models that will guide productive change demonstrated by assessment results being linked to the mission, to improvement, and to reducing a culture of fear.

The question of value of assessment is frequently linked to noting that among competing priorities there is not time for such practices. Perhaps the need to reflect on choices will reveal that time is found to undertake that which is valued. If assessment practices were valued, time would be made to engage, to actually practice assessment including designing strategies for change and improvement in student learning. It is essential to continually reinforce the notion that academic freedom is not stifled by authentic assessment methods. The content and outcomes of the courses are agreed upon, but the method of delivery is open and valued. Wergin (2003) points out that individual research programs belong to each faculty member, but the curriculum belongs to the faculty as a body. The faculty, in a culture of assessment, identify time for the practice of assessment balanced with honor of their academic freedom.

By agreeing upon and identifying needs, strengths, and philosophy of change, faculty will expand the vision of the faculty role to include larger institutional responsibility and goal setting. Faculty will increase disclosure and will ask for appropriate assistance and professional development opportunities, and an environment of asking and sharing will result. Additionally, the climate of success will include risk taking and engagement, with questions of teaching and learning encouraged and rewarded. A solution to the "solo contractor" thinking is to integrate assessment requirements into expectations for annual performance and promotion/tenure. In addition to faculty evaluation, the accomplishment of assessment and usage of results are integrated into annual performance criteria for chairs, deans, and senior administrators. Professional development can facilitate these shifts through workshops, one-on-one mentoring, and objective and demonstrated leadership designed for change and institutional accountability toward effectiveness.

Individual Change

Significant barriers to building trust for assessment also exist at the individual level, and it is at that level that a willingness to investigate new areas of teaching, learning, and assessment needs to begin, since change cannot take place in organizations without first taking place at the individual level within the organizational membership. Clark (n.d.) observes that "organizations are simply sets of relationships; relationships between and among people who hold a stake in organizing. . . . Organizations don't transform; people do." Gray (1997) amplifies this theme, and applies it to change within higher education. He says that frequently the introduction of innovations or changes such as assessment is perceived as an institution-wide event, to take place shortly after being announced by senior leaders. The reality is that the adoption of change and innovation is a process that proceeds from individual to individual, and from department to department. Thus, the role of campus leadership in this process includes the managing of trust through constancy of purpose and reliability of action. Building an organizational culture where trust is valued takes substantial change, and senior organizational leadership has to develop an effective strategy for promoting this change. This is best accomplished by consciously diagnosing the extent of change necessary and, only then, proceeding to reorient choices and actions to reflect a determination to build trust (Chatterjee, 1997).

Commitment of Resources

Knowing where and how to obtain necessary resources is indicative of an environment that supports the practice of assessment. Faculty must believe that they are able to contribute to a well-designed assessment process without having to be experts in assessment. If there is difficulty in requesting and finding data or truly authentic instruments and evidence-gathering techniques, or difficulty in interpreting the data or communicating what has been learned, change toward a more productive culture of assessment will not be facilitated. The climate for change must be leveraged to reduce barriers. Providing the essential resources may be an approach at the institutional level or within a college or department.

Inability to initiate or implement a process may be a result of not knowing how to practice assessment. One resource for a climate of success is an assessment coordinator or assessment office on campus able to assist program assessment. This person (or office, as at Clemson and Georgia Tech) is able to suggest instruments, assist in identifying appropriate measures and data, help define measures of student learning for grant proposals, and implement assessment at the institutional level that can be disaggregated to the program level and therefore used by departments as a source of feedback. Faculty know what they teach and therefore frequently believe that course grades are sufficient measures of student learning. Their perception is that course objectives are easier to assess and harder to tie to program learning outcomes. The solution is providing professional guidance and development with adequate resources, guidelines, and assistance to facilitate effective change.

Professional Development

Questions about the validity of assessment methods may stop or delay gathering or using data. A lack of knowledge about assessment processes and tools impedes collecting and analyzing data. Furthermore, assessment methods may be too complex, cumbersome, or time-consuming to maintain over time or obtain the direct assessment of desired outcomes. Rhetoric and jargon of assessment may not be meaningful or understood. All of these environmental limitations may result in developing or sustaining an "accountability" approach to the tasks of assessment: an attitude of just doing something for the benefit of getting it done. Assessment is not seen as research but compliance, an attitude frequently driven by impending accreditation or reaffirmation events.

To address these encumbrances, purposeful and intentional professional development may be necessary to move toward an active participation by the faculty. Faculty must be given the knowledge and professional development to break the inertia, to become informed about the true benefit of accountability through assessment. Learning about the progressive pedagogies and how to gain feedback on implementing and improving student performance via those pedagogies is a key to cultural change. The sheer amount of assessment data to be collected and processed may be successfully managed through appropriate leveraging of information technology resources (Hoey, 2006).

The professional development of faculty can be directed individually or in groups. Written and oral information delivered through institutional standards or guidelines, presentations, feedback, and one-on-one sessions are both intended to clearly establish the purposes of assessment: what students will learn in the context of a course, in the context of a sequence of courses, and in an entire degree program. Some resources that may be useful for the delivery are Web-based monologs, rubrics, surveys or benchmarks, in-house newsletters and seminars, travel to conferences, competitive minigrants for assessment practices, and publicizing of best practices. Faculty who have adopted a process for assessment that includes the identification of clear, measurable program objectives and outcomes are able to design and collect authentic (direct) measures of student learning. These student artifacts represent the students' demonstration of the extent to which the students know, think, or do something as a result of the teaching. These artifacts can be examined in light of previously agreed-upon criteria for success (benchmarks or standards), and judgments can be drawn regarding student learning related to the desired outcomes.

Unfamiliar language can be replaced with local nomenclature, purpose of assessment can be clarified, academic freedom can be protected, and institutions can move toward a climate of change and culture of assessment. Assessment that was once regarded as a process outside of the rhythm and processes of academic life thus becomes more integrated into known institutional cycles and processes in progressive stages of implementation. Changes will take time, however, and ongoing evaluation is necessary to demonstrate that improvements have occurred as a result of implementing modifications to sequence of courses or content delivery methods, improved methods to collect data, etc. To desire improvement, to value reaching the "best" rather than accept being "good," to strengthen higher education and the academy are all parts of the vision and a climate of success for assessment.

Practical Barriers

A number of practical barriers to assessment have been articulated in the literature base. Aschbacher (1992) found a number of barriers in her study of performance-based assessment implementation, such as an emphasis on planning learning activities rather than outcomes that might result; a reluctance to change established current practice; the difficulty of specifying meaningful criteria by which to rate student work; "assessment anxiety," or the fear of being judged; the need for training and ongoing support; the lack of a plan for developing and implementing assessment over the long term; and simply a lack of time for planning and implementing assessment.

The scope of the work involved and the need to leverage information technology appropriately have also been a focus in the literature. Ansary, Rahrooh, and Buchanan (2002) address problems of creating a process and maintaining the infrastructure that is required to validate the ABET EC2000 outcomes, the cost issues related to the resources engaged in accommodating such a process, and how these issues are anticipated to influence the participation of universities and colleges in such activities. The sheer magnitude of the work involved can also be daunting, especially in large institutions. Furlong and Vohra (2002) detail difficulties of incorporating feedback into the assessment process and strategies for analyzing and using assessment results as feedback directed toward the improvement of total program quality. Tolan and Hurny (2004) note the need to develop efficient and easily maintained assessment metrics and measures to get to the real, longitudinal data needs; upgrading organizational participants to more sophisticated uses of technology relative to assessment; and the time and cost involved in developing assessment systems.

Advances in teaching and learning have to go hand in hand with the progress in implementing assessment; innovations in both experience similar barriers. Thompson and Williams (1985) discuss barriers in the context of adopting and sustaining problem-based learning (PBL), an innovation increasingly found in schools of biomedical engineering such as at Georgia Tech. They note that several barriers to the acceptance of problem-based learning, especially in established schools, include complacency borne of time-honored tradition, a lack of meaningful rewards for faculty who develop expertise in education at the expense of a traditional research program, and the fact that a method of integrated learning such as PBL that promotes interdisciplinary thinking may be perceived as a threat to the continued viability of department-based courses.

Developing Trust in Assessment

Developing greater trust in the use of assessment strategies is important. However, other barriers to the assessment process must also be surmounted if effective, systematic assessment of student learning is to succeed. Going beyond the immediate barriers to trust in assessment, characteristics of a culture of assessment are infused with a low level of trust. The three domains of barriers to systematic assessment practices may be summarized as barriers of attitude, of knowledge, and of practice. Examples within each domain are shown in Figure 6.2.

There are general characteristics of what is needed for sustainable assessment systems to flourish. A general acceptance of the presence of ongoing evaluation is necessary; however, in practice, the level of acceptance ranges from compliance to embracing the opportunity for program improvement. The extant variance in attitudes toward sustained program assessment may either underpin in a positive way or may act to curtail the adoption of a relativistic attitude toward assessment, such as the notion that limitations exist for all methods of collecting data. This variance in attitudes may produce a lack of trust in assessment strategies and resulting data unless tempered by the realization that data collection strategies must be triangulated and that extant methods can and should be continuously reflected upon and improved. An ideal environment or culture of assessment probably does not exist, given the tremendous variation among institutions and disciplinary cultures. However, open communication continues to be an undercurrent of best practice running through many of the characteristics in a high-trust environment. Figure 6.3 contains characteristics of low- and high-trust environments as identified by Nault and Hoey (2002).

Limitations to assessment methods strap the faculty's willingness to identify one assessment strategy that provided completely trustworthy data. For instance, surveys of employers are excellent sources of information on

FIGURE 6.2
Examples of Barriers to Systematic Assessment

Domain of Barrier	Examples of Barriers
Attitudinal	• Lack of "buy in," "commitment," or "motivation" • "Indifference, resistance, and hostility" toward assessment • Assessment viewed as "administrative nonsense"
Knowledge	• Turnover in personnel resulting in loss of institutional memory • Not knowing what needed to be evaluated • Responding to a need for accountability rather than developing assessment processes through a departmentally driven process for program improvement
Practice	• Results not provided at department level where they are most useful • Data not provided from central sources in a timely manner • No evidence of change or improvement • No link between assessment results and budget allocations • Institutional leadership not supporting assessment momentum after an accrediting body leaves

student learning and the mastery of specific skills. Nevertheless, the questions may not obtain necessary details or be interpreted the same way by all employers. Figure 6.4 characterizes the strengths and weaknesses of a number of commonly used specific methods of assessment. Student artifacts provide a rich source of data for assessing student learning; however, there are at least two limitations identified to this strategy: storing and rating of the materials. To a high degree, both limitations may be overcome through electronic storage, access, and retrieval with the understanding that there may be a lack of accuracy of the data, of trust in the source of information, or of resources to undertake detailed assessment or store the materials.

The interplay of culture and change confounds the environment of trust, the acceptance of ongoing assessment, and the culture of assessment itself.

FIGURE 6.3
Summary: Aspects of Trust

Aspect of Trust in Assessment	Low-Trust Environment	High-Trust Environment
Trust in the motives	• Belief that data will be collected ostensibly for one purpose, but used somehow to punish faculty	• Linkage evident between university, college, and department plans • Purpose of assessment articulated by leadership
Trust in the questions	• "Safe" questions asked whose outcome will not require change	• Questions asked to investigate aspects of teaching and curriculum effectiveness
Trust in the methods *Trust in Specific Methods:* *See Figure 6.4*	• Inadequate methodological basis	• Sound methodological frameworks • Faculty participate in developing approaches and selecting or developing instrumentation
Trust in the data	• Low response or participation rates on surveys lead to unusable data	• Clear linkage between data source and appropriate question being asked

Lattuca, Terenzini, and Volkwein (2006) relate that many engineering faculty are positive toward the process of assessment and its being used for program improvement. Nonetheless, Hoey and Nault (2002) report that faculty typically do not report that their environment is a high-trust culture for assessment and that there is room for improvement in assessment questions, strategies, and data. Clearly, improving assessment activities is not the sole challenge of the program faculty but can be shared with other college or university constituencies in order to move toward more sustainable and meaningful assessments.

Building Trust

Davis et al. (2002), citing Stiggins (1997), specify the following elements of success for assessment in engineering education: clearly communicated purposes, such as orientation workshops and guidelines; clear and appropriate targets, such as assessing key aspects of the design process; target and method

FIGURE 6.4
Aspects of Trust as Characterized in Specific Methods of Assessment

Assessment Method	Strengths and Weaknesses
Standardized Exam or Licensure Exam	*Weakness:* Not all students take it; content of material may not map to curriculum. *Strength:* Objective
Curriculum Display or Student Artifacts	*Weakness:* Collection and storage issues; providing valid rating *Strength:* Direct measure
Performance Appraisal: Co-op Student, Supervisor Reports	*Weakness:* Variability; no control over the raters and their interpretation *Strength:* Workplace information
Accreditation Review by Discipline Peers	*Weakness:* Motives of reviewers; faculty may not interact with results *Strength:* Review by knowledgeable peers
Interview: Student Advisory Committee, Graduating Students	*Weakness:* All volunteers; self-selected; bias timing; honesty of results *Strength:* Use consultant; cross-section of students
Surveys: Exit, Career, Employer, Alumni	*Weakness:* No differentiation between departments in the data
Student Placement Data After Graduation	*Weakness:* Overall, small measure of current student knowledge; tertiary data

matching, for example, using constructed responses to assess higher-order reasoning among students; appropriate sampling, such as collecting work from multiple institutions, engineering disciplines, and course levels to ensure adequate representation; and elimination of bias and distortion, such as iterative rater calibration processes to ensure consistent application.

It is evident that engineering faculty members know exactly what the limitations are to the assessment strategies that they use. They are able to articulate, without reservation, the enhancements that would provide a stronger assessment protocol, even if they are unable to undertake the modifications for their own program. The limitations brought out include aspects of the motives, questions, methods, and data currently used in assessment, but also include barriers such as sufficient time for data collection and provision of department-level data from any centralized assessment efforts. Nault, Hoey, Leonard, and Marr (2002) observe that the more faculty members are involved in the delivery of the program, the greater the trust in assessment data that is within their ability to control. Engineering faculty members will hold greater trust in using student work for assessment purposes if provided opportunities to establish scoring rubrics to examine the projects, and if sufficient trust can be built in those individuals rating the student artifacts. Successful assessment of student learning flourishes in an environment in which the practice of assessment and the attitude toward assessment are valued and supported, and above all where the level of discussion and communication concerning student learning can be infused with trustworthy, data-based results.

Building and sustaining trust in the practices of assessment continues to be limited; however, change can be made both in the culture and in practice. First, improvement to assessment data collection and methods is critical to enhancing trust in assessment data and the use of that data for course and curriculum adjustment. Faculty are able to articulate the limitations to assessment practices as well as provide solutions. Communication is decidedly the most important feature to ensure success.

Second, ensuring that timely and relevant analyses are provided for use by faculty is vital. In cases where some assessment processes are centralized, it is important that faculty obtain information relevant to the students in their program, and that they have this information in time for it to be of use: for consideration in departmental retreats, for planning purposes, and for use in making adjustments in new courses or programs.

Third, there is a need to develop a balanced approach and appreciation of the roles of those involved in the assessment process. While faculty are entrusted with the instructional process, institutional research and assessment professionals typically have responsibility for an institution-wide approach. A shared understanding of how to proceed is needed based on commonly understood data collection protocols, relevant and interesting questions being addressed, and a clear schedule for dissemination of results being established. Such efforts will push us beyond the obstacles to effective assessment that have been the subject of this research.

Finally, a clear consensus exists that the process of assessing programs is beneficial to curriculum improvement. As educated practitioners, faculty value accurate and trustworthy processes to collect and analyze data. This culture has evolved in the past 10 years through necessity as ABET Criteria (EC2000) were implemented and institutions responded (ABET, 2006).

The National Science Foundation's Engineering Education Coalitions provided a vehicle for communication of assessment practices. Absent other ongoing efforts, it would have been predictable that the level of communication among engineering faculty with regard to the assessment of student learning would have been reduced with the termination of the NSF coalitions, yet it is imperative that engineering programs do not lose the institutional memory and forward momentum concerning assessment of student learning that has developed over the decade in which the coalitions were funded. As it has happened, opportunities to continue to sustain communication, dissemination of best practices, and sharing of approaches have arisen through venues such as the annual Best Assessment Practices conferences at Rose-Hulman Institute. This process, over time, will gradually raise levels of trust in assessment processes, augment their sustainability, and allow us to optimize curricular approaches to engineering education through trustworthy feedback gained in assessment.

Thus, while significant barriers to assessment implementation exist in engineering education, solutions are being developed and islands of best practice are gradually appearing. Strategies for overcoming pitfalls of mistrust in assessment include building high-trust organizational environments; providing sound methodological frameworks and robust instrumentation; facilitating faculty openly sharing and discussing classroom assessment information; and using broad-based, participative planning and institutional goal-setting processes, as discussed in the next chapter.

References

ABET. (2006). Criteria for accrediting engineering programs. Retrieved December 15, 2006, from http://www.abet.org/Linked%20Documents-UPDATE/Criteria%20 and%20PP/E001%2006-07%20EAC%20Criteria%205-25-06-06.pdf

Ansary, O., Rahrooh, A., & Buchanan, W. W. (2002, June). Controversial aspects of the new ABET criteria and its implementation. *Proceedings of the 2002 American Society for Engineering Education Annual Conference and Exposition*, Montreal, Quebec.

Aschbacher, P. R. (1992). *Issues in innovative assessment for classroom practice: Barriers and facilitators. Project 3.3: Alternative assessments in classroom practice.* Los Angeles: National Center for Research on Evaluation, Standards, and Student Testing. (ERIC Document Reproduction Service No. ED355280)

Chatterjee, S. R. (1997, August). *The role of corporate communication in building trust in leadership* (No. 9706). Working Paper Series. Perth, Australia: Curtin University of Technology, Curtin Business School, School of Marketing.

Clark, L. A. (n.d.). Measurement's highest purpose: Building effective performance measurement systems. Retrieved December 15, 2006, from The Performance Center website: http://www.performancecenter.org/research/Measurement%20 Purpose.html

Davis, D., Trevisan, M., McKenzie, L., Beyerlein, S., Daniels, P., Rutar, T., Thompson, P., & Gentili, K. (2002, June). Practices for quality implementation of the TIDEE "Design Team Readiness Assessment." *Proceedings of the 2002 American Society for Engineering Education Annual Conference and Exposition*, Montreal, Quebec.

Furlong, E., & Vohra, P. (2002, June). A potential barrier to completing the assessment feedback loop. *Proceedings of the 2002 American Society for Engineering Education Annual Conference and Exposition*, Montreal, Quebec.

Gray, P. J. (1997). Viewing assessment as an innovation: Leadership and the change process. In P. J. Gray & T. Banta (Eds.), *The campus-level impact of assessment: Progress, problems, and possibilities* (pp. 5–15). San Francisco: Jossey-Bass.

Hoey, J. J. (2006, March). *Leveraging information technology for assessment tracking and reporting at Georgia Tech.* Presented at the Best Assessment Processes VIII Conference, Rose-Hulman Institute of Technology, Terre Haute, IN.

Hoey, J. J., & Nault, E. W. (2001, October). *Keeping the assessment momentum.* Presented at the Southern Association of Institutional Research Annual Meeting, Panama City, FL.

Hoey, J. J., & Nault, E. W. (2002, October). *Progress in assessment obstacle analysis.* Presented at the 2002 ABET Annual Meeting, Pittsburgh.

Lattuca, L. R., Terenzini, P. T., & Volkwein, J. F. (2006). *Engineering change: A study of the impact of EC2000.* Baltimore: ABET.

Nardini, H. G. (2001). Building a culture of assessment. *ARL* 218: 11. Available at http://www.arl.org/newsltr/218/assess.html

Nault, E. W., & Hoey, J. J. (2002, August). Recent advances in assessment obstacle analysis. *Proceedings from 2002 International Conference on Engineering Education*, Oslo, Norway.

Nault, E. W., Hoey, J. J., Leonard, M., & Marr, J. (2002, August). Trust: Essential to successful assessment. *Proceedings of the 2002 International Conference on Engineering Education* (Session 6B8-18), Oslo, Norway.

Shaw, R. B. (1997). Trust in the balance. In S. K. Hacker, L. Couturier, & M. E. Hacker (Eds.), *The trust requirement in advanced manufacturing systems*. Portland: Oregon State University, The Performance Center, Department of Industrial and Manufacturing Engineering. Retrieved December 15, 2006, from http://www.performancecenter.org/research/Trust%20Requirement.html

Stiggins, R. (1997). *Student-centered classroom assessment.* Upper Saddle River, NJ: Prentice Hall.

Thompson, D. G., & Williams, R. G. (1985). Barriers to the acceptance of problem-based learning in medical schools. *Studies in Higher Education, 10*(2), 199–204.

Tolan, L. A., & Hurny, J. J. (2004, June). Resources, organizational change and data systems: Issues and problems in the implementation of outcomes assessment. *Proceedings from 2004 American Society for Engineering Education Annual Conference and Exposition*, Salt Lake City.

Wergin, J. (2003). *Departments that work: Building and sustaining cultures of excellence in academic programs.* Bolton, MA: Anker.

7

OVERCOMING RESISTANCE
TO CHANGE

Sherra Kerns and Karan Watson

"And it ought to be remembered that there is nothing more difficult to take in hand, more perilous to conduct, or more uncertain in its success, than to take the lead in the introduction of a new order of things. Because the innovator has for enemies all those who have done well under the old conditions, and lukewarm defenders in those who may do well under the new. This coolness arises partly from fear of the opponents, who have the laws on their side, and partly from the incredulity of men, who do not readily believe in new things until they have had a long experience of them."

—Machiavelli, *The Prince*

While some things have changed since the sixteenth century, the creating and sustaining of any change remains a challenge. The establishment of an effective assessment system for engineering education generally requires a pervasive, cooperative effort with attributes distinct from the individual teaching, research, and service activities otherwise required of faculty members. Making the system work often requires changing "the way we do things," and most people find change at least inconvenient and probably uncomfortable and unwelcome. Effecting change requires simultaneously affecting both individual and collective behaviors. It is not easy.

Many people believe they are good at leading change because they have a passion as well as an intellectual drive for the cause behind the change. They do not understand that passion and merit are necessary but not sufficient for most complex changes, especially those that involve a change in behavior for numerous people. Among the change agents has to be one or more who understand strategic leadership in change and maintain a focus on the complex process involved in reaching the ultimate goal. Such a person must also work to simplify and reduce complexity to create steps that allow individuals to monitor their progress and sense success on the path to the ultimate goal. However, change is not a mechanistic or linear process that tolerates much reduction of complexity; rather, it is a complex process, sometimes bordering on chaos, in which new properties emerge. If change is done well, the new properties emerge in areas and ways that support the ultimate goal, more often than not in ways somewhat different than anticipated.

The difficulty of a complex change process is compounded when it is focused on changing the behavior of faculty members of universities and colleges. Among workers, these are the people most highly trained to be skeptical and to find flaws in evidence. Faculty members' prerequisite training instills a presumption that they should question and then re-question assumptions and even the evidence that supposedly proves a point. With respect to work, they are not easily taken in by slogans or passion, and they understand that often the process of coming to a decision is as important, in the long run, as the decision. Consensus often depends on whether a good process was followed, one that was broadly inclusive, because for complex issues there are always debatable questions and trade-offs that must be made. Engineering faculty members have considerable training in attending to broad system concerns and to continuous trade-offs between effort and cost and ultimate benefits. Change is a people process, much less well behaved than the processes involving systems of things with which engineering faculty are familiar, and yet engineers will tend, at least initially, to try to model, reduce, simplify, and analyze efforts to change in the same way they work with systems. They will seek to find fault and play "the Devil's Advocate." As Tom Kelley (2005) notes in *The Ten Faces of Innovation*,

> the Devil's Advocate may be the biggest innovation killer in America today. . . . Every day, thousands of great new ideas, concepts, and plans are nipped in the bud . . . because the Devil's Advocate encourages idea-wreckers to assume the most negative possible perspective, one that sees only the downside, the problems, the disasters-in-waiting. Once those floodgates open, they can drown a new initiative in negativity. (p. 2)

And this problem is important,

> because innovation is the lifeblood of all organizations, and the Devil's Advocate is toxic to your cause. This is no trivial matter. There is no longer any serious debate about the primacy of innovation to the health and future strength of a corporation. (p. 3)

The point of these descriptions is not to promote hopelessness but to note that often the change agents behind ABET or learning-outcomes-motivated changes have been naïve in their understanding. Their experiences evince the significant need for strategic planning and leadership in the change process. They have inappropriately assumed that all that is needed to motivate wide behavioral change is a simple demonstration of "do-ability" and some data on a few gains. When this is provided, they are then surprised that, for some cases, rather than resistance subsiding or easing, it actually mounts to higher levels.

While no single short chapter can give a road map to change that will transform someone into a strategic change agent, it can introduce and overview many of the components of complex changes that should be considered, and provide some examples of how others have overcome pitfalls. We begin with resistance, or barriers to change. Resistance *always* occurs in a change process, no matter how worthy the goal. Next, we discuss the need to manage the complexity of the change process. We close with ideas on how important it is to recognize and utilize successes. Along the way, we include three scenarios[1] illustrative of some techniques for change management.

Strategies for Change Depend on Levels of Resistance

Rick Maurer has introduced a useful topological categorization for the intensity of resistance, composed of three levels (Mauer, 1996).

Level One: Resisting the Idea Itself

At resistance level one, there is a cognitive difference of opinion that may be based on misinformation or missing data for one or all parties, or it may be based on conflicting data that causes reasoning people to come to different conclusions. At this level, presentations of information and well-facilitated discussion about conclusions often diminish the resistance to a change, even when people do not unanimously agree on all the conclusions. Workshops including or followed by dialogue among those promoting a change and those being asked to change can resolve much of the resistance. In this mode, it is often useful for the change leader to also be among those who must change. Someone viewed and respected as "one of us," who sees the need or appropriateness of trade-offs to make the change can push cautious faculty past the tipping point.

Level Two: Resisting the Change Because of Deeper, Emotional Issues

At level-two resistance, the person being asked to change senses that an important value or belief is being altered by the change. In this type of resistance, the person being asked to change often has feelings of being undervalued or taken advantage of. This resistance is accompanied with distrust of the change agents; fear of isolation or being left out of the mainstream; and a focus on the lack of incentives, potential loss of respect, or belief that the change will put the person on the "wrong side" of an important issue in the opinion of some valued constituency. With this resistance level, "how to" workshops actually build the resistance, rather than soothe it. Such workshops cause the level-two resister to feel that the decisions have already been made, and made without proper consideration of the deeper issues at hand. By contrast, meetings on "what are the issues" and "where do the changes lead us" are more effective. Here we can see clearly one of the reasons that change is complex: People with level-one resistance are often frustrated by such discussions on issues and outcomes; they can begin to believe that there is not intellectual merit to the change, so, even if it is for different reasons, they begin to side with level-two resisters, believing that this change is either not worth it or should be absolutely minimized. Thus, most experienced change agents suggest that these dialogs for resistance level two must maintain some focus on the question, "What's in it for us, individually and as a group?"

Level Three: Resisting Because of Deeply Embedded Perspectives and Distrust

Level-three resistance typically arises from a history of animosity between those in favor of the change and the resister: deep-seated or longstanding differences in values and goals. The level-three resister is against any notion associated with the change. Examples include people who have concluded that ABET adds no value to programs, or that external rankings will suffer and their research productivity will be diminished by too much focus on teaching, or that anything that the change proponent has ever advocated has been a disaster for the program. This type of resistance can rarely be eliminated. The strategies for change in this case have to be creative and should never underestimate the huge resistance people have to being manipulated. Two factors are crucial in addressing this resistance: (1) choosing carefully how to express the motivating reasons for the change and (2) distributing leadership for change, so that the interpersonal level-three clash does not divert the focus from the actual change desired. It is also important that people with this level of resistance are not marginalized by exclusion or disrespect for their opinion. Often these resisters will end up marginalizing themselves by the unreasoned intensity of their resistance. Finally, it is often not important to convert everyone into being a disciple of the change at hand. Trade-offs made with stubborn resisters may well allow them to "live with the change," even if they continue to dislike it.

Achieving Change Is a Complex Process

It is useful to assume that all three types of resistance will be present at any given time, so a change agent is likely to err if she or he tries to deal with resistance a single level at a time or apply the preceding strategies sequentially. Often a single individual will move between level one and level two several times during a change process. Those individuals with level-three resistance usually work to disguise it as level-one or level-two resistance in order to put their arguments on a more rational basis, so level-three resisters can be particularly difficult to identify. Thus, the strategic change agent must develop a strategy, hopefully involving multiple change-agent colleagues who present multiple adjustable, adaptable, and reconfigurable elements to motivate and support the change as it moves forward. It is often useful for agents to provide some appropriate presentation demonstrating their understanding of the complexity of the change and their preparations, including an adaptable plan appropriate to the complexity of the change. This plan might need to address the following issues and needs:

- The organizational culture for the change is understood and valued.
- The true nature of the change being promoted is understood, and its magnitude is appreciated.

- The important dynamics and resources needed for successful change are being addressed, and immediate impediments are being resolved, where possible.
- The leadership for the change is up to the task.
- The resistance to the change is going to be addressed and not discounted.

Organizational Culture

The topic of organizational culture is a large, rich field of study; we will choose one of many models for how it might be understood. Schein's (1996) work defines the culture of a group as

> a pattern of shared basic assumptions that the group learned as it solved problems . . . that has worked well enough to be considered valid, and therefore, to be taught to new members as the correct way to perceive, think, and feel in relation to those problems. (p. 12)

He further states that descriptions and understandings of an organization's culture include three layers: the artifacts present, the espoused values, and the underlying assumptions. Often the underlying assumptions are hard to recognize (underlying!) until the particular cultural artifacts are identified and their alignments to espoused values are explored. Furthermore, culture is not defined by how any single individual feels about the organization, since, as many people working in the area of diversity have learned, each organization is understood in a variety of ways by its constituents. Counter-narratives with as much validity as the master narrative exist for every culture, and no description of an organization's culture can capture all of the diverse perspectives of the individuals within the organization. Still, the broad, general strokes used to describe an organization can at least help to frame the context of the arena for change.

Nature of the Change

Many change agents fail to recognize fully what change is being asked of people. To make a change seem manageable, they tend to oversimplify the change or portray it as a task to be executed, rather than a habit to be unlearned and replaced by a newly learned and developed habit. Evidence shows that, even in the face of overwhelming data demonstrating the benefits of changing behaviors, humans still resist or even refuse to change. It is essential that a change agent not underestimate the difficulty of changing habits; evidence shows that even when faced with a life-threatening habit, people do not easily make persistent changes in their behavior (Deutschman, 2005). While there is no absolute scale for the difficulty of change, all changes require some level of behavioral change. To categorize change, we begin by recognizing two basic dimensions: change that requires different individual behavior and change that requires individuals to change a behavior within a group. A second, useful differentiation is to characterize changes as either resequencing/restructuring commonly practiced behaviors or as requiring learning of new concepts and skills. Finally, we must understand whether we are changing the underlying assumptions for an organization's practices or changing the approaches that support the underlying assumptions. While there are numerous other considerations that might characterize the nature of a change, these three, pairwise characterizations will often allow for adequate consideration of the nature of the change.

Dynamics for Change

Even when we understand the nature of the change we want to promote and the cultural context of the organization where change will occur, we need to account for the dynamics of a change process. These dynamics include, but are not limited to, the individual and group energy available for change, the resources available to support the energy it takes to change, and the adaptable strategies needed for increasing the momentum for change, simultaneously accompanied by the need to strategically anchor changes. When organizations have just completed a major, often crisis-motivated activity, the urge to immediately embark on a complex change process, no mater how worthy, may create more resistance than would be encountered if the group were just allowed a little time to recover. In addition, we can "burn out" an important leader for change by continuously stressing him or her to lead another change before recovery from his or her last leadership effort. Sometimes, either the resources, such as time and instruction for learning new skills, or the positive incentives are lacking for trying something hard, even if it is only hard because it is new. At other times, given real or perceived organizational priorities, the change may not be able to attract the attention it warrants. Issues with resources, incentives, and priorities can all cause a change to be more difficult than it should be. Poor timing of a change can raise the intensity of resistance. Thus, strategic change agents have to evaluate how a change will fit in with other organizational initiatives and needs. Weaving a change into the fabric of other priorities and making strategic choices for when and how to expend organizational energy on a change are both critical determinants of whether a change will succeed.

The fact that ABET visits at rather predictable times helps motivate the change design dynamics associated with accreditation processes. However, motivation by fear of the next ABET visit almost always results in a somewhat rebellious reaction, followed by relaxation of efforts after ABET has gone. Continuous attention to anchoring and stabilizing a change is important: for instance, maintaining accreditation processes so that they become an underlying, characteristic community activity and an organizational priority. Without anchored change, hard-won progress will dissolve and new habits will dissipate after a crisis has passed. The entire change process may have to be re-created when the behaviors are required again, and this time with the theme from "been there, done that" playing as accompaniment.

Leadership for Change

To paraphrase French politician Georges Clemenceau: Leadership is far too important to leave in the hands of a few people in leadership. This is especially true in the face of complex change. It is nearly always necessary that titled leaders not be against the change, but it is rarely sufficient just for them to be for it. As a matter of fact, given some cultures, the nature of some changes, and the intensity of some resistance, it can be a good strategy for titled leaders to not provide too strong support for the change at hand. Leaders for change must be viewed as fair, objective, and trustworthy by the organization requiring change, and they must demonstrate sincere empathy for the different perspectives on the change held by different individuals and groups within the organization. They must be able to demonstrate that they can make judgments based simultaneously on the current realities and on the realities they want to create. Leaders must be selected to drive change with both passion and reason, but this leadership alone is not enough. The change leadership must include individuals who are anchoring the change into the organization's culture; these may be the change leaders or other members of the organization. One of the worst situations in change leadership occurs when a passionate leader who wants vast, quick changes within a culture she or he does not fully appreciate becomes embattled with a leader who was working to stabilize changes and address change dynamics, trying to achieve a lasting change. Surprisingly, it is difficult to recognize this conflict as it is happening; it is often recognized only in hindsight.

Resistance to Change

Appreciating the intensity of a change, as perceived by those who must change, is useful, but the real work in change is discovering how to motivate and manage activities that overcome the resistance. Lewin (1947) introduced a three-stage process for achieving change, beginning with "unfreezing" organizational attitudes, then moving the organization to a different state before "refreezing" or anchoring the change. Unfreezing individual attitudes and attachments to the *status quo* will require techniques appropriate to the particular situation but is invariably the first necessary step. Figure 7.1 provides an ideational map of the process of change for an individual. It depicts the initiation of change as separation from the status quo. To facilitate change, it is important to recognize and expect the normal need of individuals to hold on to the comfort of the known. In fact, the removal of this comfort elicits a sense of disillusionment or betrayal. Only when the situational anxiety created by not changing exceeds the anticipatory anxiety of having to learn a new behavior will individuals normally take action toward actually changing. For some, this does not happen and change is refused, even though the status quo is no longer available (Johnson, 1998).

Figure 7.1 also helps convey that change is a process that takes time. The amount of time will vary between individuals, so it is crucial to recognize that members of a group will not all be at the same place in their acceptance of change and their acquisition of new behaviors at any given point in time. Effective change agents must be sensitive to an individual's stages within the change process and provide the interactions appropriate and responsive to that stage. This can make group interactions especially challenging, since the information exchange useful for one person may actually disrupt the change progress of another. Reading the progress of individuals can be especially difficult in an engineering educational environment, where professional behaviors and pride about having appropriate knowledge can mask an individual's learning difficulties and impede willingness to seek or accept mentoring when change is challenging.

Tools for Change Agents

Imagining the superposition of a set of curves as depicted in Figure 7.1, each with different time axes, provides a vivid pictorial representation of the chaotic complexity of change processes due to the different attitudes and behaviors of individuals composing the group under change. Tools for change agents may be divided into two broad categories: those that inform and in-

FIGURE 7.1
Depiction of the Change Process for an Individual

Participation in Change

New Solution
Found

Status Quo

Sense of Disillusionment
or Betrayal

Searching for Solutions
(SituationalAnxiety
is greater than
Learning Anxiety)

New
Status Quo

Growth of
Resistance
(Learning Anxiety
is greater than
Situational Anxiety)

No Solution
Found

"Crisis" of Decision

Derived from Algert & Watson, 2005; reprinted with permission

struct change leadership directly and those that assess characteristics of individuals involved in organizational change, thereby informing change leadership and improving our ability to correctly identify strategies for change. Examples of change instruction tools are many.[2] One informative example is the work of John Kotter (1995) on transformation processes.

In the second category, a variety of tools has been developed to reveal the traits of individuals and thereby provide information to change agents and, hopefully, increase their effectiveness. While these tools are in general use within many organizational settings, they are not yet widely used in the academy. Many require informational workshops prior to use and during interpretation of results. Those that purport to address aspects of human potential can be considered prejudicial to those individuals who are seeking personal growth and expansion of their capabilities. For these reasons and more, the usefulness of these tools depends not only on the characteristics and capabilities of the tools but also, and probably more importantly, on the attitudes of those using them. Academics are suspect of simplistic categorization and testing that will characterize them. Using these tools is, in itself, a change in approach!

Examples of such tools are the Kirton Adaptive-Innovative Inventory (KAII), measuring respondents' tendency to be innovative or adaptive in their work styles; Myers-Briggs Type Indicators (MBTIs), assessing a person's likely psychological type; and the DiSC profile, describing the behavior patterns of individuals; there are many others. The DiSC, for instance, identifies proclivities for various roles, such as Analyzer, Implementor, Conductor, Persuader, Promoter, Relater, Supporter, and Coordinator. Note that none of these have generally negative connotations; each describes a form of positive contribution to the organization. Most of these tools can be administered via a brief Web-based questionnaire, and some, such as DiSC, provide the responder instantaneous feedback. DiSC is one example of a tool that can be used to help individuals within a group recognize their possible roles for contributions toward change. Such tools can be used to empower individual roles and to raise appropriate expectations of others regarding the preferred working styles of their colleagues.

Rising to Crisis

This is not a perfect world. Sometimes, despite best efforts, cultural modifications achieving anchored change are not possible. One or more individuals within the group may staunchly refuse to change within reasonable time and process, or the time provided for change may simply be too short to support pervasive change in the organizational culture.

Fortunately or unfortunately, most academics are familiar with "crisis mode"; in fact, many even enjoy the challenge of operating in this mode, and this preference may itself be one of the obstacles impeding change. This "let's get this out" mentality is much like cramming for a test—it can produce satisfactory results, but it is unlikely to provide deep understanding or lasting benefit.

A particular problem in handling assessment and accreditation activities in crisis mode is that these are recurring activities that can benefit from systematic supporting habits, including data gathering and analysis, the maintenance of substantive dialog with constituents, and embedded processes to guide curricular improvements. The processes associated with assessment and accreditation are best run continuously. ABET visits can be viewed as samplings of outputs from these processes. So, when crisis mode is used, these internal systems are started and stopped, resulting in the losses and maintenance issues typically associated with using any production facility in a periodic fashion.

Success Is Easy to Recognize

Change will happen differently each place and time, but the elements of Figure 7.2 are typically involved. A web of elements, including resistance to change, nature of change, leadership for change, and change dynamics, interact with one another to influence organizational culture. Intended or intentionally initiated change will invariably be superimposed on changes happening simultaneously in larger or smaller parts of the organization's environment and upon changes in the personal lives of members of the organization.

Success comes in three principal stages. Recognizing the stages of success is essential to change management; it is equivalent to a progress report. This identification allows a change leader to craft strategies appropriate for the organization's stage during the progress of change.

FIGURE 7.2
Schematic of Change Elements Impacting Organizational Culture

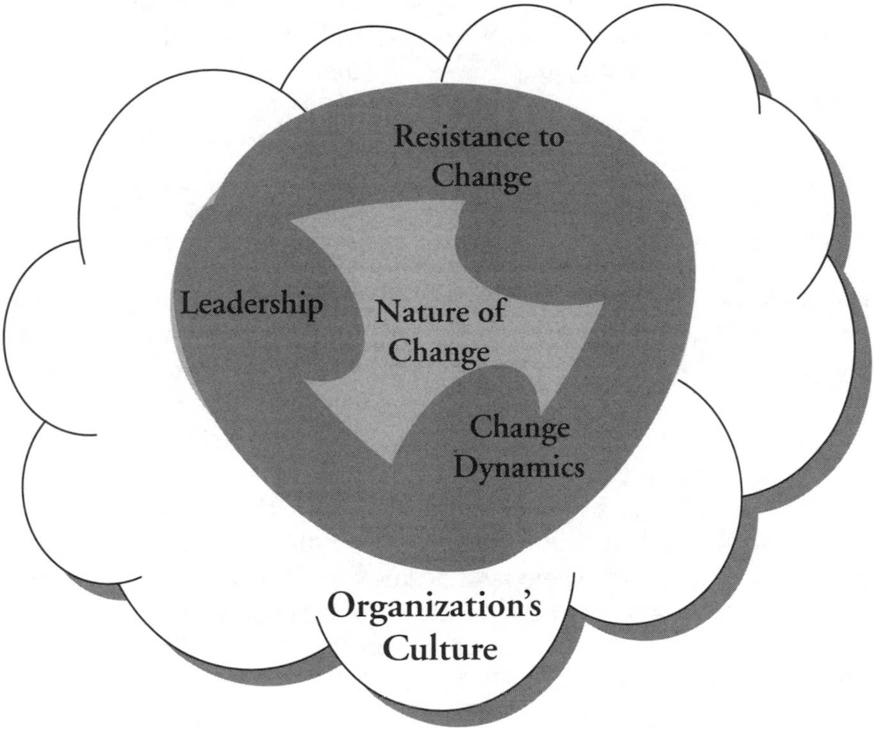

Shared Understanding of the Goal

The first stage of success is shared understanding. This does not mean that everyone has become a believer, but it does mean that everyone is "on the same page." You know where you are headed. Everyone's mental picture of the destination will be different, informed by his or her experiences and his or her position within the organization. Differences in individual values will result in different interpretations of what is most important about reaching this goal. Because of these differences in values and perceptions, rich, multi-level communication is always requisite to achieving this stage.

Dialog is essential, too. Often, the most ardent resisters will remain silent, making it difficult to determine the bases of their resistance. Providing nonjudgmental opportunities for expressions of dissent is essential to reaching shared understanding. While it may not be possible for everyone to agree that a goal is worthy, it should be possible for everyone to understand what the goal is.

Sometimes it works well to give a problem to a group of individuals and let systems for solutions emerge. During this process, it is essential to monitor progress and to monitor process, and yet provide appropriate freedoms for the group to find a solution. When this method works, buy-in is usually a minor issue because the group "owns" the solution.

SCENARIO 7.A
The Law of Conservation of Right Answers

Edgecliffe College was built on a bluff and has been operating that way ever since. While its emphasis had always been instruction in dance, its president read about the shortage of engineering talent and decided to field six new engineering programs. Fortunately, he was able to hire an exceptional faculty of 50 individuals because he'd recently won the lottery and invested the proceeds in oil.

The young faculty had little experience with ABET, so they requested a consultant. ABET of course complied, and the consultant visited and provided a detailed, complete, and accurate description of all aspects of accreditation. After the consultant left, the faculty concluded that ABET's Criterion 3 Outcomes were a bunch of hooey. They called a meeting, invited some of their colleagues from industry and other universities, and decided together to rebel and write their own list of what they wanted from their graduates.

The meeting did not result in the list they'd hoped for. While they did get lots of ideas aired, no consensus was reached. Over the next months, they together honed an agreed-upon set of Capabilities that would characterize all graduates of all Edgecliffe engineering programs. They'd done it their way!

The president told the engineering faculty that, if all programs were not ABET accredited, he would close engineering and fire any faculty who did not demonstrate proficiency in ballet *and* tap. The faculty decided that they would prepare for an accreditation visit as soon as they had their first graduates.

(Details omitted for brevity) . . . and they *had* been in consultation with their constituencies, and their list of Capabilities mapped onto Criterion 3 Outcomes, because they'd done a comprehensive job of considering what they wanted from their graduates, thereby proving that all noble and sincere searches for truth and right arrive at the same place, which must, therefore, be true and right.

A Working System to Achieve the Goal

The organization will need to develop a method for achieving its goal, to build a system based on that method, and to get that system working. Ideally, everyone has some role in the solution, even if it is that of active observer providing constructive praise and criticism. The system may be organized centrally and hierarchically or in a distributed way; responsibilities may be assigned to single individuals or assumed by groups. The particulars of the system design may be dynamic and should suit the organizational culture and take account of available resources.

Here again, communication within the organization is essential. Individuals should be aware of how the system operates and know where to go to provide system inputs and to gain access to system products. It is important that, to the extent possible, members of the organization believe that the system adds value to the whole. If there is general confidence that the system is beneficial, the anchoring of the change to the new system will strengthen with time, because people will become accustomed to using the system. It will become a habit.

SCENARIO 7.B
How to Become a Huge Success
as an Engineering Leader

Professor B. Dean Soonerlater leads the program in info-bio-nano engineering at Frontiers University. He had previously been at Old Stone College, where the faculty measures everything students do. A kind of panicked compliance attended all accreditation matters at Old Stone, and Soonerlater wants to make things better at Frontiers. Instead of amassing mountains of data that they have no time to evaluate, or gathering results suggesting changes the faculty doesn't want to make, Soonerlater has a new strategy:

- Semester 1: Engage constituents in dialog on objectives and outcomes needed for ABET. Talk and listen. Simultaneously, train three faculty in assessment and evaluation of learning outcomes, but don't worry about connecting or coordinating the two groups . . . yet.
- Semester 2: Continue dialog. Set up a luncheon with alumni, employers, and eight faculty (about 20% of department) to discuss "what our students need to know when they first go to work."
- Summer: Combine faculty from the luncheon with those trained in assessment ("The Core Corp") to *draft* learning outcomes and plan assessment and evaluation of performance.
- Semester 3: Core Corp runs test measurements of outcomes and prepares presentation of results for next semester's advisory board meeting. Also launches broad discussions with faculty.
- Semester 4: Corps holds workshop for advisors testing plans for unfurling the use of objectives and outcomes. Solicits ideas and discusses other demonstrable competencies. (Here, Soonerlater notes: Ask business leaders [1] to develop concrete advice for the faculty to help implement a successful system and [2] how they are willing to contribute to ensuring system success.)
- Semester 5: Advisory board and faculty join to tackle curricular improvement and gain feedback on what works and what doesn't. Redesign reward system, realizing faculty are going to have to do more—teach and assess—while standard program funds are not rising. Advisory board designs a system for donor support to reward innovation and achievement in supporting program educational objectives, and endows it itself.

Two years later, as Professor Soonerlater prepares for his move to dean of engineering at Successes U, he finds these notes. While cynicism has not totally disappeared, his plan has worked. Many in the faculty feel *they* forged a renaissance in educational processes and have been rewarded for their work—and many of those involved lived happily ever after.

Use of System Outputs to Guide Program Improvement

The final stage of success is using the system to guide improvements. A major factor associated with this success is the alignment of evaluation and reward structures with desired outcomes (Kerr, 1975). Put another way, "societies get the best of what they celebrate."[3]

Societies invariably involve many types of competition for rewards and a variety of individual definitions of what a reward is. For most academics, rank and compensation are valued rewards. Independence is also highly valued. When these and other rewards are not well aligned with change goals, the divergence is clear and apparent. Such divergence poses particular challenges for accreditation activities, since accreditation is not the only goal of academia. Work toward accreditation is an inherently collective endeavor within a society accustomed to rewarding individuals. The respect of peers is, however, highly valued within academia.

SCENARIO 7.C
The Bell Cow

Once upon a time there was a young farmer and an old farmer. The young farmer came to the old farmer to complain that although he had put a bell on his best milk cow because he wanted the other cows to graze with her, the others did not follow her. The elder farmer explained that you can't choose which cow the others will follow. You must watch to see which cow is followed and bell that cow.

The program in bowling alley engineering at Major U had a significant problem. Faculty members were cleanly divided into two camps: those who did research and those who taught. Each camp had great respect for its members but little for the other camp. Researchers taught graduate courses and teachers taught undergraduates. Assessment intensified the burden on the teachers.

Their brilliant chairman, who held the Brunswick High Chair in Ten Pin Engineering, approached the top researcher, Professor Bolla Spare, and convinced her that her talents could transform an otherwise drab undergraduate engineering curriculum into something inspirational, if she would only teach an undergraduate course. Honored by this compliment, and confident that she could help, Professor Spare took on the challenge.

She almost failed. Right after the midterm exam, she realized that most of the class had been lost for some time. She worked even harder, now appreciating at least some of the challenges of teaching undergraduates, and after only two offerings she created a beginning course that was attracting students from all over campus. All manner of rewards were coming her way. Not only was she feeling proud of her work; she was also being asked to design new classrooms for teaching the course and to mentor others so that they could teach additional sections, and, of course, she was given most honored faculty status and big raises by Dean Strike. Other researchers began to feel that only being great in research was no longer enough and began to join in reforming the undergraduate curriculum.

Discussions of how to involve constituents, apply quality metrics, and improve the curriculum now began to include the entire faculty. And they lived happily ever after.

It is important to recognize the cultural aspects of the department or other principal administrative unit in building a pervasive reward system that can be maintained. Examples that are sometimes useful (but may unintentionally reinforce counterproductive underlying assumptions in the culture) include the following:

- Rewarding people for good teaching by releasing them from the normal teaching load (in other words, associating excellence in an activity with release from the activity)
- A stipend or reward for innovators or early adopters of new assessments or systems that are not sustainable in the long run (in other words, rewarding innovation or change but not rewarding excellence in maintaining a well-designed system)
- An administrative title for one person involved in the change, but little/no recognition for any of the others (in other words, providing individual reward for what must be a team effort)

Even though each of these reward systems can be counterproductive to future organizational health, they can be very productive in starting or initiating maintenance of change.

Subtle changes in evaluations are necessary as well. Examples include the following:

- Have teaching evaluations account, not only for the number of courses, course level, enrollments, and student opinions on teaching, but also for evidence of teacher effectiveness in promoting student learning.
- Reward those who teach prerequisite courses based upon evidence that students do well in subsequent courses.
- Reward those selected for teaching prerequisite courses and other courses where evaluation of student program learning outcomes is focused.
- Make evident to students (with visual displays or other methods) the relationships and connections between courses, including the identification of faculty course coordinators, and an explanation of their qualifications for such responsibilities.
- Of course, clarify and demonstrate that excellence in supporting change or excellence in performance within a new system will contribute to promotion or tenure.

Specific rewards will, of course, need to be consistent with the organizational culture and values. The above list of examples is not comprehensive. Two points are of highest importance. First, rewards come in a variety of forms; significant rewards are those that are recognized by both the individuals and the group collectively as valuable. Second, both individuals and the faculty as a group will detect and respond to any misalignments between assignments and rewards; if efforts are not rewarded, their quality will decline.

Final Words

When "good things" cannot be institutionalized within an organization, the failure can usually be traced to ineffective leadership by change agents. History and human nature demonstrate that, instead of leading, people often try to win or get buy-in for short-term motivations, or they sometimes even demonstrate themselves the very pattern of resistance to learning exhibited by those resisting the desired change. Our observations for such change agents are straightforward:

- Change is hard, even if the system being implemented is simple or obviously better, because people compose the culture and people are complex, individually and as a group.
- Resistance must be appreciated, respected, and addressed, not paved over, bullied out, or ignored.
- Pace must accommodate the time required to anchor successes so that gains are not lost while moving on to subsequent changes.
- Change does not end. Once a change agent has succeeded in leading a change, he or she should expect to become a follower in the next change, which is often a change to the very system he or she led to install.

Having said this, it is important to realize that patience, persistence, and success in leading change are rewarded. Those who understand the framing of change, whether within ABET accreditation, curricula, research, or service, usually progress to be the sages of an organization, rather than the cynical and tired permanent resisters. These are the people who remember that we faculty not only have one of the most important jobs in society; we have one of the jobs most filled with fun and delight—continually washed and renewed by the new ideas and attitudes of students.

Notes

1. These scenarios are based on true stories, disguised by the authors for the purposes of generalization and their own amusement.
2. Several are summarized at www.valuebasedmanagement.net.
3. Woodie Flowers, MIT, as quoted in Conover, K. A. (1996, March 12). Retooling Inventors' Nerdy Image. *Christian Science Monitor.* Retrieved July 9, 2007, from http://www.csmonitor.com/1996/0312/12121.html.

References

Algert, N. E., & Watson, K. (2005, April 20). Systematic change in engineering education: The role of effective change agents for women in engineering. *Proceedings: Women in Engineering & Advocates Network (WEPAN)/National Association of Minority Engineering Professionals Advocates (NAMEPA) Conference*, Las Vegas, NV.

Deutschman, A. (2005, May). Change or die. *Fast Company, 94*, p. 53.

Johnson, S. (1998). *Who moved my cheese? An amazing way to deal with change in your work and in your life.* New York: G. P. Putnam's Sons.

Kelley, T. (2005). *The ten faces of innovation: IDEO's strategies for beating the devil's advocate and driving creativity throughout your organization.* New York: Doubleday.

Kerr, S. (1975). On the folly of rewarding A, while hoping for B. *Academy of Management Journal, 18*(4), 769–783.

Kotter, J. P. (1995, March/April). Why transformation efforts fail. *Harvard Business Review,* pp. 59–67.

Lewin, K. (1947). Group decision and social change. In T. M. Newcomb & E. L. Hartley (Eds.), *Readings in social psychology* (pp. 340–344). New York: Holt.

Mauer, R. (1996). *Beyond the wall of resistance: Unconventional strategies that build support for change.* Austin, TX: Bard Press.

Schein, E. (1996). *Organizational culture and leadership.* San Francisco: Jossey-Bass.

PART THREE

LEARNING ALONG THE CONTINUUM OF THE EDUCATIONAL EXPERIENCE

8

ASSESSING THE FIRST YEAR OF ENGINEERING EDUCATION

Jerome P. Lavelle and Sarah A. Rajala

Each fall, students enter colleges of engineering throughout the United States as first-year engineering students. Studies have shown that many of these students have only a vague idea of what engineering encompasses as a field of study and a career path. Yet many students choose engineering as a beginning major because of their aptitude in mathematics and sciences in high school, and in some cases because of the assumed potential salary and job opportunities associated with an engineering degree. If the goal of engineering education is to attract and retain a large and diverse population of students each year, it is important to understand the unique characteristics of engineering education in order to achieve this goal.

The challenges for engineering education are many. The first order of business is to attract students to consider engineering as a possible field of study. Because of the wide and varied aspects of engineering, it is not easy to condense what "engineering is" or what "engineers do" into a single sound bite, icon, or mental image. This fact makes it difficult to reach out to audiences of potential students. In many cases the most difficult populations to reach include those from traditionally underrepresented populations in engineering (women and ethnic minorities). First-year engineering programs are the entry point for students into the field of engineering, and students' experiences in that first year often influence their continued interest in, and success in, completing an engineering curriculum. As such, the design, evaluation, and assessment of the first-year curriculum (and students' experiences in it) are vitally important. In order to produce more engineers, engineering programs must not only attract more (and new) potential students, but keep more of those who express an initial interest.

The basis of educational assessment is to establish a planned-for outcome or goal, and to put in place methods and processes to collect data for measurement. In the first year there is a unique opportunity to both understand and influence students in their pursuit of an engineering degree. This chapter focuses on assessment as a key component in the goal toward improving the engineering educational process, especially and uniquely as it is focused in the first year. We provide herein a review of the recent initiatives undertaken in first-year engineering programs in the United States, including a review of the efforts at North Carolina State University.

A Review of Recent Initiatives

Over the past decade there has been much activity in curriculum and program renewal in engineering education, with a particular focus on the first year. Drivers of this activity have included NSF's Education Coalition initiative and ABET's Engineering Criteria 2000 (EC2000) accreditation criteria, and much has been published related to this activity in the *Journal of Engineering Education* and the *Proceedings of the Frontiers in Education Annual Conference* and *Proceedings of the ASEE Annual Conference*. Table 8.1 summarizes the literature reviewed as part of this chapter. These articles represent an excellent sampling of the recently published activities associated with first-year engineering programs. Over the past decade, most improvement initiatives in engineering education have focused on the first-year engineering course and curriculum. Table 8.1 identifies several course-based, curriculum-based, program-based, and research initiatives conducted in the first semester or first year of engineering programs around the nation. The table summarizes each of the categories of initiatives in terms of activities and assessment.

Course-Based Initiatives

One of easiest places to implement change in the first year is through an "introduction to engineering" course found in most curriculums. Most recent initiatives have involved improving a currently existing introductory course by adding or changing content. Specific initiatives have included the introduction of discipline-based (Hanesian & Perna, 1999; Holt & Ohland, 1998; Milano, Parker, & Pincus, 1996) or multidiscipline-based design projects (Orabi, 1999), the addition of a design challenge (Dolan, Whitman, & Edgar, 2005), and hands-on activities (Connor & Goff, 2001; Weber et al., 2000).

TABLE 8.1
First-Year Initiatives and Assessment

Paper	School	Objective	Detail	Assessment Methods
Hanesian & Perna (1999)	New Jersey Institute of Technology	Course-based	Design Course Introductory discipline-based courses	Course evaluations
Milano et al. (1996)	New Jersey Institute of Technology	Curriculum-based	Member Gateway EE Coalition Curriculum innovation	Survey results and student feedback evaluations
Inam & Caso (2002)	Texas A&M University		Cohort clustering	Statistical analysis of variables associated with students in clusters
Graham & Caso (2002)	Texas A&M University		Measuring concepts and competencies	Freshman attitude survey; pretest and posttest statistical analysis
Olds & Pavelich (1996)	Colorado School of Mines		Longitudinal data on educational goals	Portfolios of collected work that reflect ed. goals
Dolan et al. (2005)	University of Wyoming	Course-based	Design challenge added to first-year course	Student survey, exit interviews
McKenna & Hirch (2005)	Northwestern University	Course-based	Does freshman design course increase student confidence?	Student survey of confidence in 26 abilities (design, comm., teamwork, etc.) Replicated at the end of the semester
Orabi (1999)	University of New Haven	Course-based	Effectiveness of multidisciplinary first-year engineering course	AP involved course profile, tests, projects, oral presentations, written reports, surveys
Jansen et al. (2003)	Vanderbilt University	Course-based	Learning objectives in freshman course	Laptop-based surveys, open-ended essays, in-class activities captured with laptops (and software)

(continued)

TABLE 8.1 (Continued)

Paper	School	Objective	Detail	Assessment Methods
Demel et al. (2002)	Ohio State University	Program-based	First-year engineering program evaluation	End of qtr. surveys for faculty, program, and content; also weekly journaling logs for improvement
Freuler et al. (2002)	Ohio State University	Program-based	Evaluating freshman engineering honors program	Web-based Online Journaling System, open to address issues, and used to ask specific questions of students
Budny et al. (1997, 1998)	Purdue University	Curriculum-based	Success of freshman courses in providing foundation of persistence in engineering	Quantitative data analysis: retention, graduation, GPA, persistence, statistical analysis
Olds & Miller (2004)	Colorado School of Mines	Curriculum-based	Effect of integrated curriculum and learning community on "average" engineering student's success	Formative and summative assessment methods: student performance data (GPA, retention rates), perceptions and attitudes (surveys, journals, informal interviews, focus groups), and faculty feedback
Hutchinson et al. (2006)	Purdue University		Identify factors related to students' beliefs about their capabilities to perform tasks necessary to achieve a desired outcome	Survey instruments, sampling and statistical analysis
Ohland & Collins (2002)	Clemson University		Meta-analysis of freshman living and learning communities	Summary statistics
Hensel et al. (2005)	West Virginia University		Evaluation of changes in freshman program	Enrollment data, academic profiles, retention statistics, GPA comparisons, grades in specific courses

Study	Institution	Type	Changes to freshman program	Assessment instruments
Lo et al. (2005)	Virginia Tech			E-portfolios, reflection papers, other assessment/research instruments
Howze et al. (2005)	Texas A&M University	Curriculum-based	Tightening integration in freshman curricula	Use of control sections, student success data, common problems in exams, online instruments to assess student perceptions and confidence, open-ended questions
Barr et al. (2005)	University of Texas–El Paso	Course-based	Effects of ABET program educational objectives in freshman course	Used pre-, mid-, and postcourse survey on outcomes and learning factors
Hatton et al. (1998)	Purdue University		Measure of freshmen engineering attitude toward academic counseling	Survey data, comparison groups, statistical analysis
Rowe et al. (2005)	Vanderbilt University	Course-based	Effectiveness of the Intro Engineering Course	Pre-, mid-, postsurvey, statistical analysis, use of Refero©
Prados et al. (2005)	Nonaffiliated Study		Impact of ABET 2000	Survey data from ABET-accredited programs
Kellar et al. (2000)	South Dakota School of Mines	Curriculum-based	Evaluation of integrated first-year curriculum	Longitudinal tracking, attitudinal assessment, portfolios, faculty and study surveys
Anderson-Rowland (1998)	Arizona State University	Curriculum-based	Course sequencing on retention	Quantitative student records data

TABLE 8.1 (Continued)

Paper	School	Objective	Detail	Assessment Methods
Pendergrass et al. (2001)	University of Massachusetts–Dartmouth		Evaluation of new freshman engineering program	Use of control groups, matched comparison groups, quantitative student success data
Weber et al. (2000)	University of Tennessee	Program-based	Evaluation of freshman program	Use of control groups, student success data, attitude survey data, common exam scores, sophomore-level course success
Barlow et al. (1996)	United States Airforce Academy	Course-based	Evaluation of new freshman engineering course	Student self-reports, concept maps, faculty observations, exam questions, reflective judgment exercises, written reports
Kampe, Goff, & Connor (2005); Lo et al. (2005); Connor & Goff (2001)	Virginia Tech		Assessment of hands-on activities	Student and faculty survey data
Marra et al. (2000)	Penn State University	Course-based	Assessment of first-year engineering course	Cohort study, structured interviews, videotaping, Perry score rating, statistical analysis
Schmidt et al. (1999)	University of Maryland	Course-based	Evaluation of Intro Engineering Design course	Use of five student-based survey instruments
Richardson & Dantzler (2002)	University of Alabama	Curriculum-based	Evaluation of TIDE curricula	Student success data, GPA, and retention data
Holt & Ohland (1998)	University of Florida	Course-based	Evaluation of discipline-based Intro to Engineering course	Questionnaire and longitudinal data

Richardson et al. (1998) provide a review of how the NSF Foundation Coalition partners have implemented design projects at their schools. Often the course itself is refined in terms of a set of new learning outcomes that consider the importance of active learning, the engineering design cycle, being an effective team member, proper written and oral communication skills, problem solving, engineering ethics, etc.

Recent studies have assessed the degree to which these outcomes are being met in the course (Barlow, Havener, Kouri, Marlino, & Smith, 1996; Jansen, Brophy, Klein, Norris, & Wang, 2003; Lo et al. 2005; Rowe, Klein, & Mahadevan-Jansen, 2005; Schmidt, Yang, Wilson, & Zhang, 1999). In addition, others have looked at the extent to which ABET program educational objectives are being met in the freshman course (Barr, Kruger, & Aanstoos, 2005), the effect on intellectual development (Marra, Palmer, & Litzinger, 2000), and how the design course affects student confidence in skills critical to the study of engineering (McKenna & Hirch, 2005).

The course-based assessment initiatives utilized many different assessment instruments and strategies. Course evaluations, student surveys, exit interviews, open-ended questionnaires, longitudinal statistical tracking, concept maps, observation, reflective essays, and written reports are all used for evaluative purposes.

Curriculum-Based Initiatives

Another place to implement changes that directly affect students' experiences in studying engineering is in the first-year curriculum. Initiatives at this level require much more coordination and oversight because they involve several courses, often in more than one department and/or college. In most cases the goal is to integrate students' experiences in courses during the first year. Proponents of this approach seek to improve students' understanding of basic math and science by incorporating the learning of that material within the context of engineering. At the same time, they seek to improve the students' learning of engineering by putting it in the context of the math and science within engineering problem solving and design. In this way, integrated curricula implement this symbiotic relationship explicitly in the form of a framework for studying engineering. This approach is historically missing in engineering curricula where silos of math, science, and engineering knowledge are taught in isolation from each other. This leaves the "dot connecting" to the student and is risky because many excellent would-be engineers don't/can't connect the dots, and thus leave engineering as their educational program of study (especially those from gender and ethnic minorities in engineering).

Programs that have studied curriculum integration include those at Colorado School of Mines (Olds & Miller, 2004), Texas A&M (Howze, Froyd, Shryock, Srinizasa, & Caso, 2005), University of Massachusetts–Dartmouth (Pendergrass et al., 2001), University of Tennessee (Weber et al., 2000), South Dakota School of Mines (Budny, Bjedov, & LeBold, 1997), University of Alabama (Richardson & Dantzler, 2002), and North Carolina State University (Felder, Bernold, Burniston, Dail, & Gastineau, 1996, 1997). Others have looked at the sequencing of courses in the first-year curriculum and retention (Anderson-Rowland, 1998) and the creation of calculus-ready and not-calculus-ready tracks (Hensel, Byrd, & Myers, 2005).

Assessment of curriculum-based initiatives include student evaluations, student performance data (GPA, retention rates), perceptions and attitudes (surveys, journals, informal interviews, focus groups), faculty feedback, use of control sections, student success data, common problems in exams, online instruments to assess student perceptions and confidence, open-ended questions, quantitative student records data, longitudinal tracking, attitudinal assessment, portfolios, faculty and study surveys, course grades, and success data (GPA, retention, enrollment data).

Program-Based Initiatives

Several programs have sought to measure the effectiveness of their first year. They have looked at measuring the degree of students attaining educational goals (Olds & Pavelich, 1996), studying students' attitudes toward achieving key competencies (Graham & Caso, 2002), evaluating the program in terms of its effect on retention (Demel, Gustafson, Fentiman, Freuler, & Merrill, 2002; Freuler, Gates, Merrill, Lamont, & Demel, 2002), and assessing how well the program provides a foundation for students to persist in engineering (Budny et al. 1997; Budny, LeBold, & Bjedov, 1998).

Assessment methods for program-based initiatives include surveys of faculty; weekly journaling logs (in some cases these are Web-based); portfolios of collected work; pretest and posttest statistical analysis; longitudinal tracking; attitudinal assessment; and quantitative data analysis of retention, graduation, GPA, and/or persistence.

Research-Based Initiatives

Several first-year engineering initiatives have elements of the previous categories but are unique in some fashion. What distinguishes these programs is
their focus on educational research methods in studying an effect. At Texas
A&M University researchers (Inam & Caso, 2002) studied the effect of clus-
tering on first-year engineering student success; at Purdue studies were conducted regarding student self-efficacy beliefs and success in engineering
(Hutchinson, Follman, Sumpter, & Bodner, 2006) and students' attitudes
toward academic counseling as a component of success (Hatton, Wankat, &
BeBold, 1998). Ohland and colleagues (Ohland & Collins, 2002; Ohland &
Crockett, 2002) assimilated meta-analyses of freshman summer-bridge programs and living/learning communities. Besterfield-Sacre, Atman, and Shuman (1998) established that student attitude data can be used to evaluate
engineering programs and student success. Others (e.g., Brannan & Wankat,
2005) have conducted surveys of first-year engineering programs. Assessment
methods in this category included statistical analysis of associated variables,
comparison groups, survey instruments, and summary statistics.

Summary of Assessment in First-Year Initiatives

In reviewing the educational initiatives undertaken by first-year engineering
programs, it is clear there is a wide variety of assessment tools, methods, and
strategies employed. In general, the degree of assessment sophistication increases from course-based to curriculum-based to research-based initiatives.
On one end of the scale are course-based programs that are evaluated only on
student-supplied survey data. Other additions to this strategy include faculty
survey data and in some cases pre- and post-semester data collection. Some
initiatives add sophistications such as control groups, use of portfolios, evaluation of reflection/essay papers, and use of structured interviews and statistical analysis.

Curriculum-based programs also reflect a wide range of sophistication.
However, perhaps because of the need for planning that goes into these initiatives, often implementers consider a wider range of assessment instruments and approaches in order to judge the success of the program. In this
category one sees stronger thought placed into the design of the assessment.
Tools such as surveys, testing instruments, statistical analysis, and longitudinal data analysis are common.

In the category of research-based initiatives one finds the highest level of
significant assessment sophistication. Excellent models and applications of

both formative and summative assessment are being used in this latter category. In general, it appears that programs have moved from "let's do and ask the students what they think," early adoption modes of assessment, to more sophisticated models. However, there are issues to be aware of when using such models.

Issues in Engineering Assessment

In an excellent brief on engineering education, Moskal, Leyden, and Pavelich (2002) identify the reliability and validity of assessment tools as the two most important concepts that researchers should be aware of. In the brief, the authors summarize the important elements of each of these concepts and identify references that engineering educators can use to better their research (such as ASEE's *How Do You Measure Success? Designing Effective Processes for Assessing Engineering Education* [Huband, 1998]). Validity, which is related to the ability to measure a desired effect, is defined by the authors in the context of assessment. In addition, there is an excellent discussion on the important differences among content-, construct-, criterion-, and consequence-related evidence as it relates to validity. Reliability, which is related to the concept of consistency, is also defined along with a discussion of test and rater reliability. Both of these concepts are important as educators, implementers, and researchers seek more advanced knowledge about the effect and interactions of their engineering education initiatives. Inam and Caso (2002) describe the validity issue that they wrestled with in studying student cohorting within the freshman engineering program at Texas A&M. See chapter 4 for additional discussion of these issues.

Olds, Moskal, and Miller (2005) describe important issues related to assessment methods. They divide methods into two groups: descriptive studies and experimental studies. They discuss important ideas in descriptive designs such as surveys, interviews and focus groups, conversational analysis, observations, ethnographic studies, and meta-analyses. Included also are elements related to randomized controlled trials, matching, baseline data, posttest-only design, and longitudinal design. Engineering education initiatives' assessment plans should recognize the importance of these concepts. See chapter 10 for more discussion about formative assessment methods.

Assessment in the First-Year Engineering Program at NC State

Over the past five years we have used several assessment methods in the freshman engineering design course (called E101, Introduction to College of

Engineering and Problem Solving) at North Carolina State University. These tools include standardized surveys such as Learning and Study Strategies Inventory (LASSI), Learning Type Measure (LTM), and the Pittsburgh Freshman Engineering Attitude Survey (PFEAS); section-independent grading rubrics; peer-to-peer evaluation feedback; student journaling; and course evaluations. The course itself has been substantially changed over the past eight years. As a member of NSF's SUCCEED Coalition we began to bring the course in line with concepts being promoted for first-year courses in that time frame. The learning objectives and outcomes as well as characteristics of the course are given in several publications (e.g., Lavelle & Robbins, 2003; Spurlin, Lavelle, Rajala, & Robbins, 2003) and are summarized in Tables 8.2 and 8.3. Table 8.4 illustrates the relationship among the stated learning objectives of the course, the course content, and the method used for assessment.

TABLE 8.2
Goals, Learning Objectives, and Outcomes for the E101 Course at NC State

Goals and Objectives of the Course: This course is designed to introduce students to the field of engineering and the study of engineering as an academic discipline. The overall objective of the course is to integrate computer usage, teamwork, problem solving, and verbal/written language into a design project (within the course) and to thus develop the skills that are the foundation of a successful engineering career. An early understanding of these skills assists students throughout their undergraduate experience and beyond.

E101 Course Learning Outcomes
By the end of the semester, students will be able to do the following:

1. Solve engineering problems by working in teams
2. Understand specifics of the various engineering disciplines and about careers in engineering
3. Apply a structured design process in solving engineering problems
4. Demonstrate how and when to apply analytical methods to solve engineering problems
5. Demonstrate knowledge of the resources and opportunities on campus that assist in achieving their unique educational and life goals
6. Present engineering problems and solutions in both written and oral presentation modes

Reprinted with permission from Spurlin, Lavelle, Rajala, & Robbins (2003)

TABLE 8.3
Important Characteristics of the E101 Course at NC State

* The course carries one-semester-hour credit and is required of all entering engineering freshman students; students must pass the course to graduate.
* Students take the course for a grade (C– minimum must be earned).
* Classes meet once per week for a 2-hour active learning lecture/lab session.
* Class section sizes are limited to ~40–48 students—thus, in order to accommodate the ~1150 incoming engineering students each fall, ~25–28 sections of this course are offered.
* Classes meet in special, computer-equipped, multimedia classrooms—this setup facilitates the learning/teaching style desired and the classroom activities.
* Regular faculty from the 11 engineering departments in the College, as well as staff in the First-Year Engineering Program serve as instructors of the course.
* There is no textbook for this course: All materials are available on the course Web page and in the College of Engineering Student Handbook (which students are required to purchase).
* Student Engineering Leaders (SELs) are used to assist in achieving the goals of the course: These are upper-level engineering students who serve as TAs for the various sections of the course (one experienced SEL is designated as the Head SEL for coordination and training purposes).
* There are 15 class meetings each semester (16 weeks minus fall break week); the subject of each of the class meetings, as well as the assignment/activity for the day, is clearly articulated on the course Web page.

Previously, we described a model (Spurlin et al., 2003) developed by the NC State engineering assessment team. The key steps included the following:

1. Defining program mission, objectives, and outcomes
2. Developing an assessment plan to assess the program objectives and outcomes with linkages to curriculum issues and implementation
3. Gathering the data into a database
4. Interpreting the data to determine program effectiveness and implementing program improvements

Spurlin et al. (2003) detail the implementation and issues related to each of the four levels of the NC State Assessment Model. Particularly interesting are the results that the model produced in step four, which involved the

TABLE 8.4
E101 Mapping of Learning Outcomes to Course Content and Assessment Method

Learning Course Outcomes	Activity/Assignment/Event (Course Content)	Assessment Method

1. Solve engineering problems by working in teams	• Straw Dome Design Project
	• Semester Design Project
	  • design phases
	  • team contract
	  • project scheduling
		• Team ratings rubric
		• Design rubric
		• Course evaluation

2. Understand specifics of the various engineering disciplines and about careers in engineering	• Departmental Presentations • COE Welcome (information fair) • Department Information Sessions	• Team presentation rubrics • Course evaluation • Midterm examination
3. Apply a structured design process in solving engineering problems	• Straw Dome Design Project • Semester Design Project • all phases of design process	• Design rubric • Course evaluation

TABLE 8.4 (Continued)

Learning Course Outcomes	Activity/Assignment/Event (Course Content)	Assessment Method

4. Demonstrate how and when to apply analytical methods to solve engineering problems	• Straw Dome Design Project
	• Semester Design Project
	  • analysis of design results
	  • engineering failure
		• Design rubric
		• Course evaluation

5. Demonstrate knowledge of the resources and opportunities on campus that assist in achieving their unique educational and life goals	• Goals Assignment • Resume Assignment • Departmental Presentations • COE Welcome (information fair) • Department Information Sessions	• Examination • Course evaluation • Departmental presentation rubric

6. Present engineering problems and solutions in both written and oral presentation modes	• Straw Dome Design Project
	• Freshmen Engineering Design Day
	• Semester Design Project
	  • final written report
	  • final oral presentation
	• Resume Assignment
	• Goals Assignment
		• Design rubric
		• Oral presentation rubric
		• Course evaluation

Reprinted with permission from Spurlin, Lavelle, Rajala, & Robbins (2003) collection and interpretation of the data. Each of the course learning outcomes was given along with a summary of the current year's data and indications of how that data affected the plans for course or assessment improvement in the next cycle. The complete results of step four of the method as examined in 2001 and 2002 are reproduced in Appendix 8.A.

The Impact/Influence of ABET's EC2000 Criteria

For engineering programs, ABET accreditation is important for many different reasons, and historically the ABET seal of approval has meant different things to different program constituents. Prior to the 1990s, ABET accreditation reflected the fact that programs had certain minimum elements in place to produce quality graduates. It was with the change to EC2000 that ABET moved from being a system-describing activity to a system-changing driver in the enterprise of engineering education. Prados, Peterson, and Latucca (2005) provide an excellent synopsis of the history and context of EC2000.

A recently released study commissioned by ABET to assess the impacts of EC2000 documents the important effects. In the study, Volkwein, Lattuca, Terenzini, Strauss, and Sukhbaatar (2004) found that there have been improvements in student learning along the dimensions of EC2000. The study also suggested that changes in the system that produces engineering graduates (namely our engineering programs) have been associated with this increase in student learning. Thus, improvements in curricula and teaching methods have had an impact as faculty have incorporated the spirit of EC2000.

For first-year engineering programs, the impact of EC2000 (and other influences) has been reflected in the type of initiatives aimed at increasing student learning while recruiting, retaining, and graduating an ever more diverse student population. Thus, the very types of initiatives discussed in this chapter are indeed the types of activities that should lead and direct programs in their efforts to improve student learning.

From an assessment perspective, many opportunities exist to increase the degree to which these activities are connected to degree program learning objectives and outcomes. Data collected as part of a first-year engineering course or curricula can be used in a variety of ways to demonstrate the value-added aspect of the engineering program. Data at this level show the baseline of where the student is at the beginning, while senior-level (or exit) data can be used to show the out-the-door state. Student self-assessments and survey data, portfolios of student work, and other data all can be effectively used to collect before-versus-after data.

Conclusion and Discussion

First-year engineering programs provide an important starting point for students seeking degrees in engineering. Because such programs are the gateways to the engineering discipline there is tremendous opportunity to influence students' experiences. At the same time, the first year is an important time for students to gain a solid footing academically, personally, socially, and professionally. In the past ten years many new initiatives have been implemented in first-year engineering programs around the nation. Educators have focused activities in the first-year engineering course and curriculum in order to improve the positive impact of the first year on engineering students.

In this chapter we have reviewed the most recent initiatives, classified them in terms of activities and assessment, and discussed the activities of the first-year engineering program at North Carolina State University.

References

Anderson-Rowland, M. (1998). The effect of course sequence on the retention of freshman students: When should the intro engineering course be offered? *Proceedings of Frontiers in Education Annual Conference*, Session T3A, pp. 252–257. Retrieved September 15, 2006, from http://fie.engrng.p#.edu/fie98/

Barlow, D., Havener, A., Kouri, J., Marlino, M., & Smith, M. (1996, June). Project falcon base: A freshman engineering experience. Proceedings of American Society for Engineering Education Conference and Exposition, Session 2653, Washington, DC.

Barr, R., Kruger, T., & Aanstoos, T. (2005). Addressing program outcomes in a freshman introduction to engineering course. *Proceedings of American Society for Engineering Education Conference and Exposition*. Retrieved September 15, 2006, from http://www.asee.org/acPapers/2005-272_Final.pdf

Besterfield-Sacre, M., Atman, C., & Shuman, L. (1998). Engineering student attitude assessment. *Journal of Engineering Education, 87*(2), 133–141.

Brannan, K., & Wankat, P. (2005). Survey of first-year programs. *Proceedings of American Society for Engineering Education Conference and Exposition*. Retrieved September 15, 2006, from http://www.asee.org/acPapers/2005-236_Final.pdf

Budny, D., Bjedov, G., & LeBold, W. (1997). Assessment of the impact of the freshman engineering courses. *Proceedings of Frontiers in Education Annual Conference*, pp. 1100–1106. Retrieved September 15, 2006, from http:fie.engrng.pitt.edu/ fie97/papers/1068.pdf

Budny, D., LeBold, W., & Bjedov, G. (1998). Assessment of the impact of freshman engineering courses. *Journal of Engineering Education, 87*(4), 405–411.

Connor, J., & Goff, R. (2001). Assessment of providing in-class, hands-on, activities to Virginia Tech's first-year engineering students. *Proceedings of American Society for Engineering Education Conference and Exposition*, Session 2793. Retrieved September 15, 2006, from http://www.asee.org/acPapers/00060_2001.PDF

Demel, J., Gustafson, R., Fentiman, A., Freuler, R., & Merrill, J. (2002). Bringing about marked increases in freshman engineering retention. *Proceedings of American Society for Engineering Education Conference and Exposition.* Retrieved September 15, 2006, from http://www.asee.org/acPapers/2002–2043_Final.pdf

Dolan, C., Whitman, D., & Edgar, T. (2005). Introduction of engineering programs at the University of Wyoming. *Proceedings of American Society for Engineering Education Conference and Exposition.* Retrieved September 15, 2006, from http://www.asee.org/acPapers/2005-415_Final.pdf

Felder, R., Bernold, L., Burniston, E., Dail, P., & Gastineau, J. (1996). IMPEC: An integrated first-year engineering curriculum. *Proceedings of American Society for Engineering Education Conference and Exposition.* Retrieved September 25, 2006, from http://www.asee.org/acPapers/01353.pdf

Felder, R., Bernold, L., Burniston, E., Dail, P., & Gastineau, J. (1997). Update on IMPEC: An integrated first-year engineering curriculum at NC State University. *Proceedings of American Society for Engineering Education Conference and Exposition.* Retrieved September 25, 2006, from http://www.asee.org/acPapers/01089.pdf

Freuler, R., Gates, M., Merrill, J., Lamont, M., & Demel, J. (2002). An anonymous electronic journal system: Program assessment tool and Monday morning quarterbacking. *Proceedings of American Society for Engineering Education Conference and Exposition*, Session 2973. Retrieved September 25, 2006, from http://www .asee.org/acPapers/2002-1357_Final.pdf

Graham, J., & Caso, R. (2002). Measuring engineering freshman attitudes and perceptions of their first year academic experiences: The continuous development of two assessment instruments. *Proceedings of Frontiers in Education Annual Conference*, Session F3B. Retrieved September 25, 2006, from http://fie.engrng.pitt.edu/ fie2002/index.htm

Hanesian, D., & Perna, A. (1999). An evolving freshman engineering design program at NJIT. *Proceedings of Frontiers in Education Annual Conference*, Session 12A6. Retrieved September 25, 2006, from http://fie.engrng.pitt.edu/fie99/

Hatton, D., Wankat, P., & BeBold, W. (1998). The effects of an orientation course on the attitudes of freshman engineering students. *Journal of Engineering Education, 87*(1), 23–27.

Hensel, R., Byrd, J., & Myers, W. (2005). Designing a freshman program to support student success. *Proceedings of American Society for Engineering Education Confer-*

ence and Exposition. Retrieved September 25, 2006, from http://asee.org/acPap ers/2005-1578_Final.pdf

Holt, M., & Ohland, M. (1998). The impact of a discipline-based introduction to engineering course on improving retention. *Journal of Engineering Education, 87*(1), 79–85.

Howze, J., Froyd, J., Shryock, K., Srinizasa, A., & Caso, R. (2005). Interdisciplinary approach to first-year engineering curriculum. *Proceedings of American Society for Engineering Education Conference and Exposition.* Retrieved September 23, 2006, from http://asee.org/acPapers/2005-957_Final.pdf

Huband, F. (Ed). (1998). *How do you measure success? Designing effective processes for assessing engineering education.* Washington, DC: ASEE Professional Books.

Hutchinson, M., Follman, D., Sumpter, M., & Bodner, G. (2006). Factors influencing the self-efficacy beliefs of first-year engineering students. *Journal of Engineering Education, 95*(1), 39–47.

Inam, A., & Caso, R. (2002). Some validity concerns in non-experimental program evaluation: A case study. *Proceedings of Frontiers in Education Annual Conference,* Session T4B. Retrieved September 23, 2006, from http://fie.engrng.pitt.edu/ fie2002/index.htm

Jansen, E., Brophy, S., Klein, S., Norris, P., & Wang, M. (2003). A problem-based introductory course in biomedical optics in the freshman year. *Proceedings of American Society for Engineering Education Conference and Exposition,* Session 1609. Retrieved September 23, 2006, from http://asee.org/acPapers/2003-2507_Final.pdf

Kampe, J., Goff, R., & Connor, J. (2005). First-year hands-on design on a dime— almost. *Proceedings of American Society for Engineering Education Conference and Exposition,* Session 2625. Retrieved September 23, 2006, from http://asee.org/ acPapers/2005-1669_Final.pdf

Kellar, J., Hovey, W., Langerman, M., Howard, S., Simonson, L., Kjerengtroen, L., et al. (2000). A problem-based learning approach for freshman engineering. *Proceedings of Frontiers in Education Annual Conference,* Session F2G. Retrieved September 29, 2006, from http://fie.engrng.pitt.edu/fie2000/papers/1311.pdf

Lavelle, J., & Robbins, M. (2003). The first-year engineering course at NC State University: Design, implementation and assessment. *Proceedings of American Society for Engineering Education Conference and Exposition.* Retrieved September 29, 2006, from http://asee.org/acPapers/2003-981_Final.pdf

Lo, J., Goff, R., Lohani, V., Walker, T., Knott, T., & Griffin, O. (2005). New paradigm for foundation engineering education. *Proceedings of American Society for Engineering Education Conference and Exposition.* Retrieved September 29, 2006, from http://asee.org/acPapers/2005-1262_Final.pdf

Marra, R., Palmer, B., & Litzinger, T. (2000). The effects of a first-year engineering design course on student intellectual development as measured by the Perry Scheme. *Journal of Engineering Education, 89*(1), 39–45.

McKenna, A., & Hirch, P. (2005). Evaluation student confidence in engineering design, teamwork, and communication. *Proceedings of American Society for Engineering Education Conference and Exposition.* Retrieved September 29, 2006, from http://asee.org/acPapers/2005-564_Final.pdf

Milano, G., Parker R., & Pincus, G. (1996). A freshman design experience: Retention and motivation. *Proceedings of American Society for Engineering Education Conference and Exposition,* Session 2553. Retrieved September 29, 2006, from http://asee.org/acPapers/01325.pdf

Moskal, B., Leyden, J., & Pavelich, M. (2002). Validity, reliability, and assessment of engineering education. *Journal of Engineering Education, 91*(3), 351–353.

Ohland, M., & Collins, R. (2002). Creating a catalog and meta-analysis of freshman programs for engineering students. Part 2: Learning Communities. *Proceedings of American Society for Engineering Education Conference and Exposition,* Session 1653. Retrieved September 29, 2006, from http://asee.org/acPapers/2002-1106 _Final.pdf

Ohland, M., & Crockett, E. (2002). Creating a catalog and meta-analysis of freshman programs for engineering students. Part 1: Summer Bridge Programs. *Proceedings of American Society for Engineering Education Conference and Exposition.* Retrieved September 29, 2006, from http://asee.org/acPapers/2002-1099_ Final.pdf

Olds, B., & Miller, R. (2004). The effect of a first-year integrated engineering curriculum on graduation rates and student satisfaction: A longitudinal study. *Journal of Engineering Education, 93*(1), 23–35.

Olds, B., Moskal, B., & Miller, R. (2005). Assessment in engineering education: Evolution, approaches and future collaborations. *Journal of Engineering Education, 94*(1), 13–25.

Olds, B., & Pavelich, M. (1996). A portfolio-based assessment program. *Proceedings of American Society for Engineering Education Conference and Exposition,* Session 2313. Retrieved September 29, 2006, from http://asee.org/acPapers/01499_ Final.pdf

Orabi, I. (1999). Outcome assessment results of a multi-disciplinary first-year course at the University of New Haven. *Proceedings of American Society for Engineering Education Conference and Exposition.* Retrieved September 13, 2006, from http:// asee.org/acPapers/99conf398.PDF

Pendergrass, N., Kowalczyk, R., Dowd, J., Laoulache, R., Nelles, W., Golen, et al. (2001). Improving first-year engineering education. *Journal of Engineering Education, 90*(1), 33–41.

Prados, J., Peterson, G., & Latucca, L. (2005). Quality assurance of engineering education through accreditation: The impact of EC2000 and its global influence. *Journal of Engineering Education, 94*(1), 165–183.

Richardson, J., Corleto, C., Froyd, J., Imbrie, P., Parker, J., & Roedel, R. (2002). Freshman design projects in the foundation coalition. *Proceedings of Frontiers in*

Education Annual Conference, Session T1D, pp. 50–59. Retrieved September 13, 2006, from http://fie.engrng.pitt.edu/fie98/

Richardson, J., & Dantzler, J. (2002). Effect of a freshmen engineering program on retention and academic performance. *Proceedings of Frontiers in Education Annual Conference*, Session S2C. Retrieved September 13, 2006, from http://fie.engrng .pitt.edu/fie2002/papers/1570.pdf

Rowe, C., Klein, S., & Mahadevan-Jansen, A. (2005). Assessing a freshman course. *Proceedings of American Society for Engineering Education Conference and Exposition,* Session 3653. Retrieved September 13, 2006, from http://www.asee.org/ acPapers/2005-1774_Final.pdf

Schmidt, J., Yang, C., Wilson, O., & Zhang, G. (1999). Assessment of the teaching-learning effectiveness of a freshman design course. *Proceedings of Frontiers in Education Annual Conference*, Session 13b1. Retrieved September 13, 2006, from http://fie.engrng.pitt.edu/fie99/

Spurlin, J., Lavelle, J., Rajala, S., & Robbins, M. (2003). Assessment of an Introduction to Engineering and Problem Solving course. *Proceedings of American Society for Engineering Education Conference and Exposition.* Retrieved September 13, 2006, from http://www.asee.org/acPapers/2003-356_Final.pdf

Volkwein, J., Lattuca, L., Terenzini, L., Strauss, C., & Sukhbaatar, J. (2004). Engineering change: A study of the impact of EC2000. *International Journal of Engineering Education, 20*(2), 1–11.

Weber, F., Bennett, R., Forrester, J., Klukken, P., Parsons, R., Pionke, C., et al. (2000). The engage program: Results from renovating the first year experience at the University of Tennessee. *Proceedings of Frontiers in Education Annual Conference*, Session S2G. Retrieved September 13, 2006, from http://fie.engrng.pitt.edu/ fie2000/papers/1256.pdf

APPENDIX 8.A

ASSESSMENT OF FIRST-YEAR ENGINEERING AT NORTH CAROLINA STATE UNIVERSITY

The following sections are taken from Spurlin et al. (2003) with permission from ASEE Publications.

Step 4: Interpreting the Data to Determine Program Effectiveness and Implementing Program Improvements.

For each outcome, not only was the assessment method defined, but the faculty for this course, as a group, determined performance standards for each method. These standards were used to interpret the data and determine strengths and weaknesses. The faculty discussed the findings during an assessment meeting in the spring of 2002 and made decisions about modifications for fall of 2002. The data were collected during the fall of 2002 semester as described above. Below is a discussion about what was found from the assessment methods for each of the six learning outcomes for this course for both fall of 2001 and fall of 2002. Data was analyzed as a whole for the course, as differences between sections were nonsignificant. Comparison of the data from each semester and how changes in the course affected student learning as seen by the assessment data are discussed.

Outcome 1: By the end of the semester, students will be able to solve engineering problems by working on teams.

In the fall of 2001, the teamwork rubric was not analyzed for assessment purposes. In the fall of 2002, the teamwork rubric showed that the students felt strongest about their teammates' ability to communicate. The teams indicated that most members (75%) could listen and speak appropriately while working in their teams. The students rated 50 percent of their teammates as being able to make good contributions to the work, and 45 percent as making contributions of high quality. Each dimension of the teamwork rubric had at least 82 percent of the students rate their teammate as a "4" or "5," which exceeds the performance standard set by the faculty: "Outcome met if 75 percent of students received "4" or "5" on each dimension of the rubric." See Table 8.A.1 for results from the teamwork rubric.

As seen in Table 8.A.1, the course evaluation survey for the fall of 2001 showed that 70 percent of the students felt that the course contributed to their knowledge about working on teams and understanding the importance of teams. The faculty discussed this finding and suggested that next time the faculty should spend more time discussing teamwork. The scores from the fall 2002 course evaluation suggested that this extra time was beneficial: 79 percent of the students felt that they had learned about working on teams.

The Grading Rubric for Written Papers score on the dimension on teamwork ("Paper clearly describes team structure and issues related to teamwork") on the final design project showed that it increased from an average of 2.60 in fall of 2001 to an average of 2.73 in the fall of 2002. The findings from fall 2002 showed that the students exceeded the performance standards set by the faculty: "Outcome met if the average of 2.5 or higher on teamwork dimension."

Outcome 2: By the end of the semester, students will be able to apply a structured design process in solving engineering problems.

Assessment of outcome 2 was determined from many of the dimensions on the Grading Rubric for Written Papers. The scores from the rubric on all of the final design projects were analyzed for the fall of 2001 (see Table 8.A.2). Each dimension was scored on a scale of 1 "Poor" to 3 "Excellent." It was found that dimensions such as *Understanding Overall Design Process, Problem Identification and Working Criteria, Project Testing,* and *Drawing of Design* had a high average. The dimensions with the lowest average included *Presenting a Gantt Chart of Tasks, Identifying Solutions Alternatives, Identifying Multiple Research Sources, Writing About Project Management of Resources,* and *Summarizing Research Sources.*

Based on these finding from the fall of 2001, it was determined that students were not able to identify research sources except on the Internet; they could not differentiate between the quality of research sources, and they could not

TABLE 8.A.1
Assessment Findings and Improvement to Program Based on Outcome 1

Outcome 1: By the end of the semester, students will be able to solve engineering problems by working on teams.

Assessment Findings Fall 2001	Modifications Made for Fall 2002	Assessment Findings Fall 2002
Teamwork Rubric was used by instructor to decide if each team member should get the same grade on the final project. A few grades were modified.	For fall 2002, data on Teamwork Rubric should be collected to determine areas of weakness.	Findings from Teamwork Rubric on each dimension: I Share of tasks assumed — 4.48 II Contribution/Quality of Work — 4.21 III Team Spirit — 4.48 IV Dependability — 4.24 V Communication — 4.62 VI Overall Evaluation — 4.48
Course evaluation showed that 70% of the students felt that the course contributed to their knowledge about working on teams and understanding the importance of teams. Although this did not make the 75% criteria, this was a high rating compared to other topics.	Next time, faculty should have more discussion about *why* they need to work on teams.	Course evaluation showed that 79% of the students felt that they had learned about working on teams and 77% felt that they had an understanding of the importance of teams. This is an increase compared to the previous year.
Rubric for Final Design Project: Dimension on teamwork: Paper clearly describes team structure and issues related to teamwork: 2.60 average		Rubric for Final Design Project: Dimension on teamwork: Paper clearly describes team structure and issues related to teamwork: 2.73 average

TABLE 8.A.2

Assessment Findings and Improvement to Program Based on Outcome 2

Outcome 2: By the end of the semester, students will be able to apply a structured design process in solving engineering problem.

Assessment Findings Fall 2001	Modifications Made for Fall 2002	Assessment Findings Fall 2002
Grading Rubric for Written Papers on the Final Design Project showed the following:		Grading Rubric for Written Papers on the Final Design Project Rubric showed the following:
Highest dimensions across all students:		Comparison to fall 2001:
Dimension — *Average* Problem Identification — 2.85 Working Criteria — 2.82 Understanding Overall Design Process — 2.70 Testing Design Drawing of Design — 2.63		*Dimension* — *Average* Problem Identification and Working Criteria — 2.71 Understanding Overall Design Process — 2.73 Project Testing — 2.70 Drawing of Design — 2.69
Lowest dimensions across all students:	• Instead of stressing a specific kind of chart, such as Gantt chart, faculty may discuss any type of project scheduling tool they feel is appropriate. • Course needs to help students with identifying multiple sources of background information and how to use that information—therefore, an information literacy module will be added to next fall's course.	Comparison to fall 2001:
Dimension — *Average* Presenting a Gantt Chart of Tasks — 2.53 Identifying Solutions/ Alternatives — 2.53 Identifying Multiple Research Sources — 2.48 Writing About Project Management of Resources — 2.46 Summarizing Research Sources — 2.41		*Dimension* — *Average* Gantt Chart Dimension Changed to Project Scheduling Tool — 2.71 Identifying Solutions/ Alternatives — 2.59 Identifying Multiple Research Sources — 2.38 Writing About Project Management of Resources — 2.46 Summarizing Research Sources — 2.42

summarize the sources they found. Therefore, the faculty decided that the E101 course should include an information literacy module to help students with identifying multiple sources of background information and how to use that information.

A module was developed and delivered to the students in partnership with the university engineering librarians. The students were given hands-on practice finding information and determining how to use it. The module included a homework assignment in which students gathered references and made a summary of the sources. This specific module was piloted in the 2002 spring semester and fully implemented in fall 2002. It was speculated that this module would increase the students' ability and that the students' scores on the rubric on the fall 2002 final design papers would improve on the dimensions related to this topic.

Even though the module on information literacy was added, the students in the fall of 2002, on average, did not improve on the following rubric dimensions for the final design paper: *Identifying Solutions Alternatives, Identifying Multiple Research Sources, Writing About Project Management of Resources,* and *Summarizing Research Sources.* See Table 8.A.2 for specific data. The faculty will meet later this semester to determine other strategies for improving this outcome. Another improvement the faculty made for the fall of 2002 was in reference to the Gantt Chart of Tasks. Since the Gantt Chart of Tasks had an unacceptable low average in the fall of 2001, the faculty would not specify this tool as the tool of choice. Instead of the Gantt Chart, each faculty member in the fall of 2002 discussed the project scheduling tool or tools they thought the students should use. In fall of 2002, the project scheduling tool dimension increased to an average of 2.71 (compared to 2.53 for the Gantt Chart dimension in fall of 2001).

Outcome 3 (fall 2001): By the end of the semester, students will be able to demonstrate how and when to apply computer tools to solve engineering problems. Modified for fall 2002: *By the end of the semester, students will be able to demonstrate how and when to apply analytical methods to solve engineering problems.*

After examining the assessment data from fall 2001, the faculty of the course determined that most students had a basic knowledge of Excel and Power-Point, but that the real issue was for students to begin to understand *how to apply math, physics and other science principles* to an engineering problem. Therefore, the outcome was modified and more emphasis was placed on analytical methods during the fall of 2002. To assess this outcome, a dimension on analytical method was added to the Grading Rubric for Written Papers. This dimension asked students to explain how math, physics, and other science principles were appropriate to their engineering problem. For fall 2002, the students had an average of 2.5 on this dimension (scale from 1, "poor," to 3, "excellent"). The faculty considered this satisfactory, and it met the performance standard set by the faculty: "Outcome met if the average of 2.5 or higher on each dimension of the rubric."

Outcome 4: By the end of the semester, students will be able to present engineering problems and solutions in both written and oral presentation modes.

In the fall of 2001, the data from each of the six dimensions of the Grading Rubric for Written Papers related to writing were analyzed. The students met the faculty performance standard on these dimensions of scoring higher than 2.5 on average. See Table 8.A.3 for specific results.

In fall 2001, the Grading Rubric for Oral Presentations scores were not kept for assessment purposes. However, for the fall 2002, data from 40 teams (out of approximately 250 teams) from this rubric were kept and analyzed. The students were rated high by the faculty on all dimensions except Organization (2.4 average). See Table 8.A.3 for specific results.

Outcome 5: By the end of the semester, students will be able to understand specifics of the engineering disciplines and careers in engineering.

In the fall of 2001, the course evaluation survey asked the students to rate their knowledge about specific issues related to engineering. The data from the survey were analyzed, and it was found that this outcome was not met as determined by the performance standard for this outcome (see Table 8.A.4). The faculty determined that this outcome could be improved by placing more emphasis on these topics. In addition, the faculty conducting informational sessions were given feedback about their sessions so that they could improve them. The faculty also determined that students would learn about each discipline if they had more active learning assignments. In the fall of 2002, each team of students developed a presentation about one discipline.

TABLE 8.A.3
Assessment Findings and Improvement to Program Based on Outcome 4

Outcome 4: By the end of the semester, students will be able to present engineering problems and solutions in both written and oral presentation mode.

Assessment Findings Fall 2001	Modifications Made for Fall 2002	Assessment Findings Fall 2002
Grading Rubric for Written Papers, dimensions on WRITING, on the Final Design Project, showed that the students met performance standard for writing skills on the final paper:	No modifications needed	Grading Rubric for Written Papers, dimensions on WRITING, on the Final Design Project, showed that the students met performance standard for writing skills on the final paper:

Dimension	*Average*			*Dimension*	*Average*
Structure of paper	2.76			Structure of paper	2.71
Conclusion	2.76			Conclusion	2.66
Grammar	2.73			Grammar	2.76
Focus and flow	2.73			Focus and flow	2.63
Intro	2.73			Intro	2.73
Style	2.67			Style	2.76

Assessment Findings Fall 2001	Modifications Made for Fall 2002	Assessment Findings Fall 2002
Grading Rubric for Oral Presentations used for overall judgment and scores not kept on each team.	No modifications needed except to add more dimensions on presentation style and timing	The following are the results from 40 teams on their final design oral presentation:

					Average
				Organization	2.4
				Content Knowledge	2.9
				Grammar and Spelling	2.9
				Style	2.8
				Visual Impact of Slides	2.9
				Professionalism	2.9
				Presentation Style	2.8
				Delivery	2.8
				Transition Between Speakers	3.0
				Timelines	2.9

TABLE 8.A.4

Assessment Findings and Improvement to Program Based on Outcome 5

Outcome 5: By the end of the semester, students will be able to understand specifics of the engineering disciplines and careers in engineering.

Assessment Findings Fall 2001		Modifications Made for Fall 2002	Assessment Findings Fall 2002	
Course Evaluation asked students to rate contribution that E101 made to their knowledge of the following topics. Outcome met if percentage higher than 75%.			Course Evaluation asked students to rate degree they had learned the following topics. Outcome met if percentage higher than 75%.	
Topics	*Percentage Who Said "4 or 5"*	This outcome could be improved by more time on these topics and more active participation by students about each discipline. Next fall, each team will learn about and give a presentation about one discipline.	*Topics*	*Percentage Who Said "4 or 5"*
Engr. Design	71		Engr. Design	71
Projects	71		Projects	72
Understand Teamwork	70		Understand Teamwork	77
Teamwork	70		Teamwork	79
Engr. Failure	66		Engr. Failure	66
Engr. Disciplines	64		Engr. Disciplines	68
Engr. as a Profession	64		Engr. as a Profession	68
Communication	57		Written Communication	57
Ethics	57		Oral Communication	64
Personal/Professional Development	50		Ethics	64
Current Events	50		Personal/Professional Development	67
Problem Solving	49		Current Events	39

Outcome 5: By the end of the semester, students will be able to understand specifics of the engineering disciplines and careers in engineering.

Assessment Findings Fall 2001			Modifications Made for Fall 2002	Assessment Findings Fall 2002		
Number of students who attended information sessions on each program and their ratings of the session.			Faculty running informational sessions were given this feedback and asked to improve their sessions.	Number of students who attended information sessions on each program and their ratings of the session.		
Info Session Attended	*Number Who Attended*	*Percentage Who Rated Session "4 or 5"*		*Info Session Attended*	*Number Who Attended*	*Percentage Who Rated Session "4 or 5"*
BE	146	66		BE	99	73
CHE	84	69		BME	143	72
CE	95	63		CHE	90	74
CSC	128	67		CE	245	85
ECE	219	57		CME	55	75
IE	56	70		ENE	74	69
MTE	239	88		CSC	107	73
MAE	120	67		EE	165	65
NE	54	74		CE	153	69
TE	43	75		IE	94	85
				MTE	180	78
				MAE	200	75
				NE	139	82

The results from the course evaluation survey for the fall of 2002 showed that students' understanding of the engineering disciplines had increased, but not to the level of the performance standard. The student ratings of the informational sessions showed improvement, and most sessions met the expected performance standard. Overall, this outcome still needs work. See Table 8.A.4 for specific results.

Outcome 6: By the end of the semester, students will be able to discuss resources and opportunities on campus that assist in student's goals.

In the fall of 2001, at the end of the semester, the course evaluation surveys were collected and analyzed. These results showed that students did not feel that they had learned much about topics related to policies and procedures or about the various disciplines in engineering.

Table 8.A.5 displays complete results for outcome 6. The faculty also decided that having the students self-assess knowledge on policies and procedures was not as good as actually testing their knowledge. Therefore, for the fall 2002 course, the students took an exam on the policies and procedures. They were able to take the test only one time but could use their textbook. Of the 40 questions, 4 questions were found to be misleading or badly worded. Each of the other questions was analyzed to determine the number of students who did not get the answer correct. If more than 10 percent of the students did not get a question correct, then the faculty felt that this was an area that students may not have understood and may need some clarification on the next time the course is taught. Five questions drew incorrect responses from more than 10 percent of the students. These questions reflected the topics of

- when a student could repeat a course;
- the number of departments and majors within the College of Engineering;
- requirements for matriculation; and
- understanding their responsibility toward meeting prerequisite course requirements.

Table 8.A.6 incorporates the changes made to the assessment plan and shows the newest plan. This plan was implemented beginning fall of 2002.

TABLE 8.A.5
Assessment Findings and Improvement to Program Based on Outcome 6

Outcome 6: By the end of the semester, students will be able to discuss resources and opportunities on campus that assist in student's goals.

Assessment Findings Fall 2001	Modifications Made for Fall 2002	Assessment Findings Fall 2002
Course Evaluation asked students to rate contribution that E101 made to their knowledge of the following topics. Outcome met if percentage higher than 75%.		Course Evaluation asked students to rate degree they had learned the following topics. Only a few topics were on the course evaluation survey, as most of the topics were tested on the exam. Outcome met if percentage higher than 75%.

Topics	*Percentage Who Rated Session "4 or 5"*				*Topics*	*Percentage Who Rated Session "4 or 5"*
Matriculation	66				Course Instructor	86
Advising	61				Classroom Facilities	79
C-Wall	49				Computer Facilities	82
FYC Repeat	48					
Interns	45					
Co-op	45					
Dual Degrees	38		Lowest ratings were on these topics. Next fall, faculty need to clarify these policies and procedures.			
Minors	37					
Study Abroad	32					
Course Instructor	76					
Course SEL (TA)	78					
Classroom Facilities	75					
Computer Facilities	78					

	Faculty also determined that it would be better to test student knowledge in these areas rather than ask their opinion if they had learned about these areas.	Students in fall 2002 were given an exam about policies and procedures. Only five questions had more than 10% of the students respond incorrectly. These questions reflected
		• when a student could repeat a course;
		• the number of departments and majors were within the College of Engineering;
		• requirements for matriculation; and
		• understanding their responsibility toward meeting prerequisite course requirements.

TABLE 8.A.6
Modified Assessment Plan for E101 for Fall 2002

Course Learning Outcomes	Strategies for Implementing Outcome	Assessment Methods	Relates to ABET Criteria 3.a–k
1. By the end of the semester, students will be able to solve engineering problems by working on teams.	Team of four persons to work on the design project throughout the semester.	• Students complete a rubric about the team experience during last week of class. Outcome met if 75% of students received "4" or "5" on each dimension of the rubric. • Course evaluation: Outcome met if 75% of students feel they understand about this topic at a high level ("4" or "5" on five-point scale). • Grading rubric for written paper: Dimension on teamwork: Outcome met if the average of 2.5 or higher on this dimension.	(d) Graduates have an ability to function on multidisciplinary teams.
2. By the end of the semester, students will be able to apply a structured design process in solving engineering problems.	Design process taught. Each team will solve one problem by end of course.	• Grading rubric for written paper to assess how well they applied the design process to the project: Outcome met if the average of 2.5 or higher on each dimension of rubric.	(b) Graduates have an ability to design and conduct experiments, as well as to analyze and interpret data.

3. By the end of the semester, students will be able to demonstrate how and when to apply analytical methods to solve engineering problems.	The small design project and the final design project both incorporate how math and science principles impact the problem and design.	• Grading rubric for written paper added dimensions to assess how well students apply math and science principles to the design of their projects: Outcome met if the average of 2.5 or higher on each dimension of the rubrics.	(a) Graduates have an ability to apply knowledge of mathematics, science, and engineering. (e) Graduates have an ability to identify, formulate, and solve engineering problems.
4. By the end of the semester, students will be able to present engineering problems and solutions in both written and oral presentation modes.	Students given two opportunities to write a paper and three opportunities to do an oral presentation.	• Grading rubrics for written paper and oral presentation applied to determine student's ability in writing and oral presentations and ability to solve the problem: Outcome met if the average of 2.5 or higher on each dimension.	(g) Graduates have an ability to communicate effectively.
5. By the end of the semester, students will be able to understand specifics of engineering disciplines and careers in engineering.	Each team will investigate one discipline and give a class presentation about the discipline. Each student given multiple opportunities to visit each discipline area and discuss each discipline with professionals in the area.	• Course evaluation: Outcome met if 75% of students feel they understand this information at a high level ("4" or "5" on five-point scale). • Attendance at informational sessions will be monitored and the outcome met if at least 75% of those who attended consider the session high quality.	Not applicable
6. By the end of the semester, students will be able to discuss resources and opportunities on campus that assist in student's goals.	Class discussion and textbook readings.	• Exam on policies and procedures.	Not applicable

9

ASSESSMENT FOR IMPROVING TEACHING AND STUDENT LEARNING WITHIN A COURSE

C. Dianne Raubenheimer

T he way in which a faculty member teaches impacts the way in which students learn, and whether they adopt a "surface" or "deep" approach to learning (Prosser & Trigwell, 1999). A surface approach is characterized by an attempt by learners to reproduce information, a concern for grades and course requirements, and minimal mental effort. In contrast, a deep approach relies on relating new information to existing knowledge, the application of new information to new contexts, and the creation of meaning (Cross & Steadman, 1996). Prosser and Trigwell (1999) show that there is a clear relationship between teaching strategy and student learning, with students adopting deep approaches to learning in classrooms that are more student centered. To achieve these effects, instructors need to move away from lecture-based teaching to more participative approaches that include real-life applications of learning. In comparison, traditional courses using traditional approaches lead to a decline in a deep approach to learning (Kember, Charlesworth, Davies, McKay, & Stott, 1997).

Mertler (2003) described three steps in the instructional process: planning for teaching, delivering instruction, and assessing teaching (see Figure 9.1). Each step is dependent on the others, where the delivery of instruction should reflect the instruction planned, and assessment should assess what was delivered in terms of what the instructor did and what the students learned. The data gathered should be used to improve future planning, delivery, and assessment activities. In reality, most assessment focuses on the students and

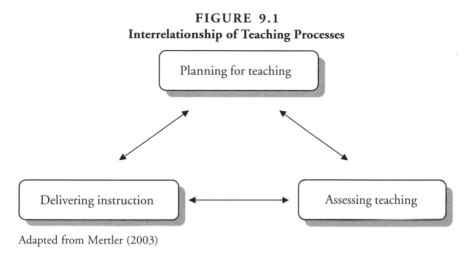

FIGURE 9.1
Interrelationship of Teaching Processes

Adapted from Mertler (2003)

not the instructor, meaning that the planning and delivery stages are not assessed and are therefore assumed to be effective. However, this is clearly not necessarily true; ineffective teaching can promote a surface approach to learning by students.

This chapter addresses the instructional process and focuses on how engineering faculty can assess and improve their own instruction using classroom assessment techniques (CATs) to gather information about student learning. This is followed by a discussion of how ongoing cycles of assessment and action research on teaching can lead to course, curriculum, and program improvement—where faculty members gain answers to some questions about teaching and identify new ones. All this can be done in ways that meet the criteria for the Scholarship of Teaching (SoT).

Purposes for Classroom Assessment

There are several purposes for classroom assessment: (a) to obtain feedback on the effectiveness of, and student satisfaction with, classroom activities and teaching, (b) to enhance teaching, (c) to track student learning, (d) to improve student learning, and (e) to increase communication and collaboration between instructor and students (Steadman, 1998).

As instructors teach, they often informally assess student learning through observation and oral questioning, gathering information for the purposes described. But for classroom assessment to be really effective, it needs to be done formally and formatively; that is, data must be gathered and analyzed systematically and used to inform future instruction. However, Dennis (2001) noted that engineering faculty who were surveyed prior to participating in a faculty development initiative had little knowledge of such assessment techniques and how to implement them. One of the purposes of this chapter is to provide strategies and examples of how formal formative classroom assessment can be undertaken in engineering courses by providing examples of how some engineering faculty have undertaken this process.

Classroom Assessment Techniques

Angelo and Cross (1993) described 50 different approaches, called classroom assessment techniques (CATs), that instructors can use to gather information about "what, how much, and how well their students are learning" (p. 3). Classroom assessment is intended not for grading but for formative assessment. These techniques are easy to implement and are intended as a means of gathering feedback early on about what and how students are learning. This allows instructional changes to be made immediately. By conducting classroom assessment, the feedback loop becomes "very short term" (Shaeiwitz, 1998a, p. 1; 1998b). One of the main benefits of using CATs instead of in-class question-and-answer sessions is that answers are elicited from all, or almost all, of the students, instead of only the typically few students who respond to instructor prompts (Marshall & Marshall, 2005). Thus, it is possible to obtain a snapshot of the group's learning, rather than that of just a few individuals.

Angelo and Cross (1993) divided CATs into three main categories: (a) techniques for assessing course-related knowledge and skills; (b) techniques for assessing learner attitudes, values, and self-awareness; and (c) techniques for assessing reactions to teachers and teaching. Each main category is divided into subcategories. It must be noted that Angelo and Cross's assessment techniques do not present an exhaustive listing, and other examples of CATs used in engineering courses are presented under these headings.

Techniques for Assessing Course-Related Knowledge and Skills

There are five subcategories in this grouping.

1. Assessing prior knowledge, recall, and understanding. One of the most commonly used CATs is the *minute paper* (Shaeiwitz, 1998b). Students are asked to write responses to variants of the questions, "What are the most important things you learned in class today?" and "What questions do you still have?" (Marshall & Marshall, 2005). The instructor can quickly review student responses and identify problem areas for review in the next session.

A review of ASEE conference and exposition proceedings from 1997 to 2005 by this author shows that, while this CAT is the most commonly cited among those using CATs, there is little description in the papers of how data were analyzed, what the results showed, or how results were used for improvement. At Virginia Tech's College of Engineering, students electronically submit minute papers from their personal laptops; Connor et al. (2004) are now developing a system for the systematic collection and storage of this data, which provides important feedback on instruction. In addition to providing immediate feedback to the instructor concerned, they intend to use the database as a teaching tool for new instructors in the college. This represents an innovative use of the data gathered in this process.

The *muddiest point* technique is a way to find out what concepts students are having difficulty with, by asking students at the end of a class session to write down what they found the most confusing (Mosteller, 1989). Birol, McKenna, Giorgio, and Brophy (2002) used this method to assess the muddiest points in new course modules in a biotechnology course and analyzed the responses to identify ineffective parts that needed change. In the aerospace engineering program, students at MIT write *muddy cards* about lectures, readings, and homework to identify the most confusing or difficult concepts. These cards are being collected and compared to lists of core concepts and associated misconceptions as part of a process of identifying student conceptual difficulties. From this, learning strategies, such as concept mapping, are used to resolve misconceptions.

A variation of the minute paper is the *attention quiz* developed by Mehta (1995, 1997), in which students answer two to four multiple-choice questions (MCQs) at the end of a class session to assess their comprehension of the main concepts covered during the lesson. The purpose of the attention quiz is to improve student attention in class, because research has shown that "students are not attending 40 percent of the time" that an instructor is lecturing (Mehta, 1997, p. 2).

Mehta (1997) extended his classroom assessment technique to the *attention retention quiz*, in which students are asked two or three questions covering content from the current lecture and one or two questions from previous sessions. A student survey showed that 96 percent of students found the attention retention quiz helped to keep their attention, 95 percent felt that it helped with retention of the material, and 88 percent perceived that it helped their understanding of the course content. At the beginning of the semester each student is given one sheet on which to answer all class quizzes. These are turned in at the end of each class session, graded, and returned to students at the beginning of the next session, at which time the instructor reviews answers and deals with problem areas. Mehta (1997) stated that it takes between seven and eight minutes to grade the papers and analyze trends. He has also experimented with an electronic system for large classes (Mehta & Schlecht, 1998) using daily homework and a quiz, whereby students complete both homework that is graded at the beginning of the session and an attention quiz at the end of class. Optical scan sheets are used in these large class sections. Data are processed and results placed on the Web, allowing students to view their own results as well as those of the whole class. It would also be possible to link the attention quizzes to the use of classroom communication systems.

In general, interactive teaching and small-group activities have been shown to have benefits to students in science, technology, engineering, and mathematics (STEM) disciplines by promoting greater academic achievement (Springer, Stanne, & Donovan, 1999) and increasing conceptual reasoning and problem solving (Crouch & Mazur, 2001). Classroom communication systems, or personal response systems, provide a way for instructors to promote a question-based approach to teaching, to increase active learning, and to enhance classroom interaction, particularly in large classes (d'Inverno, Davis, & White, 2003). The communication system can be used as a *background knowledge probe* about particular concepts or to assess conceptual understanding at intervals during class or at the end of a class. These communication systems utilize electronic transmitters that students use to respond to questions projected by the instructor onto a screen. The electronic receiver and software aggregates student responses to different answer options for the whole class. When used during class to probe student understanding of concepts just taught, immediate feedback is provided to the instructor and students, and any misconceptions and concerns can be dealt with instantly.

The effectiveness of this approach has been established in a number of disciplines (Draper & Brown, 2004), including physics (Crouch & Mazur, 2001; Dufresne, Gerace, Leonard, Mestre, & Wenk, 1996) and engineering (Nicol & Boyle, 2003), particularly when instructors initiate peer discussions—called *interactive engagement*—and invite students to discuss the questions and their individual responses. It is also particularly effective when used for contingent teaching, in which the instructor uses the process diagnostically, that is, to hone in on problem areas typically experienced by the particular audience (Draper & Brown, 2004). In a foundational mechanical engineering course, Nicol and Boyle (2003) compared two ways of using the communication system to promote interactive classwide discussion versus peer instruction, and found that small-group peer instruction and discussion preceded by individual responses was the approach students perceived to be most effective. In this way, students first identify their own understanding of the concept and then in the peer discussion must defend that answer or be prepared to revise it based on new evidence. This approach also resulted in an increase in exam scores, particularly in "raising the tail of the class" (Draper & Brown, 2004, p. 82).

Brophy, Norris, Nichols, and Jansen (2003) noted that such communication systems typically only support multiple-choice questioning, which can be set to assess student abilities at different levels of Bloom's taxonomy (Mehta & Schlecht, 1998). To provide a greater variety of question type, the Vanderbilt-Northwestern-University of Texas-Harvard/MIT (VaNTH) Engineering Research Center has developed a browser-based system that allows students to submit in-class responses to MCQs and short-answer and essay questions using their personal laptops (Brophy et al., 2003). MCQs were used to identify students' initial conceptions and to check understanding after instruction on specific concepts. The short-answer questions were perceived to be more authentic because they required students to generate their own response rather than select from a predetermined list. The instructor was able to consolidate the responses to the short-answer questions and use this for further teaching to discuss what was correct or what was missing. The system was also used to gather minute papers and muddiest points.

As a low-tech version of this approach, in the absence of a classroom response system, the instructor can also provide individual students with flash cards labeled *A, B,* and *C.* Students select and raise the card they think corresponds with the answer to the question shown by the instructor on an overhead projector. By scanning the classroom the instructor can assess how many students have the correct response. Mehta (1995) calls this the M^2 *method,* which he uses at 10- to 20-minute intervals to actively involve students during lectures.

Background knowledge probes can be used to identify students' existing conceptions prior to instruction, and then instruction can be modified to address areas of weakness. In an electrical engineering class, an instructor used diagrams of different instruments to find out what students knew about current, voltage, and resistance and how to measure these dimensions (Angelo & Cross, 1993). The instructor then used students with more knowledge to engage in peer instruction of others. At Southern Connecticut State University, Yu and Peters (2006) extended this notion by combining a background probe prior to teaching with the same assessment at the end of the semester. They mapped each course outcome to questions on a survey, then compared the differences between the results at the beginning and end of the semester, and were able to calculate the learning gains for each outcome. This indicated both learning goals that were satisfactorily achieved by students and others that needed further work in the future.

To assess students' preconceptions of fundamental physics problems, Hein and Irvine (1999) used the *folder activity*, which is a writing activity at America University in Washington, D.C., in which students write about core concepts as part of their homework assignments. These writings are submitted every two weeks, and students receive written feedback to help them to rework initial conceptions. It is also suggested that students write a reflection on the feedback received so that they can grapple with, and confront, their misconceptions. The process of articulating ideas helps with the process of confronting and dealing with flawed conceptions.

Empty outline and the *memory matrix* are two other strategies suggested by Angelo and Cross (1993), but they will not be discussed here.

2. Assessing skill in analysis and critical thinking. At West Piedmont Community College, Kiser (personal communication, November 28, 2006) used the "defining features matrix," which requires students to classify concepts according to the presence or absence of defining features, to assess their level of understanding regarding whether any given engineering problem would require an analytical or a creative approach (or a combination of both) to solve. He did this by describing the defining features of several engineering challenges and then having students select from a matrix which problem-solving strategy(ies) they would use. From the data gathered, he concluded that, while students had a good understanding of analytical approaches, they "didn't seem to understand the types of engineering problems that require a more creative approach." He used the results to hold a class discussion on the similarities and differences between the two problem-solving approaches.

Analytic memos, a simulation exercise, were used by Jenkins and Yates (2005) at University of Southern California, where students were required to write a rebuttal memo to the management of Ford. As engineers "working for the company" their task was to use cost-benefit analysis to explain why the decision to sell a particular make of car was problematic. The case was intended to highlight ethical dilemmas in engineering and led to further in-class discussion about other ethical issues in different areas of engineering.

Using *categorizing grids, pro-and-con grids,* and *content form and function outlines* are three other strategies in this category suggested by Angelo and Cross (1993).

3. Assessing skill in synthesis and creative thinking. Within this category, Angelo and Cross (1993) suggest six different strategies: the *one-sentence summary, word journals, the approximate analogy, invented dialogs, concept maps,* and *annotated portfolios.* The latter two strategies are discussed more fully in chapter 10.

The *one-sentence summary* is a way to get students to describe a phenomenon in one sentence. One uses question prompts to do this, such as asking students to explain what happens when water flows through a pipe. Students then combine the prompts into a sequential sentence. An example response is shown in Table 9.1.

4. Assessing skill in problem solving. Problem solving can be assessed through *documented problem solutions,* in which students document the process they

TABLE 9.1
An Example of the One-Sentence Summary

Context: Water flowing through a pipe	
Question	*Response*
Who or what?	Water
Does what?	Applies pressure
To what or whom?	To the pipe
When?	When it flows
Where?	Along the pipe
Why?	Because of a force on the walls
In sentence form . . .	When water flows through a pipe there is pressure in the pipe because the water applies a force on the walls of the pipe.

are engaged in as they solve problems provided. As students explain their process in writing, they become aware of how they solved the problem and how they can improve the process. Shaeiwitz (1998a) at West Virginia University uses a modification of this called *group problem solving* in which students work in groups to solve simple problems, then move to more complex ones. As students work through the process, the instructor moves around the classroom answering questions, providing input and guidance. This also gives the instructor an insight into common difficulties and misconceptions that can be discussed with the whole class.

Other methods advocated by Angelo and Cross (1993) are *problem recognition tasks, what's the principle,* and *audio- and videotaped protocols.*

5. Assessing skill in application and performance. Directed paraphrasing is a technique in which students are asked to summarize a technical concept into language that is accessible to a layperson. Tillison and Hand (2005) used this as one of the techniques to assess an environmental engineering course at Michigan Technological University, where students were asked to explain to designated audiences, within a three-minute time limit, two different scenarios regarding an aspect of a treatment technique. This enabled the instructor to assess how well the students understood the concepts and make adjustments as necessary.

Student-generated test questions is a technique in which students are told to come up with exam questions together with model answers. This helps the instructor to assess the type and level of questions students produce and how well they answer these. Shaeiwitz (1998a) tells his engineering students that the questions they generate must be problems that "test in-depth understanding or have unique features to receive maximum credit" and that "plug-and-chug" questions will only receive a score of 60 percent. He found that all students were able to produce questions that demonstrated higher-order thinking skills and was satisfied with what they had learned.

Other techniques suggested by Angelo and Cross (1993) are *application cards, class modeling,* and *a paper or project prospectus.*

Techniques for Assessing Learner Attitudes, Values, and Self-Awareness

The intention of assessment strategies in this category is to identify student values, learning strategies, and study skills, and to enhance students' self-awareness as learners and as being responsible for their own learning. Angelo and Cross (1993) identified three subcategories in this group.

1. *Assessing students' awareness of their attitudes and values.* Possible techniques include *classroom opinion polls, double-entry journals, profiles of admirable individuals, ethical dilemmas,* and course-related *self-confidence surveys* (Angelo & Cross, 1993).

Parisay (1999), in an operations research course at California State Polytechnic University, used a student *self-confidence survey* at the beginning and end of the semester to find out existing knowledge and skills and to indicate the degree of improvement made by students. This survey was useful for students to trace their own learning gains by the end of the course.

2. *Assessing students' self-awareness as learners.* The *Student Assessment of Learning Gains* (SALG) is an online, Web-based survey that instructors can use for students to rate their learning gains on particular course outcomes ("Field-Tested Learning and Assessment Guide," n.d.). The instrument, to which instructors can add their own questions, can be used to identify aspects that support student learning and others that need improvement. It can also be used for students to monitor their own progress on particular outcomes over time.

Annotated portfolios (Parisay, 1999) are a valuable tool for students to collect and display their best work. When the artifacts in the portfolio contain annotations of how that artifact relates to course outcomes and how it assisted their learning, students are encouraged to reflect on their own learning. Students in Parisay's (1999) course became "aware of their performance and/or weaknesses" (p. 4).

Felder and Silverman (1988) developed the Felder-Silverman model for assessing learning styles, which was later developed into an online instrument called the Index of Learning Styles (Soloman & Felder, n.d.). Instructors can require students to complete this instrument to identify the students' learning styles in the classroom. This falls in the category of *self-assessment of ways of learning* technique. Using the model, students identify their own learning style preferences and can work on developing those that are less well developed. Similarly, Felder and Silverman (1998) encourage instructors to find out the profile of their classes and to use teaching strategies that address all the learning style variants.

At Smith College, Riley (2006) used Web logs ("blogs") for students to journal about their experiences in a thermodynamics course and to assess students' *self-awareness as learners.* Students were provided with weekly prompts to guide their reflection about what they were learning. To rate the blogs, the authors used a rubric that assesses the extent to which students are reflective, use critical thinking, and are engaged in reflective action. They concluded that the metacognitive reflection enhanced student responsibility for learning and promoted student capacity for lifelong learning.

Other strategies include *focused autobiographical sketches, goal ranking and matching*, and *interest/knowledge/skills checklists* (Angelo & Cross, 1993).

3. *Assessing course-related learning and study skills.* In order to monitor how much time students spend out of class on different courses, Estes, Welch, and Ressler (2006) asked students to record the amount of time they spent working on a given course since the last class meeting. While their use of this strategy was to identify homework tasks that were too demanding and needed revision, this strategy can also be beneficial for students to monitor their own study habits. Angelo and Cross (1993) call this *productive study-time logs.* Other techniques include *punctuated lectures, process analysis*, and *diagnostic learning logs* (Angelo & Cross, 1993).

Techniques for Assessing Reactions to Teachers and Teaching

Angelo and Cross (1993) identified two subcategories of techniques for assessing the reaction to teachers and teaching.

1. *Assessing learner reactions to teachers and teaching. Chain notes* were used by Suri (2003) to elicit feedback about teaching in order to redesign the environment to help students learn. Chain notes are written on cards given to students at the beginning of the session. During the session a large envelope circulates the classroom on which the instructor has written a question he or she wants to find an answer to. Examples might include "What are you paying attention to right now?" and "What were you doing just before this reached you?" Students write a brief answer to the question, put it in the envelope, and pass it on. In large lecture classes, this helps to give an indication of off-task behaviors and distractions.

Electronic mail feedback can be used to provide feedback on course activities. Steward, Mickelson, and Brumm (2005) at Iowa State University used weekly e-mail journals that were focused on specific questions in an agricultural and biosystems engineering course. The instructor responded to individual e-mails as necessary, made a posting to the group, or incorporated a response into the next class session. This enabled responses to student questions about specific course content and about the application of concepts. It also provided insight into which teaching methods students perceived to be most beneficial to their learning.

In a chemical engineering course at Michigan State University, Buch (2002) used a *student management team* (SMT), which consisted of a representative group of four or five students and the instructor. The group was tasked with improving the course by collecting and analyzing classroom assessment data on instructor performance and on the structure and content of the course. The team met each week to develop the appropriate assessment strategy and decide on action items. The SMT analyzed data and made suggestions for improvement to the instructor. In this way immediate feedback and corrective actions were discussed and implemented. This strategy is similar to the *classroom assessment quality circles*, and *group instructional feedback* suggested by Angelo and Cross (1993).

Teacher-designed feedback forms can be developed by instructors to elicit specific information about reactions to instruction. Tillison and Hand (2005) used Bloom's taxonomy to design a form to elicit information covering the cognitive, affective, and psychomotor domains. They found that most of the course objectives were set at the lower levels of Bloom's taxonomy, enabling them to make changes to the anticipated course outcomes as well as to the methods for assessing the different levels of ability.

2. Assessing learner reactions to class activities, assignments, and materials. Most of the strategies already mentioned in this chapter can be used to elicit feedback from students about particular course activities, materials, and assignments. Other structured processes suggested by Angelo and Cross (1993) are the *RSQC²*, *group-work evaluations, reading rating sheets, assignment assessments*, and *exam evaluations*.

Getting Started Using CATs

For instructors to begin to assess student learning, they must first be aware of their own intentions for what they want students to learn from their class. That is, they need to be clear about their own instructional goals and course outcomes. To help an instructor assess personal instructional goals, Angelo and Cross (1993) developed a Teaching Goals Inventory (TGI). This inventory is grouped around five clusters considered important goals for student learning. The inventory helps instructors to (a) become aware of what they want to accomplish in individual courses, (b) locate CATs they can adapt and use to assess how well they are achieving their teaching and learning goals, and (c) provide a starting point for discussions of teaching and learn-

ing goals among colleagues. The inventory can be taken online at www
.uiowa.edu/~centeach/tgi/index.html.

Angelo and Cross (1993) provide a simple three-step process for implementing CATs in a classroom—(1) planning, (2) implementation, and (3)
reporting—with these steps further broken down into substeps, making a
total of nine steps in *one* classroom assessment project (CAP) cycle.

Ongoing Course Improvement Through Classroom Action Research

Action research is a classroom research process that can be used for ongoing
classroom assessment, or iterative CAP cycles. It involves successive cycles of
(a) identifying a problem or asking a question, (b) planning, (c) acting or
carrying out the plan, (d) observing and gathering data, and (e) reflecting on
results, in order to find solutions to teaching and learning problems and to
generate new research questions. Figure 9.2 illustrates the four stages of the
action research cycle.

Because the process is iterative, the research is essentially never finished,
although one may reach a point at which significant questions are answered.
However, inevitably, new questions will arise in the process of answering
others. Classroom assessment techniques represent a range of strategies for
assessing student outcomes and can be used as one component in action research to gather appropriate data (Cross & Steadman, 1996). The difference
between this approach and traditional research is that it does not end with
data analysis but leads to the generation of new questions and new actions
(Cross, 1998). Another important feature of action research is the concept of
triangulation of data, in which multiple methods (e.g., CATs, interviews,
observation of teaching protocols) are used to gather data from various stakeholders (students, instructors, and others as appropriate).

Popov (2003) changed the way a final mechanical engineering design
project was taught, and he used an action research design to evaluate the
effect on the quality of student learning. His purpose was to stimulate intrinsic student motivation and promote peer interaction. He provided several
broad topics for students to choose from, and they then had to develop a
more focused problem from these broad areas. During the semester, students
had weekly meetings with other students, as well as individual meetings (as
needed) with the instructor. A workshop was held where students presented
their design ideas for feedback, and progress reports were added as steps
toward a final report. Student work was used as one source of data, and they

FIGURE 9.2
The Four Stages in the Action Research Cycle

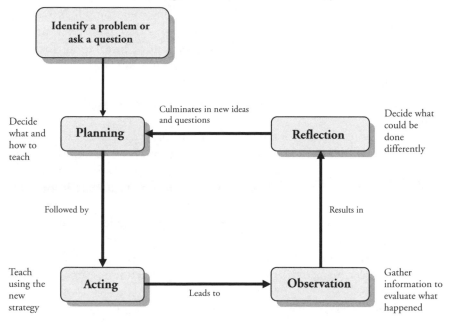

completed a student feedback questionnaire at the end of the semester. The results showed that the students had engaged in deeper levels of learning than in previous years. Reflection on the findings gave Popov indicators for future change, such as including peer and self-assessment of the presentations and providing exemplars of deep learning outcomes to students, leading him into another action research cycle.

The Scholarship of Teaching

There are many definitions of what constitutes the scholarship of teaching in universities, and these definitions tend to be used interchangeably. Experts agree that there is a lack of "broadly acceptable definitions for the scholarship of teaching, scholarly teaching, excellence in teaching, expert teacher, and research on teaching and learning" (Kreber, 2002a, p. 161). This can be attributed to the fact that faculty members hold differing conceptions about the value and purposes of the scholarship of teaching (Brew, 1999).

Boyer (1990), who coined the term "scholarship of teaching," was concerned that there is an excessive focus on research productivity at universities that has created an imbalance in the work of academics in favor of research. He thought that there should be a balance among four components in the life of scholars: (a) the scholarship of discovery, geared to inquiry for the sake of producing new knowledge; (b) the scholarship of integration, focusing on integrating new knowledge into a larger picture; (c) the scholarship of application, emphasizing the value and use of knowledge; and (d) the scholarship of teaching, involving the dissemination of knowledge as a communal act.

In the context of the United States, Schön (1995) concluded that Boyer's challenge to develop the scholarship of teaching requires a new epistemology for universities: "Like other organizations, education institutions have epistemologies. They hold conceptions of what counts as legitimate knowledge and how you know what you claim to know" (p. 27). He called for a new epistemology that requires "knowing in action" and "reflection in action," and added that this is what social psychologist Kurt Lewin (1946) meant by action research. "The new scholarship implies action research. The new categories of scholarship activity must take the form of action research" (Schön, 1995, p. 30).

Richlin (2001) distinguished between scholarly teaching and the scholarship of teaching, with the latter being embedded in the broader term of scholarly teaching. She held that scholarly teaching is geared to improving teaching and that, while it adopts a formal, systematic research process, it is not geared to public communication and often remains a private activity. In contrast, the scholarship of teaching requires publication and dissemination of the results of one's work. Similarly, Hutchings and Schulman (1999) argued that teaching excellence, in which faculty strive to be good teachers, is the responsibility of all educators, while the scholarship of teaching has four additional criteria: that it (a) becomes public, (b) is open to critical review and evaluation, (c) is in a form that members of the education community can use and build on, and (d) is geared to raising questions for investigation. In this way the products of the scholarship of teaching result in peer-reviewed information that "becomes part of the knowledge base of teaching and learning in higher education" (Richlin, 2001, p. 58). Kreber (2002b) suggested that both terms have merit and that comparisons of one another are counterproductive, because they each contribute to debates about improving teaching.

Trigwell, Martin, Benjamin, and Prosser (2000) developed a model for the development of the scholarship in teaching that is essentially a rubric for levels of engagement on four dimensions: the informed dimension, the reflection dimension, the communication dimension, and the conception dimension. This is shown in Table 9.2, which has been modified to include descriptions for cells that were blank in their original version. Using this model, faculty who are less involved in the scholarship of teaching are located at the top of the table and tend to use informal theory to drive their practice. They tend to be more teacher focused than student focused. In contrast, faculty who are more engaged in the scholarship of teaching are located at the bottom of the table. They use documented educational theories and pedagogies to guide their teaching, involve students in the learning process, engage in reflective practice, conduct classroom research, and communicate their findings to others. It is also possible for faculty to be located at different levels on each of the four dimensions.

The grid can also be used to assess the extent to which particular faculty members are engaged in the scholarship of teaching (Raubenheimer, 2004), and if used in this way, most of the examples cited in this chapter would fall within level 3 or 4 on the classification scheme. The authors surveyed in this chapter have used formal CATs to answer specific questions identified, they have interpreted and reflected on their results, their focus has been on improving teaching practices and student learning, and they have communicated their findings through written and verbal means. These practitioners have been engaged in the scholarship of teaching.

TABLE 9.2
Multidimensional Model of Scholarship of Teaching

	Informed Dimension	Reflection Dimension	Communication Dimension	Conception Dimension
1	Uses informal theories of teaching and learning	Effectively none or unfocused reflection	Does not communicate with others about teaching	Sees teaching in a teacher-focused way
2	Engages with the literature of teaching and learning generally	Limited reflection on teaching	Communicates with departmental/faculty peers (tea room, conversations, department seminars)	Sees teaching in a teacher-directed way
3	Engages with the literature, particularly the discipline literature	Reflection-in-action	Reports work at local and national conferences	Sees some teaching in a student-focused way
4	Conducts action research, has synoptic capacity and pedagogic content knowledge	Reflection focused on asking, what do I need to know about here, and how will I find out about it?	Publishes in international scholarly journals	Sees teaching in a student-focused way

Modified from Trigwell, Martin, Benjamin, & Prosser (2000), p. 163

References

Angelo, T. A., & Cross, K. P. (1993). *Classroom assessment techniques: A handbook for college teachers* (2nd ed). San Francisco: Jossey-Bass.

Birol, G., McKenna, A., Giorgio, T., & Brophy, S. (2002). Implementation of educational modules in a biotechnology course: A challenge based education approach. *Proceedings of the 2002 American Society for Engineering Education Annual Conference and Exposition.* Washington, DC: ASEE.

Boyer, E. L. (1990). *Scholarship reconsidered: Priorities of the professoriate.* New Jersey: Carnegie Foundation for the Advancement of Teaching.

Brew, A. (1999). *The value of scholarship.* Paper presented at the HERDSA Annual International Conference, Melbourne, Australia. Retrieved September 18, 2002, from http://www.herdsa.org.au/vic/cornerstones/authorframeset.html

Brophy, S. P., Norris, P., Nichols, M., & Jansen, E. D. (2003). Development and initial experience with a laptop-based student assessment system to enhance classroom instruction. *Proceedings of the 2003 American Society for Engineering Education Annual Conference and Exposition.* Washington, DC: ASEE.

Buch, N. (2002). Use of student management teams (SMTs) as a course evaluation tool. *Journal of Engineering Education, 91,* 125–131.

Connor, J. B., Lohani, V. K., Bull, E., Wildman, S. G., Magliaro, S. G., Knott, T. W., Griffin, O. H., & Muffo, J. A. (2004). An analysis of freshmen engineering: A cross-case perspective. *Proceedings of the 2004 American Society for Engineering Education Annual Conference and Exposition.* Washington, DC: ASEE.

Cross, K. P. (1998). Classroom research: Implementing the scholarship of teaching. *New Directions for Teaching and Learning, 75,* 5–12.

Cross, K. P., & Steadman, M. H. (1996). *Classroom research: Implementing the scholarship of teaching.* San Francisco: Jossey-Bass.

Crouch, C. H., & Mazur, E. (2001). Peer instruction: Ten years of experience and results. *American Journal of Physics, 69*(9), 970–977.

Dennis, N. D. (2001). ExCEEd Teaching Workshop: Taking it on the road. *Proceedings of the 2001 American Society for Engineering Education Annual Conference and Exposition.* Washington, DC: ASEE.

d'Inverno, R., Davis, H., & White, S. (2003). Using personal response system for promoting student interaction. *Teaching Mathematics and Its Applications, 221*(4), 163–169.

Draper, S. W., & Brown, M. I. (2004). Increasing interactivity in lectures using an electronic voting system. *Journal of Computer Assisted Learning, 20,* 81–94.

Dufresne, R. J., Gerace, W., Leonard, W. J., Mestre, J. P., & Wenk, L. (1996). iClasstalk: A classroom communication system for active learning. *Journal for Computing in Higher Education, 7*(2), 3–47.

Estes, A. C., Welch, R. W., & Ressler, S. J. (2006). The assessment of teaching. *Journal of Professional Issues in Engineering Education and Practice, 132,* 2–10.

Felder, R. M., & Silverman, L. K. (1988). Learning and teaching styles in engineering education. *Engineering Education, 78*(7), 674–681.

Field-tested learning and assessment guide (n.d.). Retrieved May 5, 2006, from http://www.flaguide.org/

Hein, T. L., & Irvine, S. E. (1999). Technology as a teaching and learning tool: Assessing student understanding in the introductory physics lab. *Proceedings of the 1999 American Society for Engineering Education Annual Conference and Exposition.* Washington, DC: ASEE.

Hutchings, P., & Schulman, L. S. (1999). The scholarship of teaching: New elaborations, new developments. *Change, 31,* 10–15.

Jenkins, M., & Yates, L. A. (2005). Development and assessment of a freshman seminar to address societal context. *Proceedings of the 2005 American Society for Engineering Education Annual Conference and Exposition.* Washington, DC: ASEE.

Kember, D., Charlesworth, M., Davies, H., McKay, J., & Stott, V. (1997). Evaluating the effectiveness of educational innovations: Using the study process questionnaire to show that meaningful learning occurs. *Studies in Educational Evaluation, 23,* 141–157.

Kreber, C. (2002a). Controversy and consensus on the scholarship of teaching. *Studies in Higher Education, 27,* 151–167.

Kreber, C. (2002b). Teaching excellence, teaching expertise, and the scholarship of teaching. *Innovative Higher Education, 27,* 5–23.

Lewin, K. (1946). Action research and minority problems. *Journal of Social Issues, 2*(4), 34–46.

Marshall, J. A., & Marshall, J. E. (2005). Crucial teaching strategies for engineering educators. *Proceedings of the 2005 American Society for Engineering Education Annual Conference and Exposition.* Washington, DC: ASEE.

Mehta, S. I. (1995). A method for instant assessment and active learning. *Journal of Engineering Education, 84,* 295–298.

Mehta, S. (1997). Productive, quick, enjoyable assessment. *Proceedings of the 1997 American Society for Engineering Education Annual Conference and Exposition.* Washington, DC: ASEE.

Mehta, S. I., & Schlecht, N. M. (1998). Computerized assessment technique for large classes. *Journal of Engineering Education, 87,* 167–172.

Mertler, C. A. (2003). *Classroom assessment: A practical guide for educators.* Los Angeles: Pyrczak.

Mosteller, F. (1989). The "muddiest point" in the lecture as feedback device. *On Teaching and Learning: The Journal of the Harvard-Danforth Center, 3,* 10–21.

Nicol, D. J., & Boyle, J. T. (2003). Peer instruction versus class-wide discussion in large classes: A comparison of two interaction methods in the wired classroom. *Studies in Higher Education, 28*(4), 457–473.

Parisay, S. (1999). Implementation of classroom assessment techniques and web technology in an operations research course. *Proceedings of the 1999 American Society for Engineering Education Annual Conference and Exposition.* Washington, DC: ASEE.

Popov, A. A. (2003). Final undergraduate project in engineering: Towards more efficient and effective tutorials. *European Journal of Engineering Education, 28*(1), 17–27.

Prosser, M., & Trigwell, K. (1999). *Understanding and learning in teaching: The experience in higher education.* Philadelphia: Society for Research into Higher Education & Open University Press.

Raubenheimer, C. D. (2004). *Cases of university faculty conceptions and practices of teaching, assessment and action research.* Unpublished doctoral dissertation, University of Louisville, KY.

Richlin, L. (2001). Scholarly teaching and the scholarship of teaching. *New Directions for Teaching and Learning, 86,* 57–68.

Riley, D. (2006, February). Assessing the capacity for lifelong learning. *Proceedings of the 2006 Best Assessment Practices VIII Symposium.* Terre Haute, IN: Rose-Hulman Institute of Technology, Terre Haute, IN.

Schön, D. A. (1995). The new scholarship requires a new epistemology. *Change, 27,* 26–34.

Shaeiwitz, J. A. (1998a). Classroom assessment. *Journal of Engineering Education, 87,* 179–183.

Shaeiwitz, J. A. (1998b). Closing the assessment loop. *Proceedings of the 1998 American Society for Engineering Education Annual Conference and Exposition.* Washington, DC: ASEE.

Soloman, B. A., & Felder, R. M. (n.d.). Index of Learning Styles Questionnaire. Retrieved April 6, 2006, from http://www.engr.ncsu.edu/learningstyles/ilsweb .html (see also http://www.ncsu.edu/felder-public/ILSpage.html)

Springer, L., Stanne, M. E., & Donovan, S. S. (1999). Effects of small-group learning on undergraduates in science, mathematics, engineering and technology: A meta-analysis. *Review of Educational Research, 69*(1), 21–51.

Steadman, M. (1998). Using classroom assessment to change both teaching and learning. *New Directions for Teaching and Learning, 75,* 23–35.

Steward, B. L., Mickelson, S. K., & Brumm, T. J. (2005). Continuous engineering course improvement through synergistic use of multiple assessment. *International Journal of Engineering Education, 21*(2), 277–287.

Suri, D. (2003). Classroom quality assurance using students as quality managers. *Proceedings of the 2003 American Society for Engineering Education Annual Conference and Exposition.* Washington, DC: ASEE.

Tillison, N. L., & Hand, D. W. (2005). Hands-on learning of water treatment design. *Proceedings of the 2005 American Society for Engineering Education Annual Conference and Exposition.* Washington, DC: ASEE.

Trigwell, K., Martin, E., Benjamin, J., & Prosser, M. (2000). Scholarship of teaching: A model. *Higher Education Research and Development, 19,* 155–168.

Yu, W., & Peters, K. (2006, February). Bottom up program assessment using course learning outcomes measurements. *Proceedings of the 2006 Best Assessment Practices VIII Symposium.* Terre Haute, IN: Rose-Hulman Institute of Technology.

10

USING FORMATIVE ASSESSMENT FOR PROGRAM IMPROVEMENT

Barbara M. Olds and Ronald L. Miller

I n this chapter we discuss how formative assessment can be used to help provide midcourse feedback to engineering programs as they work to continuously improve learning and teaching. We begin by briefly reviewing the theory and relevant literature on formative assessment and then describe examples of several methods that can be used to provide useful feedback for program improvement. We conclude with some caveats and cautions about formative feedback.

"Formative" and "summative" are terms often used to describe assessment activities and were originally coined by Scriven (1967). According to evaluation expert Robert Stake, "When the cook tastes the soup, that's formative; when the guests taste the soup, that's summative" (quoted in Frechtling, 2002, p. 8). The Central Michigan University Assessment Toolkit (Central Michigan University, n.d.) distinguishes between formative and summative assessment thus: "Formative assessment is often done at the beginning or during a program, thus providing the opportunity for immediate evidence for student learning in a particular course or at a particular point in a program." It can "contribute to a comprehensive assessment plan by enabling faculty to identify particular points in a program to assess learning (i.e., entry into a program, before or after an internship experience, impact of specific courses, etc.) and monitor the progress being made towards achieving learning outcomes" (Formative Assessment section). Summative assessment, on the other hand, "is comprehensive in nature, provides accountability and is used to check the level of learning at the end of the program" (Summative Assessment section).

According to Frechtling (2002), "By measuring progress, program staff can eliminate the risk of waiting until participants have experienced the entire program to assess likely outcomes. If the data collected as part of the progress [formative] evaluation failed to show expected changes, the information can be used to fine tune the project [e.g., curriculum, courses]. Data collected as part of a progress evaluation can also contribute to, or form the basis for, a summative evaluation conducted at some future date" (p. 9).

Since the adoption of new ABET criteria (ABET, 2006), most engineering educators have considered assessment primarily in its summative form, that is, measuring student outcomes (commonly ABET 3.a–k) at the end of a college career. However, formative assessment and feedback can help a program determine the impact of its activities, courses, and strategies at various intermediate points in the program and to make important midcourse corrections.

Theory and Use of Formative Assessment for Program Improvement

As originally conceived, formative assessment was designed to provide intermediate feedback to individual students at the course or curriculum levels. According to Boston (2002), this approach provides many advantages over traditional summative assessment practices by giving students direct and frequent feedback on progress toward meeting course or curricular outcomes. Data provided to students can also be used by instructors to make midterm course adjustments to address student needs. By extension, it can be used to make ongoing adjustments to an entire program.

Formative assessment is grounded in constructivist learning theory (Fosnot, 1996), in which instructors generally function as mentors and coaches who help students construct meaning as they learn, as opposed to more traditional instructors who view their role as filling students' minds with information. In the constructivist model, assessment consists of frequent formative feedback and guidance from instructors to supplement the traditional summative assessment of high-stakes tests and final grades. In addition, frequent self-reflection is often a component of well-developed formative assessments and contributes to students' ability to self-monitor knowledge construction.

Black and Wiliam (1998) have reviewed over 250 articles and determined that use of formative assessment tools at the course level resulted in statistically significant improvements in student achievement as measured by test scores. Frequent feedback can also improve student motivation, particularly when focused on progress toward meeting explicit learning objectives with clear assessment criteria (Fontana & Fernandes, 1994; Frederickson & White, 1997).

Nicol and Macfarlane-Dick (n.d.) list seven principles of good feedback practice. Although focused on classroom practice, each principle can also be used to inform program-level formative assessment. The seven principles are as follows:

1. Facilitating development of self-assessment (reflection) in learning
2. Encouraging teacher and peer dialog about learning
3. Helping define and clarify good performance (goals, objectives, expected standards of performance)
4. Providing opportunities to close the gap between current and desired performance
5. Delivering high-quality learning experiences to students
6. Encouraging positive motivational beliefs and self-esteem
7. Providing information to teachers to help shape teaching

As discussed in the following section, several well-tested tools and techniques that address the principles listed above for conducting program-level formative assessment are available to engineering educators.

Examples of Formative Assessments That Can Be Used for Program Improvement

A variety of methods that can be used for formative assessment have been developed or adapted for engineering fields. In this section we introduce and give examples of engineering applications for several of them. Our list is by no means exhaustive, but we believe that it represents a good cross-section of promising practices. We have deliberately selected what we consider to be *direct* measures of student learning. *Indirect measures*, such as surveys, which ask students to self-report about their learning, often provide useful formative feedback to programs; however, we believe that most engineering educators are familiar with such instruments, and thus we chose to focus on other informative, but less frequently used, assessments.

Concept Inventories

Increasing evidence suggests that many engineering students may have the computational skill to correctly solve homework and test problems but may still not understand the fundamental concepts underlying the models presented in their course work (Svinicki, 2004). Although conceptual understanding of important concepts has been extensively studied in science fields (Duit, 2006), until recently no systematic studies of engineering students' conceptual understanding of fundamental engineering concepts had been conducted and published. However, engineering education researchers (sometimes in collaboration with learning scientists) have begun to probe and measure students' conceptual understanding of important engineering concepts by addressing questions such as the following:

- What are the fundamental concepts in engineering?
- Which of these concepts do engineering students find most difficult to learn?
- Why are these concepts difficult?
- Do students' fundamental misconceptions about these concepts contribute to their difficulty?
- How can we create instruments that measure students' understanding of these concepts?
- How can we create instruction that helps students learn these concepts?

In an effort to grasp what concepts engineering students do not understand and why, engineering educators have recently begun to more systematically probe students' conceptual understanding, often through the use of concept inventories. These inventories are usually constructed in a multiple-choice format with the distractors (plausible wrong answers) identifying common areas of student misunderstanding. No computations or equations are required to answer the questions. The most widely used of these assessments is the Force Concept Inventory (FCI), which consists of 29 multiple-choice questions designed to assess students' conceptual framework of Newtonian and non-Newtonian mechanics (Hestenes, Wells, & Swackhamer, 1992).

The FCI has demonstrated that simple tests can be developed to help faculty identify and then work to repair student misconceptions in specific technical disciplines. The FCI has undergone extensive reliability and validity testing and analysis. Although some researchers question whether the FCI actually measures the force concept (Huffman & Heller, 1995), results from the instrument have been used to measurably improve introductory physics curricula and pedagogy at many institutions (Hake, 1998), thus making it a powerful formative feedback tool.

Efforts are now under way to develop concept inventories in engineering that will drive change in engineering education in the way that the FCI has driven change in physics instruction. Examples include inventories developed through the NSF-funded Foundation Coalition in the domains of fluid mechanics, thermodynamics, heat transfer, chemistry, materials engineering, strength of materials, electric circuits, and electric signals (Evans, 2002). In addition, other concept inventories have been or are being developed including measures of students' understanding of thermal and transport phenomena (Miller, Streveler, Nelson, Geist & Olds, 2005; Miller et al., 2006; Olds, Streveler, Miller & Nelson 2004), statistics (Steif & Dantzler, 2005), and engineering statistics (Stone et al., 2003). Figure 10.1 shows a typical question from the Thermal and Transport Concept Inventory designed to measure students' conceptual knowledge of thermal and transport processes (Miller et al., 2006).

Some engineering-focused concept inventories are currently available to engineering educators, while others are still in experimental form. The hope is that concept inventories will become assessment tools that can be used to evaluate continuous improvements in engineering programs, but caution should be taken when using them because not all have been carefully constructed using appropriate methodologies or tested for validity and reliability.

Reflective Journals

Reflective journals incorporating periodic probes and checks can be used effectively for program formative assessment. Using journaling as a classroom strategy has been reported for many years in disciplines other than engineering and with increasing frequency in engineering settings (Larson, 1991; Paris & Ayres, 1994). Yancy (1998) describes reflection as simultaneously looking forward (to goals that might be obtained) and looking backward (to see what has been accomplished). Through reflection, students can discover what they already know, what they are learning, and what they might not yet understand. From a constructivist perspective, reflective writing can help students to create more complete and robust mental models of complex ideas such as ethical dilemmas and difficult concepts. It can also help faculty ascer-

FIGURE 10.1
Example of a Concept Inventory Question in Thermal Science

Two identical closed beakers contain equal masses of liquid at a temperature of 20°C, as shown below. One beaker is filled with water and the other beaker is filled with ethanol (ethyl alcohol). The temperature of each liquid is increased from 20°C to 40°C using identical heaters immersed in the liquids. Each heater is set to the same power setting.

It takes 2 minutes for the ethanol temperature to reach 40°C and 3 minutes for the water to reach 40°C.

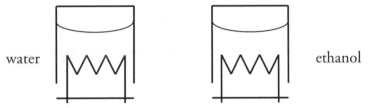

Ignoring evaporation losses, to which liquid was more energy transferred during the heating process?

    a.   Water, because it is heated longer [correct answer]

    b.   Alcohol, because it heats up faster (i.e., the temperature rises faster)

    c.   Both liquids received the same amount of energy because they started at the same initial temperature and ended at the same final temperature

    d.   Can't determine from the information given because heat transfer coefficients from the water and alcohol beaker surfaces are needed

    e.   Can't determine from the information given because heat capacities of water and ethanol are needed

tain how students function within a team, solve problems, or even design a system or component and can thus lead to program improvement.

Programs that wish to move the use of journals beyond classroom learning and assessment to a rigorous program assessment tool may do so by applying qualitative research methods, specifically drawing upon text-coding software and methodologies used in ethnographic studies. Gorman, Groves, and Catalano (2004) and Spickard-Prettyman, Qammar, and Evans (2005), for example, have used reflective journals in design classes to monitor team dynamics, intellectual growth, and individual team member opinions about team progress. Reflective journals may also be composed electronically and coded using qualitative analysis software such as N6, HyperResearch, or Ethnograph. When such tools are used, protocols can be developed to search for patterns in student responses, which will provide formative feedback at the course or program level.

Portfolios

Portfolios, which have long been employed in fields such as writing, architecture, and the arts, have more recently been used for outcomes assessment in engineering, especially electronic portfolios, or e-portfolios. They have been of particular interest to engineering programs attempting to measure the ABET "professional skills" such as teamwork, ethics, and communication. Simply stated, a portfolio is a collection of student work over time that is used to holistically assess either individual student learning or the effectiveness of a course or program. Collected work may include papers, exams, homework, videotaped presentations, projects, lab reports, design reports, and self-assessments. In some cases, students select the work to be included in their portfolio and include a reflective component on why the work was selected and how it demonstrates their mastery of a required competency. In other cases, the program may require that specific student work be included in the portfolio that can then be used to assess student progress on specific program outcomes. Portfolios are usually evaluated using scoring rubrics (see Performance Measures Using Rubrics, pp. 276–277) to provide formative feedback for program improvement.

Portfolios have several advantages: They can be used to view learning and program development longitudinally; multiple components of a curriculum can be measured simultaneously; the process of reviewing portfolios provides an opportunity for faculty exchange and development; and they may increase student participation in the assessment process (Prus & Johnson, 1994). However, portfolios also have disadvantages, the most significant of which may be the cost in evaluator time and effort. For program evaluation, this cost may be mitigated somewhat by evaluating portfolios from a representative sample of students using work products carefully selected to provide feedback on key student outcomes.

Electronic portfolios are now used in a variety of disciplines (Cambridge, 2001; Jafari & Kaufman, 2006) and they have been adopted by several engineering programs in recent years. An early adopter of e-portfolios was the Rose-Hulman Institute of Technology, which developed a Web-based portfolio system in which students submit their "best work" and include a reflective essay. Their entries, tied to the ABET criteria, are assessed electronically by faculty, who use the results to improve their programs (Rogers & Williams, 1999). Though much of the early work in the use of e-portfolios in engineering was done at smaller institutions such as Rose-Hulman, programs at larger institutions such as Virginia Tech (Knott et al., 2005) and the University of Texas at Austin (Campbell & Moore, 2003) have recently begun experimenting with them as well. Technological innovations such as iWebfolio and TrueOutcomes are making it increasingly easy to develop and maintain online portfolios.

Portfolios, whether paper or electronic, are a useful type of "authentic assessment" that can provide valuable insights and feedback for program improvement. However, like all formative assessment methods, they are not a panacea, and they must be carefully planned and implemented in order to be effective.

Concept Maps

According to Novak and Canas (2006), concept maps are "graphical tools for organizing and representing knowledge" (p. 1). A typical map includes concepts, usually enclosed in a circle or box, connected by lines showing relationships between concepts. Linking words or phrases on the lines specify the relationship between the two concepts (Novak & Canas, 2006). Concept mapping is an established assessment tool (e.g., Liu & Hinchey, 1993; Lomask, Baron, & Grieg, 1993; Wilson, 1993) geared toward measuring "knowledge integration" by students. An example concept map generated by a student describing different kinds of energy and their relationships is shown in Figure 10.2.

Concept maps are being used for assessment in many science and engineering programs. For example, Zeilik (2006) has developed and used concept maps in physics and astronomy. Besterfield-Sacre and Shuman have used concept maps in conjunction with scoring rubrics to assess industrial engineering students' conceptual knowledge of their chosen major (Besterfield-Sacre, Gerchak, Lyons, Shuman, & Wolfe, 2004); in this way they believe that they are assessing several ABET criteria, including 3.k, an understanding of modern tools and techniques. Walker and King have utilized concept maps to assess senior design abilities (Walker & King, 2003); Turns has used concept maps to assess course-level learning in courses in statistics and human factors (Turns, Atman, & Adams, 2000).

One of the issues in using concept maps as an assessment tool has been how to score them consistently. Not surprisingly, maps typically have been scored by counting concepts, links, and hierarchies. Novak believes it should

FIGURE 10.2
An Example Concept Map Showing Energy Relationships

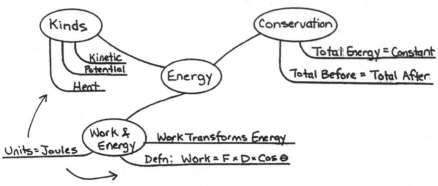

take only between 3 and 10 minutes to score a map once criteria have been defined (Novak & Gowin, 1984). Recently some increasingly sophisticated approaches have been developed that better facilitate the use of concept maps as an assessment tool. There are also software packages such as CmapTools (http://cmap.ihmc.us) that allow for the development of concept maps on the Web as well as joint construction of concept maps by learners in distributed sites (Canas et al., 2001). Software may also facilitate the use of concept maps for assessment by, for example, comparing maps developed by novices to those developed by experts.

Though concept maps are a promising method for measuring growth in students' conceptual knowledge over time and for providing formative feedback to a program about students' current state of knowledge, there are questions remaining about their use. Ruiz-Primo and Shavelson, for example, argue that more research on students' facility in using concept maps, on training techniques, and on reliability and validity is needed (Ruiz-Primo, 2004; Ruiz-Primo & Shavelson, 1996).

Measures of Intellectual Development

Most engineering programs expect that their students will develop intellectually in addition to acquiring knowledge and skills in a specific engineering discipline. However, most measures of student achievement are focused on content knowledge, process ability (e.g., design), or communication skills; students are assumed to be developing intellectually, especially in their ability to think critically, but rarely are meaningful data collected and reported that support that assumption. However, the recent movement toward outcomes assessment now encourages reliable measures of students' abilities to make reasoned decisions as they solve complex problems.

Perhaps the most recognized and valid method to quantify maturation of college students' intellectual abilities relies on developmental process models such as Perry's Model of Intellectual and Ethical Development (Perry, 1970) and King and Kitchener's Reflective Judgment (RJ) Model (King & Kitchener, 1994). These models measure students' positions along a hierarchical construct of stages representing increasingly more sophisticated ways of understanding knowledge and solving complex, open-ended problems. The standard method for evaluating students' stage of development is a structured, hour-long interview conducted by a trained expert. The interview is transcribed and then studied and rated by a second expert.

The models describe the stages people pass through as they mature in their understanding of the nature of knowledge, use of evidence, and open-ended problem solving. For example, people at RJ/Perry position 2 believe that all questions have single right answers and, thus, no problem is truly "open-ended." Students with this dualistic penchant often view professors who admit to not knowing an answer as incompetent. People at position 4 understand that there are legitimate unknowns and uncertainties, even in science and engineering, and they do use evidence reasonably well. However, they feel that there are no legitimate ways to weigh alternative possibilities and, thus, all solutions are equally valid and "everyone is entitled to their own opinion." Because all views are equally valid, students at position 4 see no reason to explore alternatives before reaching a decision: One well-argued possibility is sufficient. At position 6, the individual understands the need to use evidence and explore alternatives when solving an open-ended problem, the need for judgments based on personal and articulated standards, and the need to be open to changing circumstances.

Ideally, most students would graduate from college at a point somewhere between positions 4 and 6. Unfortunately, data collected using both models show that undergraduate college students start just above position 3 but have progressed, on average, only about 1/3 to 2/3 of a position by the time they graduate (King & Kitchener, 1994; Wise, Lee, Litzinger, Marra, & Palmer, 2001). Since data indicate that progress above level 4 is affected by education and is not simply a result of aging (King & Kitchener, 1994), it appears that most university programs do not adequately help their students reach the higher positions. However, research shows that such teaching approaches as coaching may lead to noticeable improvement in students' progress up the levels (Pavelich & Moore, 1996).

The cost of interviewing students, creating a transcript of the session, and expert scoring is high (about $150 per subject and 7 to 8 hours of time). In attempts to circumvent these disadvantages, several researchers over the years have developed paper-and-pencil (P&P) instruments to assess a person's position on the RJ or Perry models. These include measures that require short essays such as the Measure of Intellectual Development (MID) (Knefelkamp, 1975) and the Measure of Epistemological Reflection (MER) (Baxter-Magolda, 1987) as well as measures using Lickert scales, such as the Learning Environment Preferences test (LEP) (Moore, 1989) and the Reflective Thinking Appraisal (RTA) (Kitchener, 1994). More recent attempts include Cogito (Olds, Miller & Pavelich, 2000), an interactive computer program. All of these instruments have been disappointing because of the low correlation between results and standard interview results, generally in the area of 0.3 to 0.4.

Despite low correlations, P&P instruments may be valuable in certain limited circumstances. For example, if one is looking for relative changes over time with large populations, P&P instruments may provide useful data. In fact, they may be the only viable assessment instrument, given costs and time. A prime example of reasonable P&P use is Alverno College's use of the MID as one measure of total curriculum effects (Mentkowski, 2000). If the curriculum question involves smaller populations over shorter times, traditional Perry or RJ interviews should probably be used.

Performance Measures Using Rubrics

Engineering educators are being encouraged by ABET and other accrediting agencies to employ "direct" measures of student learning, such as performance appraisals, in addition to such "indirect" measures as surveys. According to Prus and Johnson (1994), a performance appraisal is preferable to most other methods to measure the application and generalization of learning to specific situations. It is particularly relevant to the goals and objectives of professional programs. Although it may be difficult to measure the quality of performances, such as on a design project, objectively, one way to reduce the disadvantage is to use scoring rubrics.

Scoring rubrics have been used for a broad range of subjects and are usually employed when a judgment of quality is required (Brookhart, 1999). In contrast to checklists, a rubric is a descriptive scoring scheme that guides the analysis of a student's work on performance assessments. These formally defined guidelines consist of pre-established criteria in narrative format, typically arranged in ordered categories specifying the qualities or processes that must be exhibited for a particular evaluative rating (Mertler, 2001; Moskal, 2000).

There are two basic types of scoring rubrics: holistic and analytic. A holistic rubric scores the process or product as a whole, without separately judging each component. In contrast, an analytic rubric allows for the separate evaluations of multiple factors with each criterion scored on a different descriptive scale.

Rubrics are intended to provide a general assessment rather than a fine-grained appraisal like the traditional 0–100 grading scale. For example, a rubric might include levels from 1 ("shows little or no understanding of key concept") to 5 ("shows full understanding of key concept; completes task with no errors"). Among the advantages of using rubrics are (1) the assessment can be more objective and consistent; (2) the amount of time faculty spend evaluating student work is reduced; (3) valuable feedback is provided to students, faculty, and the program; and (4) rubrics are relatively easy to use and explain (Georgia Educational Technology Training Center, n.d.).

Generally, rubrics are best developed starting from a desired learning outcome and working backward to less ideal outcomes, preferably using actual student work to describe in detail the rubric's various levels. The scoring system should be objective, consistent, and relatively simple, with a few criteria sets and performance levels, such as three to five evaluative criteria (Popham, 1997). Rubrics can be used to assess students' abilities to recognize and resolve ethical dilemmas (Shuman et al., 2005) or their performance on open-ended laboratory projects encompassing several ABET outcomes (Olds & Miller, 1999). Figure 10.3 shows the rubric designed to evaluate student written reports from the chemical engineering laboratory course at Colorado School of Mines (available at www.mines.edu/academic/chemeng/assess).

Conclusion

Given the increasing number of effective tools for gathering formative assessment data, do engineering programs avail themselves of the opportunity to make data-driven program improvements? Although they are not as prevalent as the summative outcomes assessments required in order for a program to receive ABET accreditation, formative assessment methods are being in-

FIGURE 10.3
Scoring Rubric for Chemical Engineering Laboratory Written Report

CSM ChE Department
Scoring Rubric for Unit Operations Laboratory Reports

Group members: _____   Lab Session: _____   Experiment: _____

Outcome	4 Exemplary	3 Proficient	2 Apprentice	1 Novice	Score
ChE graduates will be able to apply knowledge of unit operations to the identification, formulation, and solution of chemical engineering problems.	Student groups apply knowledge with virtually no conceptual or procedural errors affecting the quality of the experimental results.	Student groups apply knowledge with no significant conceptual errors and only minor procedural errors.	Student groups apply knowledge with occasional conceptual errors and only minor procedural errors.	Student groups make significant conceptual and/or procedural errors affecting the quality of the experimental results.	

Outcome				
ChE graduates will be able to design and conduct experiments of chemical engineering processes or systems, and they will be able to analyze and interpret data from chemical engineering experiments.	Student groups design and conduct unit operations experiments with virtually no errors; analysis and interpretation of results exceed requirements of experiment and demonstrate significant higher-order thinking ability.	Student groups design and conduct experiment with virtually no errors; analysis and interpretation of results meet requirements of experiment and demonstrate some higher-order thinking ability.	Student groups design and conduct experiment with no significant errors; results are analyzed but not interpreted; very limited evidence of higher-order thinking ability.	Student groups design and conduct experiments with major conceptual and/or procedural errors; no evidence of significant analysis and interpretation of results; fail to meet requirements of the experiment; demonstrates only lower-level thinking ability.
ChE graduates will demonstrate an ability to communicate effectively in writing.	Written report is virtually error-free, presents results and analysis logically, is well organized and easy to read, contains high-quality graphics, and articulates interpretation of results beyond requirements of the experiment.	Written report presents results and analysis logically, is well organized and easy to read, contains high-quality graphics, contains few minor grammatical and rhetorical errors, and articulates interpretation of results that meets requirements of the experiment.	Written report is generally well written but contains some grammatical, rhetorical, and/or organizational errors; analysis of results is mentioned but not fully developed.	Written report does not present results clearly, is poorly organized, and/or contains major grammatical and rhetorical errors; fails to articulate analysis of results meeting requirements of the experiment.

creasingly used by engineering educators, as attested to by the examples cited in this chapter.

As with all educational assessments (formative or summative), several cautions and caveats are worth noting. For formative program assessment to be effective, the most important lesson to remember is that those who will benefit from the information (students, faculty, and course coordinators) must receive it in a timely and meaningful way in order for this to happen. Also, programs should avoid the temptation to start collecting assessment data before developing clear objectives, outcomes, and assessment processes. Assessment novices should look for campus resources to help start the assessment process effectively. Many institutions have assessment expertise on campus, perhaps in the psychology or education departments. Finally, faculty should remember that the quality of results is more important than the quantity. Programs should focus on their most important objectives and collect and interpret results that will be of the most value in improving the program.

References

ABET. (2006). *Criteria for accrediting engineering programs.* Retrieved July 30, 2006, from http://www.abet.org

Baxter-Magolda, M. B. (1987). Comparing open-ended interview and standardized measures of intellectual development. *Journal of College Student Development, 28,* 443–448.

Besterfield-Sacre, M., Gerchak, J., Lyons, M., Shuman, L. J., & Wolfe, H. (2004). Scoring concept maps: An integrated rubric for assessing engineering education. *Journal of Engineering Education, 93*(2), 105–115.

Black, P., & Wiliam, D. (1998). Assessment and classroom learning. *Assessment in Education, 5*(1), 7–74.

Boston, C. (2002). The concept of formative assessment. *Practical Assessment, Research & Evaluation 8*(9). Retrieved March 15, 2006, from http://PAREonline.net/getvn.asp?v=8&n=9

Brookhart, S. M. (1999). The art and science of classroom assessment: The missing part of pedagogy. *ASHE-ERIC Higher Education Report 27*(1). Washington, DC: The George Washington University Graduate School of Education and Human Development.

Cambridge, B. L. (Ed.). (2001). *Electronic portfolios: Emerging practice in student, faculty, and institutional learning.* Sterling, VA: Stylus.

Campbell, M. I., & Moore, C. (2003). Web-based engineering portfolio system. *Proceedings of the 2003 American Society for Engineering Education Annual Conference and Exposition.* Retrieved July 30, 2006, from http://www.asee.org/conferences/v2search.cfm

Canas, A. J., Ford, K. M., Novak, J. D., Hayes, P., Reichherzer, T., & Suri, N. (2001). Online concept maps: Enhancing collaborative learning by using technology with concept maps. *The Science Teacher, 68*(4), 49–51.

Central Michigan University (n.d.). CMU assessment toolkit. Retrieved July 30, 2006, from http://www.provost.cmich.edu/assessment/toolkit/formativesumma tive.htm.

Duit, R. (2006). *Bibliography: Students' and teachers' conceptions and science education.* Kiel, Germany: Institute for Science Education.

Evans, D. L. (2002). Tools for assessing conceptual understanding in the engineering sciences. *Proceedings of the 32nd ASEE/IEEE Frontiers in Education Conference.* Retrieved July 30, 2006, from http://fie.engrng.pitt.edu/fie2002/index.htm

Fontana, D., & Fernandes, M. (1994). Improvements in mathematics performance as a consequence of self-assessment in Portuguese primary school pupils. *British Journal of Educational Psychology, 64*(3), 407–417.

Fosnot, C. T. (1996). Constructivism: A psychological theory. In *Constructivism: Theory, perspectives, and practice.* New York: Teachers College Press.

Frechtling, J. (2002). *The 2002 user-friendly handbook for project evaluation.* [Electronic version]. Washington, DC: The National Science Foundation.

Frederickson, J. R., & White, B. J. (1997, March). *Reflective assessment of students' research within an inquiry-based middle school science curriculum.* Paper presented at the annual meeting of the American Educational Research Association, Chicago.

Georgia Educational Technology Training Center. (n.d.). Assessment rubrics. Retrieved July 30, 2006, from http://edtech.kennesaw.edu/intech/rubrics.htm

Gorman, M. E., Groves, J. F., & Catalano, R. K. (2004). Societal dimensions of nanotechnology. *IEEE Technology and Society Magazine, 23*(4) 55–62.

Hake, R. (1998). Interactive-engagement vs. traditional methods: A six-thousand-student survey of mechanics test data for introductory physics courses. *American Journal of Physics, 66,* 64–74.

Hestenes, D., Wells, M., & Swackhamer, G. (1992). Force concept inventory. *The Physics Teacher, 30,* 141–158.

Huffman, D., & Heller, P. (1995). What does the force concept inventory actually mean? *The Physics Teacher, 33,* 138–143.

Jafari, A., & Kaufman, C., (Eds.). (2006). *Handbook of research on ePortfolios.* Hershey, PA: Idea Group.

King, P. M., & Kitchener, K. S. (1994). *Developing reflective judgment.* San Francisco: Jossey-Bass.

Kitchener, K. S. (1994). *Assessing reflective thinking within curricular contexts.* Report to Fund for the Improvement of Post-Secondary Education (FIPSE), Washington, DC. (Contract: P116B00926. ERIC Clearing House No. ED415751)

Knefelkamp, L. L. (1975). Developmental instruction: Fostering intellectual and personal growth of college students (Doctoral dissertation, University of Minnesota, 1974). *Dissertation Abstracts International, 36,* 1271A.

Knott, T. W., Lohani, V. K., Loganathan, G. V., Adel, G. T., Wolfe, J. L., Paretti, M. C., et al. (2005). Using electronic portfolios in a large engineering program. *Proceedings of the 2005 American Society for Engineering Education Annual Conference and Exposition.* Retrieved July 30, 2006, from http://www.asee.org/confer ences/v2search.cfm

Larson, R. L. (1991). Using portfolios in the assessment of writing in the academic disciplines. In P. Belanoff & M. Dickson (Eds.), *Portfolios: Process and product.* Portsmouth, NH: Boyton/Cook.

Liu, X., & Hinchey, M. (1993). The validity and reliability of concept mapping as an alternative science assessment. *The Proceedings of the Third International Seminar on Misconceptions and Educational Strategies in Science and Mathematics.* Ithaca, NY: Misconceptions Trust.

Lomask, M. S., Baron, J. B., & Grieg, J. (1993). Assessing conceptual understanding in science through the use of two- and three dimensional concept maps. *The Proceedings of the Third International Seminar on Misconceptions and Educational Strategies in Science and Mathematics.* Ithaca, NY: Misconceptions Trust.

Mentkowski, M. (2000). *Learning that lasts: Integrating learning, development and performance in college and beyond.* San Francisco: Jossey-Bass.

Mertler, C. A. (2001). Designing scoring rubrics for your classroom. *Practical Assessment, Research & Evaluation, 7*(25). Retrieved July 30, 2006, from http://PARE online.net/getvn.asp?v=7&n=25

Miller, R. L., Streveler, R. A., Nelson, M. A., Geist, M. R., & Olds, B. M. (2005). Concept inventories meet cognitive psychology: Using beta testing as a mechanism for identifying engineering student misconceptions. *Proceedings of the 2005 American Society for Engineering Education Annual Conference and Exposition.* Retrieved July 30, 2006, from http://www.asee.org/conferences/v2search.cfm

Miller, R. L., Streveler, R. A., Olds, B. M., Chi, M. T. H., Nelson, M. A., & Geist, M. R. (2006). Misconceptions about rate processes: Preliminary evidence for the importance of emergent conceptual schemas in thermal and transport sciences. *Proceedings of the 2006 American Society for Engineering Education Annual Conference and Exposition.* Retrieved July 30, 2006, from http://www.asee.org/confer ences/v2search.cfm

Moore, W. S. (1989). The learning environment preferences: Exploring the construct validity of an objective measure of the Perry scheme of intellectual development. *Journal of College Student Development, 30,* 504–514.

Moskal, B. M. (2000). Scoring rubrics: What, when and how? *Practical Assessment, Research & Evaluation, 7*(3). Retrieved July 30, 2006, from http://PAREon line.net/getvn.asp?v=7&n=3

Nicol, D., & Macfarlane-Dick, D. (n.d.). Rethinking formative assessment in HE:

A theoretical model and seven principles of good feedback practice. Retrieved June 25, 2006, from http://www.enhancementthemes.ac.uk/uploads/documents/NicolMacfarlane-Dickpaper-revised.pdf

Novak, J. D., & Canas, A. J. (2006). The theory underlying concept maps and how to construct them. Technical Report IHMC Cmap Tools 2006-01, the Florida Institute for Human and Machine Cognition. Retrieved July 30, 2006, from http://cmap.ihmc.us/Publications/ResearchPapers/TheoryUnderlyingConcept Maps.pdf

Novak, J., & Gowin, D. B. (1984). *Learning how to learn.* New York: Cambridge University Press.

Olds, B. M., & Miller, R. L. (1999, Spring). Using portfolios to assess a ChE program. *Chemical Engineering Education,* 110–114.

Olds, B. M., Miller, R. L., & Pavelich, M. J. (2000). Measuring the intellectual development of students using intelligent assessment software. *Proceedings of the 30th ASEE/IEEE Frontiers in Education Conference.* Retrieved July 30, 2006, from http://fie.engrng.pitt.edu/fie2000/authors/O.htm

Olds, B. M., Streveler, R. A., Miller, R. L., & Nelson, M. A. (2004). Preliminary results from the development of a concept inventory in thermal and transport science. *Proceedings of the 2004 American Society for Engineering Education Annual Conference and Exposition.* Retrieved July 30, 2006, from http://www.asee.org/conferences/v2search.cfm

Paris, S. G., & Ayres, L. R. (1994). *Becoming reflective students and teachers with portfolios and authentic assessment.* Washington, DC: American Psychological Association.

Pavelich, M. J., & Moore, W. S. (1996). Measuring the effect of experiential education using the Perry model. *Journal of Engineering Education, 85,* 287–292.

Perry, W. G., Jr. (1970). *Forms of intellectual and ethical development in the college years.* New York: Holt, Rinehart and Winston.

Popham, W. J. (1997). What's wrong—and what's right—with rubrics. *Educational Leadership,* 72–77.

Prus, J., & Johnson, R. (1994, Winter). Assessment and testing, myths and realities. *New Directions for Community Colleges,* p. 88.

Rogers, G. M., & Williams, J. M. (1999). Asynchronous assessment: Using electronic portfolios to assess student outcomes. *Proceedings of the 1999 American Society for Engineering Education Annual Conference.* Retrieved July 30, 2006, from http://www.asee.org/conferences/v2search.cfm

Ruiz-Primo, M. A. (2004). Examining concept maps as an assessment tool. In A. J. Canas, J. D. Novak, & F. M. Gonzalez (Eds.), *Concept maps: Theory, methodology, technology. Proceedings of the First International Conference on Concept Mapping.* Pamplona, Spain: Universidad Publica de Navarra. Retrieved July 30, 2006, from http://cmc.ihmc.us/CMC2004Programa.html

Ruiz-Primo, M. A., & Shavelson, R. J. (1996). Problems and issues in the use of concept maps in science assessment. *Journal of Research in Science Teaching, 33*(6), 569–600.

Scriven, M. (1967). The methodology of evaluation. In R. W. Tyler, R. M. Gagne, & M. Scriven (Eds.), *Perspectives of curriculum evaluation.* Chicago: Rand, McNally.

Shuman, L. J., Olds, B., Besterfield-Sacre, M., Wolfe, H., Sindelar, M., Miller, R., & Pinkus, R. (2005, May). Using rubrics to assess students' ability to resolve ethical dilemmas. *Proceedings of the 2005 Industrial Engineering Research Conference,* Atlanta, GA.

Spickard-Prettyman, S., Qammar, H., & Evans, E. (2005). Using a vertically integrated team design project to promote learning and an engineering community of practice. *Proceedings of the 2005 American Society for Engineering Education Annual Conference and Exposition.* Retrieved July 30, 2006, from http://www.asee.org/conferences/v2search.cfm

Steif, P. S., & Dantzler, J. A. (2005). A statistics concept inventory: Development and psychometric analysis. *Journal of Engineering Education, 94,* 363.

Stone, A., Allen, K., Reed Rhoads, T., Murphy, T. J., Shehab, R. L., & Saha, C. (2003). The statistics concept inventory: A pilot study. *Proceedings of the 2003 Frontiers in Education Conference.* Retrieved November 29, 2006, from http://fie.engrng.pitt.edu/fie2003/index.htm

Svinicki, M. (2004). *Learning and motivation in the postsecondary classroom.* Bolton, MA: Anker.

Turns, J., Atman, C., & Adams, R. (2000). Concept maps for engineering education: A cognitively motivated tool supporting varied assessment functions. *IEEE Transactions on Education, 43*(2), 164–173.

Walker, J., & King, P. (2003). Concept mapping as a form of student assessment and instruction in the domain of bioengineering. *Journal of Engineering Education, 92*(2), 167–177.

Wilson, J. M. (1993). The predictive validity of concept mapping: Relationships to measures of achievement. *The Proceedings of the Third International Seminar on Misconceptions and Educational Strategies in Science and Mathematics.* Ithaca, NY: Misconceptions Trust.

Wise, J., Lee, S. A., Litzinger, T. A., Marra, R. M., & Palmer, B. (2001). Measuring cognitive growth in engineering undergraduates: A longitudinal study. *Proceedings of the 2001 American Society for Engineering Education Annual Conference and Exposition.* Retrieved July 30, 2006, from http://www.asee.org/conferences/v2search.cfm

Yancy, K. B. (1998). *Reflection in the writing classroom.* Logan: Utah State University Press.

Zeilik, M. (2006). Classroom assessment techniques: Concept mapping. *Field-Tested Learning Assessment Guide.* Retrieved July 30, 2006, from http://www.flaguide.org/cat/minutepapers/conmap7.php

II

THE CAPSTONE EXPERIENCE AT THE BACCALAUREATE, MASTER'S, AND DOCTORATE LEVELS

David G. Meyer

The goal of this chapter is to provide an overview of the various capstone design-related assessment methodologies that have been developed in response to ABET criteria, along with some guidance (based on the collective wisdom of the engineering education community) as to the appropriateness and relative effectiveness of these various measures. Much of this wisdom can also be applied to assessment of graduate-level capstone experiences.

Assessment of Capstone Experiences Within Baccalaureate Programs

According to ABET (2006), "Students must be prepared for engineering practice through the curriculum culminating in a major design experience based on the knowledge and skills acquired in earlier course work and incorporating appropriate engineering standards and multiple realistic constraints" (p. 3). Often called a "capstone design" or "senior design" course, the culminating design experience in an undergraduate engineering curriculum assists undergraduates as they transition from students of theory to practicing engineers. It is in this setting that they begin to truly understand the relationships between different aspects of their chosen engineering disciplines, as well as the necessary balance between scientific theory and design practice. Gravander, Neely, and Luegenbiehl (2004) characterized this accordingly: "The major design experience needs to introduce students to the messiness of 'the real world,' a sense of ambiguity and uncertainty that is an essential component to humanities, social science, and management course content" (p. 4). Indeed, a key feature of the culminating design experience is a problem space that encompasses multiple engineering disciplines, ambiguity, unconstrained variables, and a direct impact on the world's social and economic fabric.

A useful working definition of an "ideal senior design project" (here, in the context of electrical and computer engineering) is provided by Gesink and Mousavinezhad (2003):

> It would be a project that would require the development of a component, product, or system that has the potential for satisfying a real need. What is a real need? Here, a real need would be one that had been identified/encountered by a practicing engineer employed by a local firm where the firm would be in the business of designing, developing and/or manufacturing engineering components, products or systems. Further, the firm would be willing to sponsor the project. (p. 2)

Virtually all accredited undergraduate engineering degree programs feature some form of capstone design experience. Many involve teamwork; require demonstration of communication skills; develop an awareness of professional responsibility; and typically require the design, construction, debugging, and, ultimately, the delivery of a device or system. As documented in ABET (2006), engineering programs must demonstrate that their students have successfully attained all of the ABET-listed outcomes (commonly referred to as "Criteria 3.a–k of EC2000") by the time they graduate.

In this context, a capstone course must provide students with a major design experience based on the knowledge and skills acquired in earlier course work, and incorporate appropriate engineering standards and multiple realistic constraints. Although not explicitly required, most engineering capstone design experiences incorporate many, if not all, learning outcomes (Criteria 3.a–k). Most experiences are team based and therefore include outcomes related to teamwork skills (based on Criterion 3.d). The experience may also reinforce students' understanding of ethical and professional responsibility (based on Criterion 3.f) and their ability to communicate effectively (based on Criterion 3.g). Realistic constraints (e.g., economic, environmental, social, political, ethical, health and safety, manufacturability, sustainability) should be employed as well (based on Criterion 3.c).

According to Currin (2002), "major effort must be put into properly identifying learning outcomes" associated with capstone design. Crafting program outcomes "which allow for curriculum flexibility yet are detailed enough to produce meaningful results is the true challenge to be faced by engineering educators" (p. 7). Proper outcome assessment cannot take place until this challenge is met.

According to ABET (2004), there must be processes in place that demonstrate that students have achieved the outcomes listed in Criterion 3.a–k to an acceptable level by the time they graduate. Each program must have an assessment process in place that produces documented results, and evidence must be given that the results are applied to the further development and improvement of the program. Evidence officially sanctioned by ABET includes, but is not limited to, the following: student portfolios, including design projects; nationally normed subject content examinations; alumni surveys that document professional accomplishments and career development activities; employer surveys; and placement data of graduates. Other forms of evidence do not appear to be as credible, including student self-assessment, opinion surveys, and course grades. These guidelines are also important when developing and implementing assessment for capstone design experiences.

According to Currin (2002), effective outcomes assessment tools share key characteristics. First, effective tools should be easy to administer. Second, they should clearly identify the learning outcome (i.e., activity or skill students can effectively demonstrate at the end of their academic program that they could not at its beginning) that is specifically being assessed. Third, effective tools should produce quantifiable results. Finally, effective tools are those that produce results that can be easily communicated with others.

National Surveys of Design Course Methodologies

A national survey of design courses and assessment was reported by McKenzie, Trevisan, Davis, and Beyerlein (2004). The purpose of this study was to obtain a better understanding of the nature and scope of assessment practices within undergraduate capstone design courses across engineering disciplines and, in particular, the extent to which current practices align with ABET EC2000 expectations. As part of this study, survey participants were asked to identify which of the Criterion 3 expectations they believed were appropriate for assessment using a capstone design project, and which of these competencies they actually evaluated. On average, 80 percent of the respondents reported that all Criterion 3 outcomes *could* be assessed within the capstone experience, while 70 percent indicated that they actually *had* assessed each of the "a–k" outcomes in their capstone project courses. The outcome reported as most appropriate to assess in a capstone course was "an ability to communicate effectively" (Criterion 3.g), indicated by 97 percent of the respondents. Other outcomes indicated as highly appropriate to assess in a capstone course included "identify, formulate, and solve engineering problems" (Criterion 3.e); "use the techniques, skills, and modern engineering tools necessary for engineering practice" (Criterion 3.k); and "design a system, component, or process to meet desired needs" (Criterion 3.c). The competency deemed least appropriate for assessment in a capstone course— endorsed by only 56 percent of the respondents—was "a recognition of the need for life-long learning" (Criterion 3.i), followed closely by "a knowledge of contemporary issues" (Criterion 3.j)—endorsed by 59 percent of the respondents. Regardless of the preferences specified, faculty indicated that all of the outcomes should be assessed more extensively than is current practice.

Also reported in the study by McKenzie et al. (2004) were the types of assessments faculty had used in their capstone courses. Oral presentations and final written reports were the most popular, as indicated by 94 percent and 91 percent of faculty respondents, respectively. Other types of assessments frequently used were intermediate written reports (77%) and peer/self-assessments (68%). Faculty also reported using a number of other measures, including student surveys, journals (self-reflection entries), alumni surveys, notebooks, log books, user manuals, and exit surveys. Fewer than 15 percent of the faculty respondents reported assessing students using portfolios, focus groups, or interviews. Others reported a "functionality requirement" for the completed device or system.

The nature of assessments used by instructors of capstone courses varies. According to McKenzie et al. (2004), 40 percent of the faculty respondents claimed their assessment measures were "detailed in nature based on careful analysis of student performance against course objectives." Examination of artifacts revealed that scoring rubrics were typically subjective in nature: That is, a specific assessment may have been based on a grading scale of 1 to N, but lacked clear performance criteria associated with the various levels of proficiency.

Findings reported by McKenzie et al. (2004) suggest uncertainty on the part of many faculty members concerning sound assessment practices, including use of appropriate assessment strategies. Faculty identified several ways they wanted to improve the quality of their capstone assessments. About one half of the respondents felt the measures should be more objective, wanting to develop more detailed scoring guidelines/rubrics and desiring clearer performance criteria. A significant number of respondents also wanted to increase the variety of assessment instruments.

Other interesting findings reported by McKenzie et al. (2004) include the duration of the capstone design experience at various institutions. Approximately one third of the respondents reported a duration of a half academic year or less (one semester or one quarter). The majority (57%) indicated their capstone projects were a full academic year (spanning multiple semesters or quarters). Virtually all of the respondents (92%) attributed a great deal of importance to their capstone course.

A survey of current ABET "best practices" was reported by Mayes and Bennett (2005). In this survey, respondents were queried about their measurement methods for objectives and outcomes, methods for engaging faculty in the assessment process, the degree of college oversight, and methods for ensuring that continuous improvement processes are in place. The two "best practices" most commonly cited by the respondents were (a) ensuring that a continuous improvement process is in place, and that assessment efforts have resulted in changes; and (b) establishing an "ABET committee," comprising representatives from each department or program, for the purpose of coordinating assessment efforts and disseminating best practices.

According to Mayes and Bennett (2005), most respondents indicated that their institutions provided each department/educational unit a fair amount of latitude in developing their own specific assessment tools and practices. Reportedly, however, the colleges coordinate or administer various surveys (alumni, senior students, employers) and gather assessment information for general education and core courses.

Respondents to Mayes and Bennett (2005) indicated that the most successful measures they had used for outcomes were related to students' course work, along with data gathered through senior surveys. The use of a capstone experience course, then, can become a major source of student's course work. According to Mayes and Bennett (2005), portfolios are not widely used and are viewed by most respondents to be unmanageable due to the large amount of data that must be collected and evaluated. Programs using portfolios as a means of assessment tend to be small or in fields where the portfolios are directly applicable to future employment (e.g., graphic arts and architecture). However, for those programs that want to begin to develop a portfolio system, the course work developed in a one- or two-capstone course series can be a useful basis for a portfolio system.

General Overview of Assessment Methodologies

An overview of methodologies that are available for use in assessing undergraduate engineering programs is provided by Shuman et al. (2000). All of the issues discussed in this section are related to designing appropriate assessment for capstone experiences in both undergraduate- and graduate-level education. Cited in the work by Shuman et al. are the growing number of national assessment "repositories" that can be adapted for use in a variety of different programs, including those available from National Institute for Science Education (NISE; www.wcer.wisc.edu/archive/nise/), American Society for Engineering Education (ASEE; www.asee.org/), and Electrical and Computer Engineering Department Head Association (ECEDHA; www.ecedha.org/), among others. A major contribution of the "Engineering Education Assessment Methodologies and Curricula Innovation" (2006) research group (see www.engrng.pitt.edu/~ec2000/), formed by the authors, is the development of what they refer to as a "buffet of attributes" from which engineering educators can pick and choose instruments that can be used in the measurement of courses or programs. Splitting outcomes into a series of attributes facilitates the use of triangulation to validate measures and instruments. The outcome "ability to work on multidisciplinary teams" could, for example, be assessed the following ways: using closed-form questionnaires (students' self-assessment of teaming abilities), peer ratings, or observations of the project team by a trained evaluator.

Shuman et al. (2000) have provided a very useful matrix of candidate assessment methodologies and their potential applications. Outcomes related to capstone design can potentially be measured using various combinations of these methodologies attributed to the ABET 3.a–k outcomes. Assessment methodologies included in this matrix are portfolios, surveys, questionnaires, interviews, focus groups, competency measurement, student journals, concept maps, verbal protocols, intellectual development, and authentic assessment.

Portfolios. Portfolios are identified by Shuman et al. (2000) as a strong candidate for outcomes assessment, particularly with respect to EC2000 outcomes related to design, technical communications skills, and contemporary issues. Traditional portfolios, however, are generally time-consuming to maintain and evaluate, which has motivated research on discovering ways in which electronic portfolios ("e-portfolios") can provide a more efficient solution.

Surveys, questionnaires, and interviews. Closed-form questionnaires are identified by Shuman et al. (2000) as a practical method for evaluating student or alumni attitudes about engineering, aspects of their education, and their self-assessed abilities/competencies. Open-ended surveys and (one-on-one) structured student interviews can be used to elicit in-depth information about complex issues, while focus groups can be used to identify the attitudes and perceptions a group of individuals has relative to a particular subject or concept. Open-ended surveys and student interviews can be utilized in conjunction with focus groups to help formulate instruments aimed at assessing specific learning outcomes. A good application would be in the assessment of professional and ethical issues in undergraduate engineering capstone courses.

Competency-based assessment. Competency-based surveying, according to Shuman et al. (2000), can be used as a means for quantifying performance relative to specific knowledge, skills, and abilities. This highly flexible assessment method can be used to construct instructor–student, student–student (peer), or self-assessment instruments. Computerized surveys such as Team Developer can be effectively used for this purpose (McGourty & DeMeuse, 2000).

Student journals. Student journals, although primarily used as a formative assessment tool, can also be used for more formalized summative assessment of student learning (e.g., asking students to describe their thought process in solving an open-ended design question). According to Shuman et al. (2000), journals can provide information about student learning processes and students' ability to construct knowledge. Research questions include how student journals can provide information on EC2000 outcomes and how a large number of journals can be efficiently screened to provide valid assessment data.

Concept mapping. Concept maps, according to Shuman et al. (2000), are a graphical assessment tool that can be used to assess students' ability to formulate and solve engineering problems or to apply their knowledge of math, science, and engineering. Verbal protocol analysis is a tool that can be used to understand some of the EC2000 process-related outcomes (e.g., ability to design a system, component, or process).

Authentic assessment. To measure how well engineering students can apply classroom knowledge and skills to realistic design problems, authentic assessment and performance-based assessment methods can be used. According to Shuman et al. (2000), the key to authentic assessment is to "create a context in which the student can individually or collaboratively demonstrate an ability to apply a well-developed problem-solving strategy," which might involve "problem definition, gathering relevant information, generating solution alternatives, choosing the optimum solution given implicit and explicit constraints, assessing and improving the proposed solution, and effectively reporting results. . . ." Some of the outstanding research issues associated with authentic assessment cited include "development of well-designed scoring rubrics and methods for ensuring inter-rater reliability" along with "guidelines . . . which help faculty choose tasks that are good candidates for collecting authentic assessment data in engineering courses" (p. 9).

Examples of Capstone Design Assessment Practices

This section references work by those around the country who give practical examples of assessment practices in undergraduate capstone design. Table 11.1 summarizes the studies discussed in this section.

In contrast to the methods discussed above, a different approach to measuring capstone design-project outcomes is described by Sobek and Jain (2004). Here, the focus was on quality measurements (in the context of an industrial sponsor), specifically toward the development of two distinct instruments intended to measure the *quality* of a design outcome: the *Client Satisfaction Questionnaire* (CSQ) and the *Design Quality Rubric* (DQR). This is in contrast to a more traditional process-based evaluation (involving some combination of written reports, presentations, lab notebooks, or evaluator judgment) that typically excludes "client/sponsor satisfaction" as a metric in determining course grades. The evaluation tools developed as part of this study were therefore purposefully designed to be free of process attributes. The underlying goal was to develop an assessment system for capstone design projects that "evaluates each project based on its outcome quality rather than the process that students used" (p. 3).

According to Sobek and Jain (2004), the most significant client satisfaction metrics include quality (the percentage of design objectives met) and overall satisfaction (in particular, how well students were able to apply their knowledge of math, science, and engineering). Design quality metrics include requirements (functionality); feasibility (manufacturability, marketability, application); creativity (originality, novelty, innovation); simplicity (reliability, serviceability, practicality, ergonomics, safety); aesthetics

TABLE 11.1

Summary of Examples for Assessing Undergraduate Capstone Design

What Was Measured	Tools for Measurement	Reference
Quality of design outcomes and other quality design metrics	*Client Satisfaction Questionnaire* and *Design Quality Rubric* are available in this reference	Sobek & Jain (2004)
Teaming skills as well as technical competence	Company evaluations, status reports, student self-assessments, peer evaluations, and oral reports; *Sample Team Member Evaluation Form* and *Peer Evaluation Form* are available in this reference	Brackin & Gibson (2002)
Design knowledge (i.e., students' knowledge of what constitutes the design process) including problem solving, teamwork, and communication skills (3.d, 3.e, and 3.g)	Author-developed instruments; currently, the *Design Team Knowledge Assessment* forms and the *Team Design Skills Growth Survey* can be found on TIDEE website: www.tidee.cea.wsu.edu/resources/assessments.html	Caso, Lee, Froyd, & Kohli (2002)
Quantitative and qualitative indicators that demonstrate achievement of outcomes, including 3.a–k and design constraints	Authors developed set of instruments to map to set of outcomes, including surveys, self-assessment assignment, and peer assessment, using rubrics; *Peer Assessment Form for Final Project Presentation* and *Team Member Assessment Form* can be found in this reference	Davis (2004)

TABLE 11.1 (Continued)

What Was Measured	Tools for Measurement	Reference
Capstone course structure and content	Review of portfolios; surveys completed by students; the *Outcomes-Based Student Assessment Survey* (available in this reference)	Berg & Nasr (2002)
Engineering design process	Evaluation of each individual student's design notebook via website	Meyer (2005)
Ability to apply knowledge obtained in earlier course work and to obtain new knowledge necessary to design and test a system, component, or process to meet desired needs (3.c)	Rubrics on developed criteria used with a series of written reports	Meyer (2005)
Multidisciplinary team skills (3.d)	Students' judgments of developed criteria related to finished device functionality	Meyer (2005)
Awareness of professional and ethical responsibility (3.f)	Rubrics on developed criteria used with a series of written reports	Meyer (2005)
Ability to communicate effectively (3.g)	Rubrics on developed criteria used with oral presentations and the final written report	Meyer (2005)

(packaging, style); and professionalism (workmanship, craftsmanship, technical excellence).

Methods of assessing student learning in capstone design projects sponsored by industry were reported by Brackin and Gibson (2002). Here the emphasis was on expanding the project evaluation beyond the design report to include teaming skills as well as technical competence. Instruments used included company evaluations, status reports, student self-assessments, peer evaluations, and oral reports (in addition to the traditional design report) to quantify students' performance—both as team members and as design engineers. The focus was on assessing teaming skills and technical competence over multiple trials.

A method for assessing design *knowledge* (i.e., students' knowledge of what constitutes the design process) was reported by Caso, Lee, Froyd, and Kohli (2002). Reported was a method for assessing individual students' knowledge of team design processes midprogram (instead of only during the final stages of their undergraduate education). The instrument developed focuses on three aspects of the team-based design process: (1) the design problem-solving process, (2) the function and operation of a team in a design project, and (3) the qualities of the communication required in a team-based design project. Data collected enabled a comparison between freshman-level students and senior-level students who had completed capstone design. These authors work with the Transferable Integrated Design Engineering Education (TIDEE) consortium (see www.tidee.cea.wsu.edu/about-TIDEE/index.html). Assessment instruments can be found on its website and include the Design Team Knowledge Assessment forms and its Team Design Skills Growth Survey.

An illustration of how ABET EC2000 assessment can be conducted within the framework of a capstone design course sequence (rather than on specific project topics themselves) was cited by Davis (2004). An excellent variety of assessment techniques were detailed that provide both quantitative measurements and qualitative indicators that can be used to demonstrate achievement of outcomes (as well as to improve the design course sequence and the curriculum as a whole). A "mapping" of instruments and criteria was provided, along with an algorithm for course grade determination. A copy of this program's *Peer Assessment Form for Final Project Presentation* and the program's *Team Member Assessment Form*, along with other detailed assessment instructions, are available from Davis (2004).

An example of how "nontraditional" learning outcomes, not classically taught as part of the engineering curriculum, have been achieved was reported by Berg and Nasr (2002). To address various aspects of EC2000 Criterion 3, the capstone course structure and content were modified. In addition, two outcome assessment methods were developed: (1) review of student portfolios by the course coordinator, department assessment team, and an independent review panel; and (2) outcome surveys completed by students at the end of the course. Their *Outcomes-Based Student Assessment Survey* related to 3.a–k and other program outcomes is available from www.asee.org/acPapers/2002-643_Final.pdf (Berg and Nasr, 2002).

Instruments that can be used for quantitative assessment of a capstone design course were reported by Meyer (2005). In this study, five learning outcomes specific to the capstone design course were identified:

1. An ability to apply knowledge obtained in earlier course work and to obtain new knowledge necessary to design and test a system, component, or process to meet desired needs (related to ABET 3.c)
2. An understanding of the engineering design process (related to ABET 4)
3. An ability to function on a multidisciplinary team (related to ABET 3.d)
4. An awareness of professional and ethical responsibility (related to ABET 3.f)
5. An ability to communicate effectively, in both oral and written form (related to ABET 3.g)

The method reported by Meyer (2005) for assessing outcome 2 was a multitiered evaluation of each individual student's design notebook. The breakthrough here was to create group accounts and team websites that hosted each member's online laboratory notebook. Adoption of this approach allowed the course staff to conveniently check on team progress as well as individual contributions. Further, the Web-based approach allowed students to include hyperlinks in their notebook entries to photos of prototyping setups, source code for testing various interfaces, video demos of project specific success criteria fulfillment, and PDFs of data sheets used in the design.

According to Meyer (2005), the method utilized for assessing outcome 3 was simply a measure of the finished device's functionality (called the "project-specific success criteria," since in this course each team completed a different project). To this end, each team was required at the outset to formulate five project-specific "functionality specifications" for its design, which would ultimately be used to judge the degree to which the finished product had been successfully completed. Rubrics used to evaluate the oral presentations and final written report provided the quantitative evaluation of outcome 5.

The assessment procedure reported by Meyer (2005) for assessing outcomes 1 and 4 was the creation of a series of design component and professional component written reports (that served as precursors of corresponding sections in the final written report). Each team member was assigned to complete one design component (e.g., schematic design, printed circuit board design, packaging design, or software design) and one professional component (reliability and safety analysis, ethical and environmental impact analysis, component select and design constraint analysis, or patent liability analysis). Grading rubrics were developed for each report, and a fixed threshold of 60 percent (minimum) was applied to the score received to document successful demonstration of the associated learning outcome. Students who did not "pass" a given outcome were required to revise their reports and resubmit them. Successful demonstration of all five learning outcomes was required to receive a passing grade for the capstone design course.

Not All Capstone Experiences Are Created Equal

In a study completed by Schnettler (2006) of the top 25 (doctorate-granting and nondoctorate-granting) electrical and computer engineering degree programs, a large variation was discovered with respect to practical implementations of the "culminating design experience" mandated by ABET. One of the most surprising revelations, no doubt due to the inherent flexibility of EC2000, was the emergence of two distinct approaches: "capstone" and "capstone certified."

As defined by Schnettler (2006), a capstone culminating design experience is one in which every student takes a "dedicated" (so-named) senior design course (or sequence of courses). Such a course (or sequence) is essentially 100 percent design oriented in content, and often addresses a number of professional practice skills (per Criterion 3.c) as well as provides students with opportunities to develop their oral/written technical communication skills (per Criterion 3.g). By way of contrast, a capstone-certified culminating design experience is one in which an upper-division content-focused course (e.g., computer architecture, signal processing, robotics, wireless communications) is used in place of a "dedicated" senior design course. Although most courses used for this purpose feature significant projects, they are typically content focused (rather than primarily design focused) and include little in the way of professional practice. Further, such courses often fail to include an analysis of realistic constraints: the specifications for the task to complete (design, simulation, etc.). Finally, many such courses do not require either a written report or an oral presentation as a deliverable. Schnettler's (2006) analysis revealed that fully one half of the capstone-certified programs had neither a professional practice component nor a technical writing component.

While all of the top 25 nondoctorate-granting electrical and computer engineering degree programs were found by Schnettler (2006) to be of the capstone variety, only about one third of the top 25 doctorate-granting ECE degree programs featured dedicated senior design courses. The remaining programs utilized a wide variety of capstone-certified courses to fulfill the role of culminating design experience. Clearly, there are significant differences between the learning outcomes associated with these two very different approaches to capstone design and how they might effectively be assessed. Potential issues pertaining to use of capstone-certified courses as "surrogate" culminating design experiences appear to be acknowledged by ABET (2005). During ABET's 2005 orientation for team chairs and institutional representatives, ABET (2005) listed factors related to Criterion 4 that influence the quality of the major design experience: (a) no culminating experience (analysis or research instead of design), (b) multiple capstone courses with widely varying quality, and (c) design experience that does not address multiple constraints.

Is EC2000 Working as Expected?

According to Mayes and Bennett (2005), the issue of "evaluators maintaining a consistent approach to evaluation in light of vaguely defined criteria has already come to light in the feedback received to date" (p. 4). A five-year study completed by Kimble-Thom and Thom (2005) has provided empirical evidence that the EC2000 Criterion 3 outcomes are lacking in specificity. The results obtained indicate "the efforts placed on how to teach engineering design courses have not addressed the more causal factor of what to teach. A lack of specificity and metrics regarding academic outcomes of senior design courses, and a divergence in learning constructs are observed" (p. 1).

To its credit, ABET itself is attempting to practice continuous improvement. A study was commissioned through the Center for the Study of Higher Education at Penn State to assess whether students are learning the skills necessary and acquiring knowledge consistent with ABET EC2000 criteria (Volkwein, Lattuca, Terenzini, Strauss, & Sukhbaatar, 2004). The underlying goal of this study was to determine the impact of changes precipitated by EC2000 (including the edict for a culminating design experience and its associated assessment) on student experiences and learning outcomes. Findings reported by Volkwein, Lattuca, Harper, and Domingo (2006) related to this same study of ABET criteria show that ABET accreditation criteria are important drivers in promoting curricular changes. In comparing the differences between 1994 and 2004 graduates, the study found that current engineering graduates are "engaged in more collaborative learning activities in the classroom, interact more with faculty, and are more actively involved in co-curricular activities such as engineering design competitions and student chapters of professional organizations" (Volkwein et al., 2006, p. 14). Current graduates also "report significantly higher levels of ability in all of the student learning outcomes specified in the EC2000 criteria" (p. 14).

Findings reported by Volkwein et al. (2006) also reveal that both engineering programs and faculty activities have been influenced by EC2000. In general, programs "increased their emphasis on curriculum topics associated with EC2000 as well as the emphasis on active learning strategies." Over 75 percent of the program chairs surveyed reported "moderate or significant increases in their program's emphases on communication, teamwork, use of modern engineering tools, technical writing, lifelong learning, and engineering design" (p. 9). Also as a result of EC2000, engineering faculty are reportedly "more engaged in assessment activities and in professional development activities related to teaching and assessment" (p. 14).

While the preponderance of evidence suggests that "EC2000 is working as expected," it is important to note that "additional external and internal influences also shape engineering programs" (Volkwein et al., 2006, p. 14). Significant external influences on engineering education that have emerged over the period of the Penn State study (1994–2004) include the Internet and World Wide Web, ubiquitous sources of online information (and search engines such as Google), online collaboration tools, simulation and visualization software, powerful personal computers, and classroom computer-graphics projectors. It is reasonable to assume that these collective advances in educational technology have also been important drivers in promoting curricular changes.

Assessment of Capstone Experiences Within Advanced Degree Programs

Although the assessment strategies discussed in this chapter have mostly illustrated assessment processes in undergraduate education, much of the theory and approaches are relevant to graduate-level education. However, in contrast to the array of tools and strategies reported for assessing undergraduate engineering programs, very few have been disseminated for advanced degree programs. The ABET (2006) general criteria for advanced-level programs consist of a single phrase that only vaguely refers to program outcomes: "an engineering project or research activity resulting in a report that demonstrates both mastery of the subject matter and a high level of communication skills" (p. 14).

A more detailed list of graduate student learning outcomes was reported by American Public University System (APUS; 2006). The five criteria listed are

- Academic skill
- Communication
- Critical thinking
- Information literacy
- Lifelong learning

According to APUS (2006), learning outcomes assessment for graduate students is conducted at the institutional, degree program, and classroom level. At the institutional level, surveys and interviews are used to evaluate the effectiveness of students achieving desired learning outcomes. At the degree program level, students' learning is assessed based on the skills, values, and knowledge they are expected to know upon graduation; subject-specific standardized national testing is used to measure student learning at the degree program level. Writing rubrics are also used to evaluate whether students are achieving desired learning outcomes at the degree program level. Finally, at the classroom level, student learning is assessed on the skills, values, and knowledge that students are expected to know at the completion of a course.

Chapter 5 gives an overview of how to assess graduate programs. The following discussion relates to the capstone experiences in graduate education, specifically theses and dissertations. A useful source for assessment of dissertations and rubrics can be found in the Amercian Association of University Professors (AAUP) publication "How to Grade a Dissertation" (Lovitts, 2005). Examples of rubrics used to assess theses or dissertations can be found on the Internet. For examples of rubrics, see the following websites, among others:

- www.und.nodak.edu/dept/datacol/assessment/unsecure/0405/ EE_gr.pdf
- www.fis.ncsu.edu/grad_publicns/program_review/ assessment_pilot.htm
- www.waldenu.edu/c/Files/DocsResearchCenter/ Thesis_Rubric_QN_Empiric al.doc

These and other rubrics used to assess theses or dissertations included the following dimensions; these dimensions can be used to formulate rubrics, as appropriate to an institution's needs:

- The thesis/dissertation has a logical organization.
- The writing and grammar are clear and correct.
- The purpose is described logically, critically.
- The literature review supports and justifies the thesis/dissertation.
- The theory that is applied or developed is logically interpreted.
- The theory and literature review align with the question being asked.
- The material is presented in a clear manner.
- The theoretical or experimental design is well developed/sound.
- The student discusses the methods' advantages and disadvantages.
- The amount and quality of data or information are sufficient.
- Data collection was done correctly.
- The results are intelligently interpreted, based on this field.
- The interpretations are properly summarized.
- The student conveys implications and applications for the discipline.
- The student cogently expresses insights gained from the study.
- The thesis/dissertation work could be published.
- The work advances the field.
- The student communicates research clearly in both written and oral forms.
- The work is original.

Summary and Conclusions

There appear to be two significantly different variants of "culminating design experiences" currently being sanctioned by ABET: (a) bona fide capstone design ("senior design") courses that span one or more terms and (b) so-called "capstone-certified" courses (senior-level subject-specific content courses that feature a significant design project). Encompassed in these two basic variants are a wide range of professional components ("soft skills") and their requisite assessment. For the capstone-certified courses, assessment methodology is most likely very similar to that used for lower-division "content" courses; however, most involve project teams and some form of written report or deliverable (e.g., a software simulation study or a "paper" design) that would provide a deeper context for assessment.

For "dedicated" capstone design courses—where teamwork, technical communication skills, and project deliverables are paramount—outcome assessment is notably different. Here, as documented in this chapter, we find a range of instruments being used in practice, including direct methods, such as reports, presentations, and project success criteria satisfaction, and indirect methods, such as surveys and peer evaluations. Direct methods, leading to quantifiable scores (which can also serve as the basis for course grade determination), are generally preferable, but almost always require more work on the part of the course staff. As documented by Jenkins and Kramlich (2002), there is a distinct lack of universal agreement on "what works and what doesn't"—even within a college or an educational unit of a given institution.

As underscored in Shuman et al. (2000), "one challenge that every engineering program faces involves achieving faculty consensus on the meaning and translation of the outcomes. A second, closely related task is to convert the desired outcomes into useful metrics for assessment" (p. 10). For better or worse, the "openness" (or perhaps vagaries) of the lack of guidelines for graduate-level education and ABET guidelines for undergraduate education have promulgated a plethora of outcome assessment methodologies, particularly relative to the culminating design experience. As documented in the literature, many assessment strategies have been employed in capstone design courses, yet uncertainty persists concerning sound practices; discovering those that work "best" has proven to be nontrivial. However, effective application of outcome assessment can truly drive curricular improvements and promote student learning.

References

Accreditation Board for Engineering and Technology Programs (ABET). (2004). Guidelines for criterion 3. Retrieved October 19, 2005, from http://www.abet.org

ABET. (2005, July 14). EAC orientation for team chairs and institutional representatives. Retrieved May 30, 2006, from http://www.abet.org

ABET. (2006). Criteria for accrediting engineering programs. Retrieved May 30, 2006, from http://www.abet.org

American Public University System (APUS). (2006). Graduate student learning outcomes. Retrieved May 30, 2006, from http://www.apus.edu

Berg, R. M., & Nasr, K. J. (2002). Achieving those difficult ABET program educational outcomes through a capstone design course. *Proceedings of the American Society for Engineering Education Annual Conference and Exposition.* Retrieved May 30, 2007, from http://www.asee.org/acPapers/2002-643_Final.pdf

Brackin, M. P., & Gibson, J. D. (2002). Methods of assessing student learning in capstone design projects with industry: A five-year review. *Proceedings of the American Society for Engineering Education Annual Conference and Exposition.* Retrieved May 30, 2007, from http://www.asee.org/acPapers/2002-1597_Final.pdf

Caso, R., Lee, J. H., Froyd, J., & Kohli, R. (2002). Development of design assessment instruments and discussion of freshman and senior design assessment results. *Proceedings of Frontiers in Education Annual Conference.* Retrieved May 30, 2007, from http://fie.engrng/pitt.edu/fie2002/index.htm

Currin, T. R. (2002). The capstone design course and its failure to serve as an effective outcome assessment tool. *Proceedings of the American Society for Engineering Education Annual Conference and Exposition.* Retrieved May 30, 2007, from http://www.asee.org/acPapers/2002-1213_Final.pdf

Davis, K. C. (2004). Assessment opportunities in a capstone design course. *Proceedings of the American Society for Engineering Education Annual Conference and Exposition.* Retrieved May 30, 2007, from http://www.asee.org/acPapers/2004-521_Final.pdf

Engineering education assessment methodologies and curricula innovation. (2006). Retrieved May 30, 2006, from http://www.engrng.pitt.edu/~ec2000

Gesink, J., & Mousavinezhad, S. H. (2003). An ECE capstone design experience. *Proceedings of the American Society for Engineering Education Annual Conference and Exposition.* Retrieved May 30, 2007, from http://www.asee.org/acPapers/2003-2282_Final.pdf

Gravander, J. W., Neely, K. A., & Luegenbiehl, H. C. (2004). Meeting ABET Criterion 4—From specific examples to general guidelines. *Proceedings of the American Society for Engineering Education Annual Conference and Exposition.* Retrieved May 30, 2007, from http://www.asee.org/acPapers/2004-1025_Final.pdf

Jenkins, M. G., & Kramlich, J. C. (2002). Assessment methods under ABET EC2000 at the University of Washington—Lessons learned: What works and what doesn't. *Proceedings of the American Society for Engineering Education Annual Conference and Exposition.* Retrieved May 30, 2007, from http://www.asee.org/acPapers/2002-2032_Final.pdf

Kimble-Thom, M. A., & Thom, J. M. (2005). Academic and industrial perspectives on capstone course content and the accompanying metrics. *Proceedings of Frontiers in Education Annual Conference*. Retrieved May 30, 2007, from http://fie.engrng.pitt.edu/fie2005/index.htm

Lovitts, B. E. (2005). How to grade a dissertation. Retrieved May 30, 2007, from http://www.aaup.org/AAUP/pubsres/academe/2005/ND/Feat/lovi.htm

Mayes, T. S., & Bennett, J. K. (2005). A survey of current ABET best practices. *Proceedings of the American Society for Engineering Education Annual Conference and Exposition*. Retrieved May 30, 2007, from http://www.asee.org/acPapers/2005-2041_Final.pdf

McGourty, K., & DeMeuse, K. (2000). *The team developer: An assessment and skill building program*. New York: J. Wiley.

McKenzie, L. J., Trevisan, M. S., Davis, D. C., & Beyerlein, S. W. (2004). Capstone design courses and assessment: A national study. *Proceedings of the American Society for Engineering Education Annual Conference and Exposition*. Retrieved May 30, 2007, from http://www.asee.org/acPapers/2004-644_Final.pdf

Meyer, D. G. (2005). Capstone design outcome assessment: Instruments for quantitative evaluation. *Proceedings of Frontiers in Education Annual Conference*. Retrieved May 30, 2007, from http://fie.engrng.pitt.edu/fie2005/index.htm

Schnettler, N. J. (2006). *The ECE culminating design experience: Analysis of ABET 2000 compliance at leading academic institutions*. Unpublished master's thesis, Purdue University, West Lafayette, IN.

Shuman, L., Besterfield-Sacre, M. E., Wolfe, H., Atman, C. J., McGourty, J., Miller, R. L., et al. (2000). Matching assessment methods to outcomes: Definitions and research questions. *Proceedings of the American Society for Engineering Education Annual Conference and Exposition*. Retrieved May 30, 2007, from http://www.asee.org/acPapers/20408.pdf

Sobek, D. K., & Jain, V. K. (2004). Two instruments for assessing design outcomes of capstone projects. *Proceedings of the American Society for Engineering Education Annual Conference and Exposition*. Retrieved May 30, 2007, from http://www.asee.org/acPapers/2004-434_Final.pdf

Volkwein, J. F., Lattuca, L. R., Harper, B. J., & Domingo, R. J. (2006, May). *The impact of accreditation on student experiences and learning outcomes*. 46th Annual Association for Institutional Research Forum, Chicago.

Volkwein, J. F., Lattuca, L. R., Terenzini, P. T., Strauss, L. C., & Sukhbaatar, S. (2004). Engineering change: A study of the impact of EC2000. *International Journal of Engineering Education, 20*(3), 318–328.

PART FOUR

THE FUTURE

12

THE FUTURE OF ASSESSMENT

Mary Besterfield-Sacre and Larry J. Shuman

O ur focus is engineering education, since this is our primary field of work. However, any discussion of future assessment methodology should be applicable to other STEM fields. Certainly many of the techniques described in this chapter originated in these fields.

The future direction (and methodology) of engineering education assessment is largely predicated on those stakeholders who have been its drivers:

- Industry has traditionally influenced the direction of engineering education in order to best meet workplace requirements.
- ABET has melded industry and academic requirements into accreditation criteria. Once focused on counting courses and other tangible assets, ABET now views assessment as documenting how programs are functioning and the effectiveness of planned changes.
- The National Science Foundation (NSF), through its ability to set a national research agenda, has had a major influence on the development of assessment methodologies for engineering and other STEM disciplines.

Hence, industry has placed demands on engineering programs to produce graduates with certain desired skills and abilities. ABET has introduced an overall quality assurance check, while NSF, particularly in the past decade, has included engineering education assessment as part of its overall research agenda. Given this summarized description of how the three interrelate as background, we suggest that to best see where engineering education assessment is headed, it is instructive to examine not only how it reached its current state, but how that has paralleled industry's development of quality measures. Consequently, we propose to view the development of engineering education assessment as being complementary to (but lagging behind) the development of quality measurement. Further, although assessment in engineering education has primarily been directed at quality assurance, this is not its only function. Thus, we can better forecast the next developments in engineering education assessment by looking at where quality measurement is today.

We discuss the future of engineering education assessment by first describing its history in parallel with the history of quality measurement. We then examine certain methodologies currently in practice and, in combination with some emerging assessment techniques that have the potential to capture important aspects of student learning, project how these will influence the future of engineering education assessment. We end with our projection of how ABET will incorporate the next generation of engineering education assessment.

History of Assessment

An Abbreviated History of Quality Measurement in Industry and Service

Industry, a motivator for changes in engineering education (and consequently accreditation), has called for the application of total quality management (TQM) principles to education for a considerable time. To some extent, engineering administrators have been listening.

Figure 12.1 provides an overview of the parallel developments of quality measurement and engineering education assessment: The left half summarizes the history of quality measurement in industry; the right half summarizes the history of engineering education assessment. The field of quality originated in the 1920s with the development of control charts and acceptance sampling procedures (Montgomery, 2005). However, their use did not move much beyond academia and research laboratories until World War II, when Bell Labs first developed military standards for the U.S. War Department. It would take another 15 years before military standards would be used as a quality standard for materiel and procurement. However, the seed was planted. By the end of the war, both the American Society for Quality Control (ASQC) and the International Standards Organization (ISO) had been formed. Although quality measurement was being developed by U.S. researchers, its major impetus came when Deming (and shortly thereafter,

Juran)[1] was invited to Japan to provide statistical quality control expertise and education to a fledgling postwar Japanese industry. Concomitantly, in the late forties Genichi Taguchi in Japan introduced design of experiments (DOE) to build quality into products and processes (in contrast to the United States, where DOE use focused on agriculture).

By the early sixties, statistical quality control (SQC) was being widely taught in U.S. engineering schools, while in Japan, due to the influence of Deming and others, it was being used to dramatically improve manufacturing capabilities. By the midseventies, DOE texts were being published with a focus on engineering and science, and their use was becoming more prevalent in industry. Ten years later, the U.S. TQM movement accelerated. This was due in no small part to the "Japanese Miracle," much of which could be attributed to the ability of Japanese industry to successfully adapt the SQC techniques that Deming and Juran introduced and that the Japanese modified to take advantage of their culture. At this point, U.S. manufacturers, especially automobile manufacturers, were forced to recognize that Japan was able to produce products at lower cost and substantially higher quality than U.S. counterparts. In response, the United States began to copy Japanese methodologies.

In 1987, ISO 9000 was introduced to provide standards for quality management systems. Such standards are updated every five years and administered by accreditation and certification bodies. In the nineties, a major quality measurement advent was the development and consequent spread of Motorola's "six-sigma initiative." Also at this time, a group of leading U.S. companies led by Motorola, IBM, Procter and Gamble, Ford, American Express, and Xerox encouraged engineering and business deans to utilize TQM methodologies to improve their educational process (Robinson et al., 1991). Major companies partnered with a select group of universities, and trained relatively large cohorts of faculty in these techniques. Four industry–university conferences were held to further promote the spread of TQM into higher education. The decade closed with the ASQC changing its name to the American Society of Quality (ASQ) to emphasize that it encompassed all aspects of quality; concomitantly, ISO 9000 was updated.

We map these events into three quality measurement eras as shown in Figure 12.1: "Acceptable to Ship", "Monitoring Product and Process," and "Building Quality Into Products and Processes." Although there is overlap, the three generally depict how quality measurement has changed over a 90-year period. In the first era, "Acceptable to Ship," the predominant form of quality measurement for U.S. manufacturers was acceptance-sampling pro-

FIGURE 12.1

Parallels Between the Progress of Quality Control and Assessment in Engineering Education

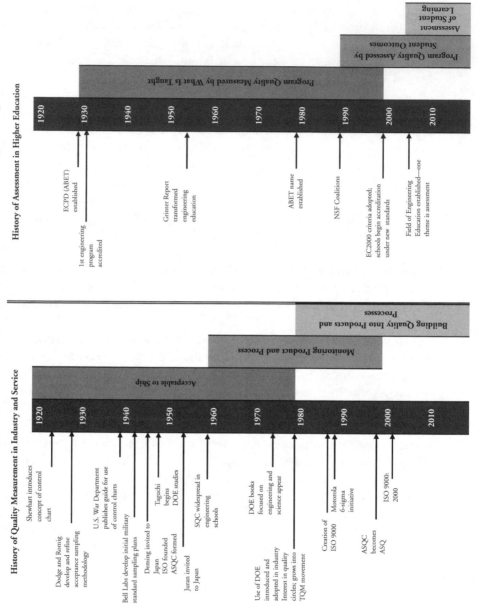

cedures. Its major shortcoming was that quality measurement occurred *after* the product had been made, and hence it was viewed as an additional cost. The second period, "Monitoring Product and Process," was marked by the use of control charts for both quality and process control. Now quality was thought of as adding value to the product. By using statistical procedures to determine when a process was trending out of control, a firm could better focus on producing a quality product. Out-of-control processes could be rectified before a poor finished product was produced. This then led to the current period, "Building Quality Into Products and Processes." Today, quality-oriented firms have adopted an approach that calls for designing (and often redesigning) quality directly into their products and processes.

An Abbreviated History of Assessment in Engineering Education

In contrast, assessment in engineering education has had only two primary periods: "Program Quality Measured by What Is Taught" and "Program Quality Assessed by Student Outcomes" (see the right half of Figure 12.1). These periods are defined by ABET's evolution. As shown, the Engineers Council for Professional Development (ECPD) was established in 1932, as the result of surveys conducted by the various professional organizations. Its purpose was "for upbuilding [*sic*] engineering as a profession" (see www.abe t.org/history.shtml for the history of ABET). Four years later, the first engineering programs were accredited. Following World War II, there were calls for major changes in engineering education. One landmark event was the publication of the Grinter Report (Grinter, 1955), which emphasized the need for thrusts in engineering science and engineering design as well as the recognition of professional responsibilities toward society. In response, engineering curricula were changed to include the science and design course work needed for accreditation. In 1980, the ECPD was renamed the Accreditation Board for Engineering and Technology, more accurately describing its emphasis on accreditation; in 2005 the name was officially shortened to ABET, Inc.

During the early nineties a series of reports emerged that again recognized serious deficiencies in engineering education and called for major reforms (Augustine & Vest, 1994; Bordogna, Fromm, & Ernst, 1993; NRC, 1995; NSF, 1995; Pister, 1993). A concerned NSF began to address engineering curriculum reform by funding eight engineering education coalitions involving over 60 institutions. These coalitions had as a major goal the design, implementation, evaluation, and dissemination of innovative, effective curricula for undergraduate engineering education.

At the same time, recognizing that current accreditation criteria were stifling innovation, a group of engineering deans and educators with encouragement from industry began the process that led to the new criteria and the beginning of the period of "Program Quality Assessed by Student Outcomes." Prados (1997) noted that major drivers behind the new criteria included a shift from defense to commercial competition impacting engineering employment, exploding information technology growth, corporate downsizing, outsourcing of engineering services, and the globalization of manufacturing and service sectors. Employers were emphasizing that success as an engineer required more than strong technical capabilities. Engineers also needed communication skills, the ability to lead and work effectively in a team, and an understanding of the nontechnical forces that affect engineering decisions. This required a new engineering education paradigm built around active, project-based learning; horizontal and vertical integration of subject matter; the introduction of mathematical and scientific concepts in the context of application; close interaction with industry; broad use of information technology; and a faculty devoted to developing emerging professionals as coaches rather than knowing dispensers of information (Prados, 1997).

The result was the outcome-based ABET criteria, adopted on November 2, 1996, and put into full use in 2000. Originally called "Engineering Criteria 2000" (EC2000), this revolutionary approach to accreditation was a paradigm shift from *what is taught* to *what was learned*. At its core was a continuous improvement process informed by the mission and goals of each institution and program. Without the inflexibility of earlier accreditation criteria, ABET could now support program innovation rather than stifle it. It also meant that ABET would encourage the development of new assessment processes that would lead to subsequent program improvement. A key component was Criterion 3 and its set of 11 required outcomes, 5 of which are considered "hard" skills, and the other 6 referred to as professional skills (Shuman, Besterfield-Sacre, & McGourty, 2005).

In addressing assessment, a number of transitions have occurred over these two periods. During the first, assessment was focused on the program's various courses offered and the work that was required of students rather than on their abilities or achievements. For each course the evaluator would review samples of students' records and work. In other words, it was similar to the period of "Acceptable to Ship." Now, with "Program Quality Assessed by Student Outcomes," evaluators examine what students should be learning and have learned. As a consequence, assessing student outcomes (i.e., the products of the program) has substantially evolved over the past 10 years. During the "early" years of EC2000, many programs measured the 11 outcomes via *indirect* assessments; the most widely used were focus groups and simple surveys (Besterfield-Sacre, Atman, & Shuman, 1998) involving program constituents, with an emphasis on students and alumni (who also represented industry). Although such assessments have been useful for obtaining student perceptions and some limited industry feedback, it was quickly recognized by the engineering education community and ABET that these were not the most viable techniques.

One result has been a call for *direct* measures for both the "hard" and professional outcomes. Included among these direct measures are performance appraisals (i.e., projects, capstone design courses) and simulations, both of which are typically coupled to rubrics to obtain the actual measurements (McGourty, et al., 2002). Specific instruments also have been developed or adopted from other educational settings to address certain outcomes. These include, but are not limited to, the "Team Developer" (now the "Professional Developer") to measure teamwork (3.d) (McGourty & De Meuse, 2000; McGourty, Reynolds, Besterfield-Sacre, Shuman, & Wolfe, 2003; McGourty, Sebastian, & Swart, 1998; McGourty, Shuman, Chimka, Besterfield-Sacre, & Wolfe, 2001), the Intercultural Development Inventory (IDI) to measure cultural sensitivity (3.h) (Bennett, 1986, 1993), and the Self-Directed Learning Readiness Scale (SDLRS) as a surrogate measure for lifelong learning (3.i) (Litzinger, Lee, & Wise, 2004; Litzinger, Wise, & Lee, 2005).

This current period is similar to the period of "Monitoring Product and Process," where the quality of the product (i.e., the student outcomes) is actively measured. We believe that such active assessment processes are improving engineering education. This is supported by a recent study commissioned by ABET and funded by the NSF (Lattuca, Terenzini, & Volkwein, 2006). We see this period evolving into one that focuses on ensuring the quality of learning: the period of "Assessment of Student Learning" that would be similar to "Building Quality Into Products and Processes." This projected evolution will create a greater need for viable, reliable, direct measures of student outcomes. The following describes how we think some of these measures might evolve.

The Next Age of Assessment

As engineering educators develop stronger expertise in measuring student outcomes, we will enter a new era in quality measurement. This "Assessment of Student Learning" period will focus on the various processes students use to achieve the outcomes. This movement toward *process measurement* will address engineering student cognition and the dimensions of learning. In doing so, assessment will be concerned with measuring students' abilities to retain knowledge and skills and to transfer that knowledge to new problems. There will also be a focus on adaptation to new engineering environments. These *in-process learning* measurements will go beyond embedded or interim assessments, that is, determining if a course is fulfilling its curriculum goals by assessing students via a simple evaluation instrument (e.g., test, quiz, or report).

Further, many outcomes are actually process rather than product oriented. For example, effective teamwork has more to do with the students' interactions and teaming capabilities (given the environment and purpose) and less to do with the resultant product. For outcomes that can be measured in product-oriented terms (e.g., 3.a and 3.k), assessment will be tied to student learning that occurs (or does not occur or occurs incorrectly).

Transition to this third period of engineering education assessment already has begun, as evidenced by three occurrences in the research community: First, in January 2005, the *Journal of Engineering Education* made a well-planned move to be the flagship archival record for scholarly research in engineering education, whereas *Advances in Engineering Education* has emerged as an academic journal focused on publishing proven engineering education innovation. Second, the NSF has redirected its engineering education funding toward research on understanding how students *learn* engineering. Third, after considerable discourse, a research agenda was developed for engineering education (Steering Committee of the National Engineering Education Research Colloquies, 2006). One of its five areas for research is assessment research.

In-Process Learning Assessment Tools—Current and Emerging

We suggest that innovations in assessment will result from extending tools and concepts that have been initially designed to facilitate various student learning processes. These include concept maps, model eliciting activities

(MEAs), concept inventories, adaptive expertise, behavioral assessment, and reflective journals. Although many of these originated as pedagogical interventions or formative assessments, we see promise for their being developed into rigorous and usable assessment tools aimed at capturing in-process learning. One reason for this is the increased interaction between engineering educators and learning scientists, anthropologists, educational psychologists, and assessment experts. This positive dynamic introduces engineering researchers to new assessment tools and educational researchers to engineering education.

These assessment methods can be categorized into four aspects of student learning: problem solving, transference of learning, how learning is organized and misconceptions, and behaviors and attitudes. We have selected exemplar assessment tools and/or pedagogical methods for each area and describe how they may be further developed for use in process assessment.

Focus on Problem Solving—Model Elicitation Activities (MEAs)

Mathematics education researchers developed MEA theory and practice to observe the development of problem-solving competencies and the growth of mathematical cognition (Lesh, 1998). MEAs are client-driven, open-ended problems designed to be model eliciting and thought revealing. They require students to mathematize (e.g., quantify, organize, dimensionalize) information and structure in context. Six principles for designing MEAs (Lesh, Hoover, Hole, Kelly, & Post, 2000) have been adapted to the development of contextual mathematical modeling activities for engineering courses (Diefes-Dux, Hjalmarson, Zawojewski, & Bowman, K., 2006; Diefes-Dux, Moore, Zawojewski, Imbrie, & Follman, 2004; Hjalmarson, Diefes-Dux, Bowman, & Zawojewski, 2006): model construction, reality (Bransford, Brown, & Cocking, 2000), generalizability, self-assessment, model documentation, and effective prototype.

What started as a tool to help researchers study problem solving was documented as a methodology that also helped students become better problem solvers (Lesh, 1998; Lesh & Doerr, 2003; Lesh & Kelly, 1997). In addition, MEAs became a tool for helping instructors and researchers become more observant and sensitive to the design of situations that engaged learners in productive mathematical thinking (Lesh, 2002). The focus on the use of modeling to study cognitive processes in problem solving has led to a continual testing and updating of the theories and implementation of MEAs in engineering curriculum. It is these characteristics that suggest that MEAs can become a valuable methodology to assess problem solving.

Indeed, the attributes of MEAs support the development of the abilities and skills stated in ABET's Criterion 3. Studies by Diefus-Dux et al. with first-year engineering students indicate that MEA tasks can be effective learning exercises (Diefes-Dux et al., 2004; Moore & Diefes-Dux, 2004). Their work has focused on refining design principles for posing MEAs within engineering contexts. As such, MEAs can provide innovative assessment opportunities, especially when MEA exercises are combined with scoring rubrics.

Hamilton, Lesh, Lester, and Yoon (in press) also are developing a series of reflection tools (RTs) that help students record significant aspects of strategies they used and how their group functioned. Students then can use this information to reflect on or discuss the effectiveness of roles, strategies, and types of engagement. Hamilton and associates look for RTs to help students briefly record significant aspects about what they have done so that they can use this information to engage in discussions about the effectiveness of various roles, strategies, and levels and types of engagement. Although RTs have served as an observational device for research, they have great promise as an assessment device for mapping out the strategies students used and when they used them, thus providing a framework for capturing student thinking during problem solving. When fully developed, the MEA approach could be used to measure the in-process learning that occurs for such product outcomes as problem formulation (3.f) and teamwork (3.d), among others.

Focus on Transference—Adaptive Expertise

Adaptive expertise is a theoretical foundation of the *How People Learn* (HPL) framework (Bransford et al., 2000). Pandy, Petrosino, Austin, and Barr (2004) point out that experts' knowledge is connected and organized around the major principles of the expert's discipline. Adaptive experts not only have knowledge that is well organized but also display the ability to transfer knowledge, skills, and values to new situations. This is reiterated by Bransford et al. (2000). Hence, the development of adaptive experts should be an educational objective, although it may not be until later in the student's career that he or she becomes an adaptive expert (Martin, Rayne, Kemp, Hart, & Diller, 2005).

Fisher and Peterson (2001) point out that people who have developed expertise in a particular area are able to think effectively about problems in that field. They propose that the purpose of undergraduate (engineering) education should be at least to initiate the development of expertise within students. They have identified four constructs that comprise adaptive expertise: *Multiple Perspective* is the willingness to use a variety of representations and approaches when working in the domain. *Metacognition* is the learner's use of various techniques to self-assess his or her understanding and performance. *Goals and Beliefs* describe student views of learning goals and expertise. *Epistemology* describes how individuals perceive the nature of knowledge. Together, these constructs constitute a cognitive approach to assist students. Fisher and Peterson propose that assessing adaptive expertise may offer a more useful reflection of student development than more traditional "content only" evaluations. Such a scheme would acknowledge the importance of other types of growth (rather than the simple acquisition of content knowledge) necessary to prepare graduates for careers in engineering.

The Vanderbilt–Northwestern–U of Texas–Harvard/MIT (VaNTH) Engineering Research Center (ERC) for Bioengineering Education Technologies has adapted the HPL framework and the "STAR-legacy cycle" (Schwartz, Lin, Brophy, & Bransford, 1999), a framework designed to support expert knowledge development. Of interest here are two steps toward developing adaptive expertise: "challenges" and "test your mettle." Challenges are given up front to motivate learners. They are designed to capture the students' curiosity while placing technical content within a real-world context. "Mettle" exercises are designed to assess students' understanding of basic concepts. To exhibit expertise, the learner must be able to apply (i.e., transfer) knowledge to solve problems in a variety of contexts by recognizing similar underlying concepts that govern the situation.

Pandy et al. (2004) describe three biomechanics challenges and two "mettle" exercises as well as "adaptive expertise assessments" that could be used by programs to assess students' progress in meeting criteria 3.a, 3.e, and 3.k. They quantified student achievement using questionnaires designed to measure changes in factual knowledge, conceptual knowledge, and transfer. A second example is given by Martin et al. (2005), who focus on bioengineering ethics. These studies provide enterprising faculty with exercises and assessment instruments that are adaptable for assessing in-process learning for certain ABET outcomes. We anticipate that the VaNTH ERC will provide a series of assessment exercises and instruments to the engineering public (see www.VaNTH.org for more information).

Focus on Organization of Learning and Misconceptions—Concept Maps and Inventories

This area focuses on how students organize their knowledge. Specifically, do students correctly learn their discipline and properly frame it cognitively so that they use it in practice? Concept maps and concept inventories can examine this from macro and micro perspectives. Concept mapping is an established assessment tool (Liu & Hinchey, 1993; Lomask, Baron, & Grieg, 1993; Wilson, 1993) designed to measure conceptual organization, or how students have organized the knowledge they have learned (or not learned). These maps are simply graphical organizers for thoughts, theories, and/or concepts in a particular discipline or subject area. Understanding is schematically represented by creating a hierarchy of ideas or concepts linked together through branches of subconcepts, with interrelationships indicated by additional branches or cross-links (Novak & Gowin, 1984).

While these maps can be used to determine if students' learning is on track with what is intended, the difficulty in using them for assessment has been in their scoring. Novak, who originally developed concept maps, believes that a competent evaluator can relatively quickly check if propositions (i.e., two or more concepts connected by labeled links) are valid and then determine if the super-/subordinate nature of the concepts makes sense. He feels it should take between 3 and 10 minutes to score a map once criteria have been defined (Zeilik, 2004). Maps usually are scored by counting concepts, links, and hierarchies. Recently some more sophisticated approaches have appeared that better facilitate their use as an outcome assessment tool. Besterfield-Sacre, Gerchak, Lyons, Shuman, and Wolfe (2004) used concept maps in conjunction with scoring rubrics to assess industrial engineering students' conceptual knowledge of their chosen major, purportedly assessing several criteria including 3.k. Walker and King (2003) utilized concept maps to assess senior design abilities; Turns, Atman, and Adams (2000) used them to assess learning in courses in statistics and human factors.

Concomitantly, concept inventories for various engineering subject areas have been developed to measure a crucial dimension of learning: conceptual understanding. The ability to understand and apply fundamental concepts from the scientific and mathematical disciplines is foundational to engineering and technology practice. There is ample evidence that science and engineering undergraduates do not easily acquire an understanding of such fundamental, small-scale phenomena as heat, light, diffusion, chemical reactions, and electricity (Duit, 2004; Garnett & Hackling, 1995; Reiner, Slotta,

Chi, & Resnick, 2000); there is also evidence that traditional assessment methods of student achievement including grades do not predict students' degree of conceptual understanding (Miller, Streveler, & Olds, 2002).

During the past 35 years, researchers have begun to identify conceptual shortcomings in engineering and science and have developed inventories to cull these misconceptions (e.g., statics, heat transfer, strength of materials, fluid mechanics, thermodynamics, statistics, and signals). The Force Concept Inventory (Hestenes, Wells, & Swackhamer, 1992), now used widely in physics, was the first of these inventories and motivated the development of the others. (See chapter 10 for additional information on concept maps and inventories.)

To date, concept maps and inventories have been used as *formative* assessment tools. We anticipate that validated measures of maps and inventories can address up front where students begin to stray in their learning processes. Next-generation concept map and inventory assessments must be sensitive enough to see where deviations in conceptual organization and understanding begin, hence allowing for corrections to take place before they become embedded. In this way, concept maps and inventories may become an in-process learning assessment of criterion 3.a.

Focus on Behaviors and Attitudes—Behavioral Observation and Reflective Journals

This focus is on valuation aspects of learning. In particular, behavioral observation and reflective journals can capture aspects of students' attitudes and behaviors, which, in turn, affect how they learn and acquire many of the outcomes. Rich, in-depth assessment methods such as behavioral observation (Brereton, Greeno, Lewis, Linde, & Leifer, 1993; Bucciarelli, 1994) are desirable because they enable us to investigate engineering learning and thus evaluate students at the higher-level learning domains. Reflective exercises have been used as a strategy for understanding students' attitudes and behaviors as they learn (Larson, 1991; Paris & Ayres, 1994). Yancy (1998) describes reflection as both looking forward and looking backward; hence, educators can evaluate what students already know, what they are learning, and what might not be understood.

Although behavioral observations and reflective journaling are effective at capturing process-oriented outcomes (teamwork, solving ethical dilemmas, etc.), they are expensive to administer relative to effort and resources. With further research, we believe both methodologies can be extended to produce practicable, economical assessments. For example, industry has learned that activities can be assessed using statistical methods that "sample" the observable environment. Work sampling and related methods (Aft, 2000; Hendricks, 1974) use probability theory to reduce the amount of time necessary to observe events or activities that do not occur in a systematic manner, without loss of information. Besterfield-Sacre, Newcome, Shuman, and Wolfe (2004) are bridging this gap by extending such traditional methods to the observation of intervals that capture the cognitive, behavioral, and affective domains of student learning. They have developed this methodology and performed work sampling for outcomes 3.c, 3.d, and 3.f.

Further, reflective writing can become a rigorous tool by applying qualitative research techniques and text-coding software. Educators have used reflective "diaries" to monitor engineering design teams on their learning progress and team functioning (Gorman, Groves, & Catalano, 2004; Spickard-Prettyman, Qammar, & Evans, 2005). Coding schemes have been developed for assessing students' progress toward a design solution along several dimensions (e.g., technical design issues, decision-making processes). Assessment research should overcome these methodological hurdles and lead to practical metrics for tracking how students' actions and reflections impact learning.

Conclusion: Potential Future of Assessment

We see engineering education assessment entering into a new period focused on student learning that is analogous to industry's current period of "Building Quality Into Products and Processes." This should follow naturally as the three drivers—industry, ABET, and the NSF—continue to encourage conceptual learning, understanding, retention, and transference as desirable (and eventually required) engineering education outcomes. There are already signs that the simplistic measures engineering programs are using for accreditation (e.g., surveys combined with embedded test questions), while sufficient now, soon will be inadequate if the engineering graduate is assessed in terms of his or her individual ability to address a growing array of complex problems with strong societal implications (e.g., sustainable energy, reduced carbon emissions, water availability, security, and low-cost products for the developing world). Already as a first step to educate better learners, research, primarily funded by NSF, is ongoing to understand how students learn. As China and India continue to produce large numbers of well-trained engineers willing to work for substantially less money than their U.S. counterparts, and modern telecommunications enable engineering tasks to be performed throughout the world, we foresee industry demanding more from our graduates, further motivating the need for improved learning. Again, those same three drivers will come together to pull (or help push if engineering educators lead the way) assessment into a new era.

We also see ABET expanding the current minimum set of outcomes. For example, it is clear to us, and an increasing number of national experts and engineering ethicists, that engineers must consider the wider, long-term ramifications of their professional decisions. Luegenbiehl (2003) has proposed that

> taking a broader perspective on their own work be included as an ethical duty for engineers. . . . engineers can be ethically required to take into account the particular local contexts for which their designs are intended, the effects of the rapid spread of their designs throughout the world, and the effects of their work on the variety of human values as they exist in varying forms in different societies. In other words, engineers have a responsibility to consider not only the immediate use for which their work is intended, but also its broader effects. (p. 8)

Thus we see Criterion 3.f, "an understanding of professional and ethical responsibility," being expanded to consider the impact of engineering solutions on the society at risk.

We also see innovation and sustainability being added as outcome criteria. The growing recognition of the earth's limited resources and the consequent need to create sustainable alternatives will require engineers to take new approaches to the design of products and systems. Europe and Japan are ahead of the United States with respect to a focus on sustainability and reusability. As interest grows, we anticipate a point at which sustainability will be a routine design constraint. Another change will be the inclusion of innovation. Every national panel that has considered the offshoring of high-end work has called for a renewed focus on innovation. To retain our competitive edge and standard of living, we will need to produce engineers who are more creative and who routinely think outside the box.

Assuming that there will be renewed emphasis on considering the societal impact of engineering decisions, sustainability, and producing more innovative graduates, assessment methodologies, informed by learning science, will be needed to ensure that we are producing quality engineering graduates. This is where engineering assessment is headed. We have presented a spectrum of assessment methods, many still under development, but all with promising potential. A number are being developed through the joint efforts of engineering education researchers and learning scientists. We can expect more such collaboration given the strong encouragement of the NSF and a number of engineering education centers. It is also being fostered by a number of other entities. For example, the Foundation Engineering Education Coalition provided a major impetus to the development of concept inventories. The VaNTH Engineering Research Center has promoted the "How People Learn" philosophy with its motivating challenges and comprehensive assessment of learning. And, finally, the *Journal of Engineering Education* has continued to publish serious, educational research studies authored jointly by engineering educators and learning scientists.

Note

1. Drs. W. Edwards Deming (1900–1993) and Joseph M. Juran (1904–) are considered two statisticians most responsible for the creation and development of the discipline of quality as we see it today. Although other experts exist, these two persons are considered foremost gurus in the field of quality control, assurance, and management. Further information can be found at their institutions' websites, www .deming.org/index.html (Deming) and www.juran.com/index.cfm (Juran), both retrieved January 29, 2007.

References

Aft, L. (2000). *Work measurement and methods improvement.* New York: John Wiley & Sons.

Augustine, N., & Vest, C. (1994). Engineering education for a changing world. Retrieved January 15, 2007, from http://www.asee.org/resources/beyond/green Report.cfm

Bennett, M. J. (1986). A developmental approach to training for intercultural sensitivity. *International Journal of Intercultural Relations, 10*(2), 179–195.

Bennett, M. J. (1993). Towards ethnorelativism: A developmental model of intercultural sensitivity. In M. Paige (Ed.), *Education for the intercultural experience.* Yarmouth, ME: Intercultural Press.

Besterfield-Sacre, M. E., Atman, C. J., & Shuman, L. J. (1998). Engineering student attitudes assessment. *Journal of Engineering Education, 87*(2), 133–141.

Besterfield-Sacre, M., Gerchak, J., Lyons, M. R., Shuman, L. J., & Wolfe, H. (2004). Scoring concept maps: An integrated rubric for assessing engineering education. *Journal of Engineering Education, 93*(2), 105–115.

Besterfield-Sacre, M., Newcome, E., Shuman, L. J., & Wolfe, H. (2004, May). Extending work sampling to behavioral and cognitive concepts. *Proceedings of the*

IIE Annual Conference and Exposition 2004 Industrial Engineering Research Conference, Houston, TX.

Bordogna, J., Fromm, E., & Ernst, E. W. (1993). Engineering education: Innovation through integration. *Journal of Engineering Education, 82*(1), 3–8.

Bransford, J. D., Brown, A. L., & Cocking, R. R. (2000). *How people learn: Brain, mind, experience and school.* Washington, DC: National Academy Press.

Brereton, M., Greeno, J., Lewis, J., Linde, C., & Leifer, L. (1993, September). An exploration of engineering learning. *Proceedings of the Fifth International Conference of Design Theory and Methodology,* Albuquerque, NM.

Bucciarelli, L. L. (1994). *Designing engineers.* Cambridge, MA: The MIT Press.

Diefes-Dux, H. A., Hjalmarson, M., Zawojewski, J., & Bowman, K. (2006). Quantifying aluminum crystal size. Part 1: The model-eliciting activity. *Journal of STEM Education: Innovations and Research, 7*(1&2), 51–63.

Diefes-Dux, H. A., Moore, T., Zawojewski, J., Imbrie, P. K., & Follman, D. (2004). A framework for posing open-ended engineering problems: Model-eliciting activities. *Proceedings of the 30th ASEE/IEEE Frontiers in Education Conference.* Retrieved January 15, 2007, from http://fie.engrng.pitt.edu/fie2004/

Duit, R. (2004). *Bibliography: Students' and teachers' conceptions and science education.* Kiel, Germany: Institute for Science Education. Retrieved January 15, 2007, from http://www.ipn.uni-kiel.de/aktuell/stcse/stcse.html

Fisher, F. T., & Peterson, P. L. (2001). A tool to measure adaptive expertise in biomedical engineering students. *Proceedings of the 2001 American Society for Engineering Education Annual Conference and Exposition.* Retrieved January 15, 2007, from http://www.asee.org/acPapers/01035_2001.PDF

Garnett, P. J., & Hackling, M. (1995). Students' alternative conceptions of chemistry: A review of research and implications for teaching and learning. *Studies in Science Education, 25*(69), 69–96.

Gorman, M. E., Groves, J. F., & Catalano, R. K. (2004). Collaborative research into the societal dimensions of nanotechnology: A model and case study. *IEEE Technology and Society Magazine, 23*(4), 55–62.

Grinter, L. E. (1955). Report of the committee on evaluation of engineering education. *Journal of Engineering Education, 44,* 25–60. Retrieved January 15, 2007, from http://www.asee.org/resources/beyond/The-Grinter-Report-PDF.pdf

Hamilton, E., Lesh, R., Lester, F., & Yoon, C. (in press). The use of reflection tools to build personal models of problem-solving. In R. Lesh, E. Hamilton, & J. Kaput (Eds.), *Models and modeling as foundations for the future in mathematics education.* Mahwah, NJ: Lawrence Erlbaum. Retrieved January 15, 2007, from http://www.crlt.org/Project_specific_documents/ComplexReasoning/Reflection Tools.pdf

Hendricks, G. C. (1974). *Effects of behavioral self observation on elementary teachers and students* (Technical Report No. 121). Stanford University, CA: Stanford Center for Research and Development in Teaching.

Hestenes, D., Wells, M., & Swackhamer, G. (1992). Force concept inventory. *The Physics Teacher, 30,* 141–158.

Hjalmarson, M., Diefes-Dux, H. A., Bowman, K., & Zawojewski, J. (2006). Quantifying aluminum crystal size. Part 2: The model-development sequence. *Journal of STEM Education: Innovations and Research, 7*(1&2), 64–73.

Larson, R. L. (1991). Using portfolios in the assessment of writing in the academic disciplines. In P. Belanoff & M. Dickson (Eds.), *Portfolios: process and product.* Portsmouth, NH: Boyton/Cook.

Lattuca, L., Terenzini, P. T., & Volkwein, J. F. (2006). *Engineering change: A study of the impact of EC2000, Executive summary.* Baltimore: ABET. Retrieved January 15, 2007, from http://www.abet.org/papers.shtml

Lesh, R. (1998). The development of representational abilities in middle school mathematics: The development of students' representations during model eliciting activities. In I. E. Sigel (Ed.), *Representations and student learning.* Mahwah, NJ: Lawrence Erlbaum.

Lesh, R. (2002). Research design in mathematics education: Focusing on design experiments. In L. English (Ed.), *International handbook of research design in mathematics education, 2002.* Mahwah, NJ: Lawrence Erlbaum.

Lesh, R., & Doerr, H. M. (2003). *Beyond constructivism: Models and modeling perspectives on mathematics teaching, learning, and problem solving.* In R. Lesh & H. M. Doerr (Eds.), Mahwah, NJ: Lawrence Erlbaum.

Lesh, R., Hoover, M., Hole, B., Kelly, A., & Post, T. (2000). Principles for developing thought-revealing activities for students and teachers. In A. Kelly & R. Lesh (Eds.), *Handbook of research design in mathematics and science education.* Mahwah, NJ: Lawrence Erlbaum.

Lesh, R., & Kelly, A. (1997). Teachers' evolving conceptions of one-to-one tutoring: A three-tiered teaching experiment. *Journal for Research in Mathematics Education, 28*(4), 398–430.

Litzinger, T. A., Lee, S. H., & Wise, J. C. (2004). Assessing readiness for self-directed learning. *Proceedings of the 2004 American Society for Engineering Education Conference and Exposition.* Retrieved January 15, 2007, from http://www.asee.org/acPapers/2004-649_Final.pdf

Litzinger, T. A., Wise, J. C., & Lee, S. H. (2005). Self-directed learning readiness among undergraduate engineering students. *Journal of Engineering Education, 94*(2), 215–221.

Liu, X., & Hinchey, M. (1993). The validity and reliability of concept mapping as an alternative science assessment. *The Proceedings of the Third International Seminar on Misconceptions and Educational Strategies in Science and Mathematics.* Ithaca, NY: Misconceptions Trust.

Lomask, M. S., Baron, J. B., & Grieg, J. (1993). Assessing conceptual understanding in science through the use of two- and three dimensional concept maps. *The*

Proceedings of the Third International Seminar on Misconceptions and Educational Strategies in Science and Mathematics. Ithaca, NY: Misconceptions Trust.

Luegenbiehl, H. C. (2003, June). Themes for an international code of engineering ethics. *Proceedings of the 2003 ASEE/WFEO International Colloquium*, Nashville, TN.

Martin, T., Rayne, K., Kemp, N. J., Hart, J., & Diller, K. R. (2005). Teaching for adaptive expertise in biomedical engineering ethics. *Science and Engineering Ethics, 11*(2), 257–276.

McGourty, J. M., & De Meuse, K. (2000). *The team developer: An assessment and skill building program.* New York: J. Wiley.

McGourty, J. M., Reynolds, J., Besterfield-Sacre, M., Shuman, L. J., & Wolfe, H. (2003). Using multi-source assessment and feedback processes to develop entrepreneurial skills in engineering students. *Proceedings of the 2003 American Society for Engineering Education Annual Conference & Exposition.* Retrieved January 15, 2007, from http://www.asee.org/acPapers/2003-1082_Final.pdf

McGourty, J., Sebastian, C., & Swart, W. (1998). Development of a comprehensive assessment program in engineering education. *Journal of Engineering Education, 87*(4), 355–361.

McGourty, J. M., Shuman, L. J., Besterfield-Sacre, M., Atman, C. J., Miller, R., Olds, B., Rogers, G., & Wolfe, H. (2002). Preparing for ABET EC 2000: Research-based assessment methods and processes. *International Journal of Engineering Education, 18*(2), 157–167.

McGourty, J. M., Shuman, L. J., Chimka, J., Besterfield-Sacre, M., & Wolfe, H. (2001). Multi-source feedback processes and student learning styles: Measuring the influence on learning outcomes. *Proceedings of the 2001 American Society for Engineering Education Conference and Exposition.* Retrieved January 15, 2007, from http://www.asee.org/acPapers/00715_2001.PDF

Miller, R. L., Streveler, R. A., & Olds, B. M. (2002). How chemical engineering seniors think about mechanisms of momentum transport. *Proceedings of the 2002 American Society for Engineering Education Annual Conference and Exposition.* Retrieved January 15, 2007, from http://www.asee.org/acPapers/2002–317_Final.pdf

Montgomery, D. C. (2005). *Introduction to statistical quality control* (5th ed.). Hoboken, NJ: Wiley.

Moore, T., & Diefes-Dux, H. A. (2004). Developing model-eliciting activities for undergraduate students based on advanced engineering content. *Proceedings of the ASEE/IEEE 30th Frontiers in Education Conference.* Retrieved January 15, 2007, from http://fie.engrng.pitt.edu/fie2004/index.htm

National Research Council (NRC). (1995). *Engineering education: Designing an adaptive system.* Washington, DC: National Academy Press.

National Science Foundation (NSF). (1995). *Restructuring engineering education: A focus on change* (Report 9565, NSF). Washington, DC: Division of Undergraduate Education, Directorate for Education and Human Resources. Retrieved January 15, 2007, from http://www.nsf.gov/pubs/stis1995/nsf9565/nsf9565.txt

Novak, J., & Gowin, D. B. (1984). *Learning how to learn.* New York: Cambridge University Press.

Pandy, M. G., Petrosino, A. J., Austin, B. A., & Barr, R. E. (2004). Assessing adaptive expertise in undergraduate biomechanics. *Journal of Engineering Education, 93*(3), 211–222.

Paris, S. G., & Ayres, L. R. (1994). *Becoming reflective students and teachers with portfolios and authentic assessment.* Washington, DC: American Psychological Association.

Pister, K. S. (1993). A context for change in engineering. *Journal of Engineering Education, 82*(2), 66–69.

Prados, J. W. (1997). The editor's page: Engineering criteria 2000—A change agent for engineering education. *Journal of Engineering Education, 86*(2), 69–70.

Reiner, M., Slotta, J. D., Chi, M. T. H., & Resnick, L. B. (2000). Naive physics reasoning: A commitment to substance-based conceptions. *Cognition and Instruction, 18*(1), 1–35.

Robinson, J. D., III, Akers, J. F., Artzt, E. L., Poling, H. A., Galvin, R. W., & Allaire, P. A. (1991). An open letter: TQM on the campus. *Harvard Business Review, 69*(6), 94–95.

Schwartz, D. L., Lin, X., Brophy, S., & Bransford, J. D. (1999). Toward the development of flexibly adaptive instructional designs. In C. M. Reigeluth (Ed.), *Instructional design theories and models, vol. II* (pp. 183–213). Mahwah, NJ: Lawrence Erlbaum.

Shuman, L. J., Besterfield-Sacre, M., & McGourty, J. (2005). The ABET "professional skills"—Can they be taught? Can they be assessed? *Journal of Engineering Education, 94*(1), 41–55.

Spickard-Prettyman, S., Qammar, H., & Evans, E. (2005). Using a vertically integrated team design project to promote learning and an engineering community of practice. *Proceedings of the 2005 American Society for Engineering Education Annual Conference and Exposition.* Retrieved January 15, 2007, from http://www.asee.org/acPapers/2005-1475_Final.pdf

Steering Committee of the National Engineering Education Research Colloquies. (2006). The research agenda for the new discipline of engineering education. *Journal of Engineering Education, 95*(4), 259–261.

Turns, J., Atman, C., & Adams, R. (2000). Concept maps for engineering education: A cognitively motivated tool supporting varied assessment functions. *IEEE Transactions on Education, 43*(2), 164–173.

Walker, J., & King, P. (2003). Concept mapping as a form of student assessment and instruction in the domain of bioengineering. *Journal of Engineering Education, 92*(2), 167–177.

Wilson, J. M. (1993). The predictive validity of concept mapping: Relationships to measure of achievement. *The Proceedings of the Third International Seminar on Misconceptions and Educational Strategies in Science and Mathematics.* Ithaca, NY: Misconceptions Trust.

Yancy, K. B. (1998). *Reflection in the writing classroom.* Logan: Utah State University Press.

Zeilik, M. (2004). Concept mapping. *Field-Tested Learning Assessment Guide (FLAG).* Retrieved January 15, 2007, from http://www.flaguide.org/cat/minute papers/conmap1.php

GLOSSARY

Compiled by C. Dianne Raubenheimer

ABET evaluator: An individual or a set of individuals who review a given program for ABET accreditation purposes.

academic program: "More than a collection of courses; it is designed to focus on outcomes that are emphasized repeatedly, in multiple courses, throughout the students' studies" (chapter 1, p. 4).

accreditation-focused evaluation: An evaluation that focuses on the standards or requirements for accreditation or licensing (Patton, 1997).

action research: A research method that faculty can use to conduct classroom-based research. It involves iterative cycles of identifying a problem, designing a way to address the problem, gathering data, and reflecting on the data to establish if the change was effective.

alternative assessments: Classroom setting assessments that (1) allow students to demonstrate the ability to directly apply learned knowledge and skills and (2) reflect higher levels of real-world application without using paper-and-pencil tests (Mertler, 2003). Examples include portfolios, performance tasks, and student interviews.

analytic rubric: A scoring guide used to divide a whole task into subcomponents. They are criterion referenced and are used to assess summative or formative performance along several different dimensions (e.g., from excellent to poor). There are usually multiple detailed parts to the rubric, each focusing on particular competencies or outcomes (Taggart, Phifer, Nixon, & Wood, 2001). Also called a *task-specific rubric*.

artifact: A piece of student work that provides evidence of achievement for a particular outcome or set of outcomes.

assessment: "Assessment is the systematic collection, review, and use of information about educational programs undertaken for the purpose of improving student learning and development" (Palomba & Banta, 1999, p. 4).

assessment process: The combined activities of assessment including developing objectives and outcomes, collecting and interpreting evidence, and using results for decision making.

assessment task: A task assigned to students that is aligned to course outcomes, allowing students to demonstrate their knowledge, skills, and attitudes.

authentic assessment: "Assessment tasks that specifically address real world applications of knowledge and skills" (Mertler, 2003, p. 70). This is also called *embedded assessment.*

authentic learning: Learning that provides students with the opportunity to engage with, explore, discover, discuss, and construct concepts and relationships in contexts that involve real problems and projects that are relevant and interesting to the learner (Visible Knowledge Project, 2002).

benchmark: A detailed description of a specific level of performance expected of students at a particular age, academic level, or development level. A measurement of group performance against established standards at defined points along the pathway toward the standard. Subsequent measurements of group performance use the benchmarks to measure progress toward achievement (New Horizons for Learning, 2002).

Bloom's taxonomy: This taxonomy provides a way of categorizing the level of abstraction of outcomes and questions, including exam questions. There are six levels in the taxonomy in increasing levels of cognitive demand: knowledge, comprehension, application, analysis, synthesis, and evaluation (Bloom, Krathwohl, & Masai, 1984).

capstone assessment: Measurement of student achievement of integrated skills and outcomes for the program.

classroom assessment techniques (CATs): Methods that can be used for (1) assessing student course-related knowledge and skills; (2) assessing learner attitudes, values, and self-awareness; and (3) for assessing reactions to teachers and teaching (Angelo & Cross, 1993).

classroom research: "A promising approach to professional development because its emphasis on carefully observing students in the process of learning, combined with collecting data and reflecting on its implications for teaching, adds to faculty knowledge about teaching and learning in the specific disciplines. Combines the best features of professional development and teacher evaluation, both of which are central concerns of the assessment movement" (Angelo & Cross, 1993, p. 379).

concept maps: Drawings or diagrams showing the mental connections students make between a major concept the instructor focuses on and other concepts they have learned (Angelo & Cross, 1993).

continuous improvement: The use of program assessment data to improve and further develop a program through a documented plan (ABET, 2006).

conventional or traditional assessment: Conventional or traditional assessment refers to paper-and-pencil testing (multiple-choice, true/false, matching, short answer) that typically must be completed within a defined period of time (Coalition of Essential Schools Network, 1998).

course-based assessment: Use of student work produced for course work that can be used for program assessment. It is also called *embedded assessment* or *authentic assessment*.

course objectives: Broad statements concerning desired student knowledge or performances that are designed to reflect accomplishments that the course is preparing students to achieve.

course outcomes: Statements concerning demonstrations of what students should know and be able to do at the end of a course.

criterion-referenced assessments: Assessments or tests constructed to determine whether or not the target has attained mastery of a skill or knowledge area (National Science Foundation, 2002).

deduction: Inference by reasoning from the general to the specific.

difficulty index (p): Proportion of students who answered an item correctly (Kubiszyn & Borich, 1990).

direct assessment: Direct observations or examinations of students' knowledge and skills assessed against measurable learning outcomes. Techniques include tests, exams, quizzes, demonstrations, and reports. They show what students know and are able to do and provide evidence of student learning (Rogers, 2006a).

discrimination (D) index: Measure of the extent to which a test item discriminates or differentiates between students who do well on the overall test and those who do not do well on the overall test (Kubiszyn & Borich, 1990).

evaluation: "Evaluation assists sense making about policies and programs through the conduct of systematic inquiry that describes and explains the policies' and programs' operations, effects, justifications, and social implications. The ultimate goal of evaluation is social betterment, to which evaluation can contribute by assisting democratic institutions to better select, oversee, improve and make sense of social programs and policies" (Mark, Henry, & Julnes, 2000, p. 3).

evidence: Another term for data.

external validity: Refers to the degree of confidence one has in generalizing findings beyond the situation studied (Patton, 1997).

faculty-developed tests: Written or oral exams that are not commercially produced or standardized (Burke, 1999).

faculty evaluator: The individual or set of individuals within a given program who are responsible for the collection, analysis, and interpretation of data with the purpose of improving student learning.

focus groups: Group discussion/interview process conducted with 7 to 12 idividuals who share some characteristics that are related to a particular research or evaluation question. The group discussions are conducted by a *trained* moderator (several times, if possible) to identify trends/patterns in perceptions among groups of individuals. The moderator's purpose is to provide direction and set the tone for the group discussion, encourage active participation from all group members, and manage time. Careful and systematic analysis of the discussions yields information that can be used to evaluate and/or improve the desired outcome (Northern Illinois University, n.d.).

formative: Formative assessment focuses on how a program can be improved and typically occurs at the beginning and intermediate phases of a program or project. The intention is to collect data for a specific time period and to use the information to improve implementation, solve unanticipated problems, and make sure participants are progressing toward the desired outcomes (Patton, 1997).

holistic rubric: Holistic rubrics are criterion referenced, meaning they show what a student knows, understands, or can do in relation to specific performance objectives of the instructional program. They provide an overall impression, are intended as a summative assessment of the task, and are less detailed than analytic rubrics (Taggart et al., 2001). Also called a *generic rubric.*

indirect assessment: Indirect assessments establish perceptions about the extent of and/or value of learning experiences, often reported by learners. They assess opinions and thoughts of students and other constituents about students' learning, knowledge, and skills. Methods include surveys and questionnaires, as well as interviews and focus groups (Rogers, 2006a).

induction: The process of deriving general principles from specific instances.

informal assessment: Spontaneous assessments that often occur unnoticed, including teacher observations and teacher questions (Angelo & Cross, 1993).

learner centered: "Focuses the primary attention of teachers and students on observing and improving learning, rather than on observing and improving teaching" (Angelo & Cross, 1993, p. 4).

learner–content interaction: How students reflect, process, and analyze new information during the course and integrate this new information into existing knowledge structures.

learner–instructor interaction: Communication between the student and instructor in a course, which may include information other than instructional material (e.g., online courses allow for a more personal relationship to develop).

learning style: The manner in which a learner perceives, interacts with, and responds to the learning environment. Components of learning style are the cognitive, affective, and physiological elements, all of which may be strongly influenced by a person's cultural background (Ohio State University, n.d.).

metacognition: The term used by cognitive psychologists to describe students' awareness and understanding of their own skills, performance, and habits (Angelo & Cross, 1993).

norm-referenced test (NRT): A standardized test in which a student's results are compared to scores of students in the same grade or age group obtained by a broad sampling. This is helpful in comparing students to their peers, often on a nationwide basis (National Science Foundation, 2002; North Central Regional Educational Laboratory, 1989.

objective testing: Testing that measures the participant's knowledge of objective facts (which have correct answers) (Questionmark Corporation, 2007).

observation: The act of making and recording actions and taking a measurement.

paradigm: "A worldview built on implicit assumptions, accepted definitions, comfortable habits, values defended as truths, and beliefs projected as reality" (Patton, 1997, p. 267).

performance-based assessment: Assessments based on settings designed to emulate real-life contexts or conditions in which students apply specific knowledge or skills (Questionmark Corporation, 2007).

performance criteria or metric: Indicators of performance or those elements that you will look for to determine student success. It is a standard of judgment on which a decision is made. Statements are specific and measurable, identifying the performances required to meet the outcome. Suggests success or lack of success in reaching the desired outcome and should be confirmable by evidence (Rogers, 2006b).

performance task: A performance task is designed to measure particular outcomes by providing a student the opportunity to demonstrate his or her abilities and to apply knowledge and skills. Typically it is accompanied by an explicit scoring system (Burke, 1999).

portfolio: Samples of student work, typically selected by the student based on guidelines prepared by the teacher (Mertler, 2003).

portfolio assessment: The process for assessing a portfolio (file or folder) into which students place appropriate artifacts to demonstrate that they have met particular outcomes. There are a variety of methods to assess portfolios, including holistic or analytical rubrics.

primary trait rubric: Primary trait rubrics are criterion referenced and are established for particular tasks based upon the trait or traits that are most essential to a good performance (Taggart et al., 2001).

problem-based learning: A term used to describe a number of different approaches to teaching and learning in which the prime focus is on a problem or problems rather than a discipline or body of knowledge.

product: The tangible evidence of a performance task undertaken by students. This is also known as an *artifact*.

program educational objectives: Broad statements concerning desired student knowledge or performances that are specifically designed to reflect the career and professional accomplishments that the program is preparing graduates to achieve in the first few years after graduation (ABET, 2006; Rogers, 2006b).

program outcomes: Statements that describe what students are expected to know, think, and be able to do by the time of graduation. These relate to the skills, knowledge, and behaviors that students acquire in their matriculation through the program (ABET, 2006). These are the same as *learning outcomes* or *intended outcomes*.

qualitative: Qualitative research and evaluation is typically used to answer questions about the complex nature of phenomena, often with the purpose of describing and understanding the phenomena from the participants' point of view. The qualitative approach is also referred to as the *interpretive, constructivist,* or *postpositivist* approach (Leedy & Ormrod, 2001).

qualitative item analysis: A nonnumerical method for analyzing test items not employing student responses but considering test objectives, content validity, and technical item quality (Kubiszyn & Borich, 1990).

quantitative: Quantitative research and evaluation is used to answer questions about relationships among measured variables with the purpose of explaining, predicting, and controlling phenomena. This approach is sometimes called *the traditional, experimental,* or *positivist* approach (Leedy & Ormrod, 2001).

quantitative item analysis: A numerical method for analyzing test items employing student-response alternatives or options (Kubiszyn & Borich, 1990).

rating scale: A scale that uses descriptive words along a continuum that indicate levels of performance. At each point in the continuum, qualities of performance are described. They are often associated with quantitative values in rubrics.

recognition items: True-false, matching, and multiple-choice items are called *objective items,* but they are also referred to as recognition items because the test taker needs only to "recognize" the correct answer (Kubiszyn & Borich, 1990).

reliability: A measure of the extent to which an instrument yields consistent results over time when the object being measured has not changed. It includes interrater reliability, internal consistency reliability, and test-retest reliability (Leedy & Ormrod, 2001).

rubrics: Specific sets of criteria that clearly define for both student and teacher what a range of acceptable and unacceptable performances looks like. They are used as scoring guides to define descriptors of ability at each level of performance and assign values to each level. Levels referred to are proficiency levels that describe a continuum from excellent product to unacceptable product (System for Adult Basic Education Support, 2006).

scoring guide: A detailed set of criteria and guidelines to be used for scoring student work. It may include rubrics, instructions for use, and samples of student work.

senior project: Projects carried out during the senior year, such as capstone design projects. These are a type of performance task requiring students to integrate knowledge.

SOLO taxonomy: The SOLO (Structured of the Observed Learning Outcome) taxonomy, which is based on the study of outcomes in a variety of academic content areas, is used to classify the student learning outcomes for the student work gathered, as well as outcomes observed during the classroom observation. "As students learn, the outcomes of their learning display similar stages of increasing structural complexity. There are two main changes: *quantitative,* as the amount of detail in the student's response increases, and *qualitative,* as the amount of detail becomes integrated into a structural pattern" (Biggs, 2003).

stakeholders: People who have a stake or a vested interest in assessment data and evaluation findings (Patton, 1997).

standardized testing: Norm-referenced tests, typically administered by an external, neutral body.

summative: Summative evaluation provides data to support judgments about the worth of a program, usually so a decision can be made about the merit of continuing the program. Typically a summative evaluation occurs at the end of a specified period and focuses on measuring performance against a set of preestablished standards, criteria, or outcomes (Patton, 1997).

survey: "A popular form of data collection, especially when gathering information from large groups, where standardization is important. Surveys can be constructed in many ways, but they always consist of two components: questions and responses" (National Science Foundation, 2002).

Teaching Goals Inventory (TGI): A questionnaire intended to help faculty identify and rank the relative importance of their teaching goals (Angelo & Cross, 1993).

test: Refers to a more structured oral or written evaluation of student achievement (Burke, 1999).

testing: Any kind of activity that results in some type of grade or comment being entered in a checklist, grade book, or anecdotal record (Burke, 1999).

triangulation of data: Using more than one source of data, for example, students, instructor, other faculty, administrators.

triangulation of methods: Using more than one method to gather data, for example, survey, observation, student artifacts.

unintended consequences: Any unplanned or unanticipated outcomes that occur as a result of implementing an assessment or evaluation. For example, the use of student test scores as part of the teacher evaluation data may result in test score pollution practices and more use of teaching-to-the-test activities accompanied by less reliance on the district curriculum guide for planning instructional activities and lessons (The Evaluation Center, 2004).

validity: This is a measurement of whether the instrument measures what it is purported to measure. It includes face validity, content validity, construct validity, and criterion validity (Leedy & Ormrod, 2001).

values: Principles, standards, or qualities considered worthwhile.

References

ABET. (2006). *Criteria for accrediting applied science programs.* Retrieved August 31, 2006, from http://www.abet.org/Linked%20Documents-UPDATE/Criteria%20and%20PP/R001% 2006–07 %20ASAC%20Criteria%205–24–06.pdf

Angelo, T. A., & Cross, K. P. (1993). *Classroom assessment techniques: A handbook for college teachers* (2nd ed). San Francisco: Jossey-Bass.

Biggs, J. (2003). *Teaching for quality learning at university.* New York: Open University Press.

Bloom, B. S., Krathwohl, D. R., & Masai, B. B. (1984). *Taxonomy of educational objectives: The classification of educational goals.* New York: Longman.

Burke, K. (1999). *How to assess authentic learning.* Arlington Heights, IL: SkyLight Professional Development.

Coalition of Essential Schools Network. (1998). *Defining assessment.* Retrieved May 19, 2006, from http://www.essentialschools.org/cs/resources/view/ces_res/124

The Evaluation Center. (2004). *Teacher evaluation kit: Complete glossary.* Retrieved May 19, 2006, from http://www.wmich.edu/evalctr/ess/glossary/glossary.htm

Kubiszyn, T., & Borich, G. (1990). *Educational testing and measurement.* Glenview, IL: Scott, Foresman, Little, Brown Higher Education.

Leedy, P. D., & Ormrod, J. W. (2001). *Practical research: Planning and design* (7th ed.). Upper Saddle River, NJ: Merrill Prentice Hall.

Mark, M. M., Henry, G. T., & Julnes, G. (2000). *Evaluation: An integrated framework for understanding, guiding, and improving policies and programs.* San Francisco: Jossey-Bass.

Mertler, C. A. (2003). *Classroom assessment: A practical guide for educators.* Los Angeles: Pyrczak.

National Science Foundation. (2002). *The 2002 user friendly handbook for project evaluation.* Arlington, VA: Author.

New Horizons for Learning. (2002). *Assessment terminology: A glossary of useful terms.* Retrieved September 21, 2006, from http://www.newhorizons.org/strategies/assess/terminology.htm_

North Central Regional Educational Laboratory. (1989). *Pencils down!* Retrieved April 25, 2006, from http://www.ncrel.org/sdrs/areas/issues/methods/assment/as6penc2.htm

Northern Illinois University. (n.d.). *Assessment terms.* Retrieved May 5, 2006, from http://www.niu.edu/assessment/Resources/Assessment_terms.htm

Ohio State University. (no date). *Commitment to Success Program (CSP): Glossary.* Retrieved May 23, 2006, from http://ftad.osu.edu/CSP/glossary.html

Palomba, C. A., & Banta, T. W. (1999). *Assessment essentials: Planning, implementing, and improving assessment in higher education.* San Francisco: Jossey-Bass.

Patton, M. Q. (1997). *Utilization-focused evaluation: The new century text* (3rd ed.). Thousand Oaks, CA: Sage.

Questionmark Corporation. (2007). *Testing and assessment glossary*. Retrieved May 5, 2006, from http://www.questionmark.com/us/glossary.htm#N

Rogers, G. (2006a). Direct and indirect assessments: What are they good for? *Community Matters, 4*, p. 3.

Rogers, G. (2006b). *The language of assessment: Humpty Dumpty had a great fall*. Retrieved May 19, 2006, from http://www.abet.org/Linked%20Documents-UP DATE/Assessment/Assessment%20Tips3.pdf

System for Adult Basic Education Support (SABES). (2006). *Glossary of useful terms*. Retrieved May 19, 2006, from http://www.sabes.org/assessment/glossary.htm

Taggart, G. L., Phifer, S. J., Nixon, J. A., & Wood, M. (2001). *Rubrics: A handbook for construction and use*. Lanham, MA: Scarecrow Press.

Visible Knowledge Project. (2002). *Glossary*. Retrieved May 19, 2006, from http://crossroads.georgetown.edu/vkp/resources/glossary/authenticlearning.htm

Editors

JONI E. SPURLIN, PhD, is the University Director of Assessment and Associate Director for Assessment at University Planning and Analysis, North Carolina State University. Since 1991, she has provided leadership and expertise to faculty, administrators, and staff in the development of tools for assessment, institutional effectiveness, and planning processes at several institutions. She has evaluated and worked with department chairs and faculty on improving outcomes assessment for engineering, computer science, liberal arts, education, business, and allied health programs. For five years she worked with engineering faculty to establish effective assessment processes related to ABET and university program review. Beginning in 2005, Dr. Spurlin started providing assessment direction on university projects including NC State's Quality Enhancement Plan, "LITRE: Learning in a Technology-Rich Environment," as well as on administrative, college, and departmental efforts in assessment. She has consulted with numerous institutions on assessment and has published in journals and conferences. Her research focuses on the development of effective assessment methods to improve student learning and retention.

SARAH A. RAJALA, PhD, is the James Worth Bagley Chair and Head of the Department of Electrical and Computer Engineering at Mississippi State University. Previously, she was Professor in the Department of Electrical Engineering at North Carolina State University and served as Director of the Industry/University Cooperative Research Center for Advanced Computing and Communication from 1993 to 1996, associate dean for academic affairs from 1996 to 2002, and associate dean for research and graduate programs from 2002 to 2006. Dr. Rajala's research interests and expertise include engineering education, assessment, and the analysis and processing of images and image sequences. She has authored or coauthored over a hundred papers in these areas and has had contributions published in 13 books. Dr. Rajala has received numerous awards for her research and professional contributions, including the Presidential Award for Excellence in Science, Mathematics, and Engineering Mentoring in 2000, Fellow of the Institute of Electrical and Electronic Engineers in 2001, and Fellow of the American Society for Engineering Education (ASEE) in 2007 for her contributions to engineering education.

JEROME P. LAVELLE, PhD, is Assistant Dean of Academic Affairs in the College of Engineering and Associate Professor in the Edward P. Fitts Department of Industrial and Systems Engineering at North Carolina State University. Dr. Lavelle's teaching and research areas include engineering management, project management, cost engineering, engineering economics, leadership, teamwork and personality, and engineering education. He is a member of ASEE and the Institute of Industrial Engineers (IIE). Previous to his career in academia, he was a member of technical staff (MTS) with AT&T Bell Laboratories in Columbus, Ohio. Dr. Lavelle is an ABET evaluator with IIE and coauthor of *Engineering Economic Analysis, 9th Edition* with Newnan and Eschenbach.

Advisory Board

MARY BESTERFIELD-SACRE, PhD, is an Associate Professor of Industrial Engineering and Fulton C. Noss Faculty Fellow at the University of Pittsburgh. She received her BS in engineering management from the University of Missouri–Rolla, her MS in industrial engineering from Purdue University, and a PhD in industrial engineering at the University of Pittsburgh. Prior to joining academia, she worked as an engineer with ALCOA and the U.S. Army Human Engineering Laboratory. Dr. Besterfield-Sacre's research interests include engineering education assessment and product innovation, K-12 systems modeling, and quality control and assurance. In the area of assessment and evaluation, Dr. Besterfield-Sacre has written numerous conference and journal papers and has given many workshops and presentations. Her research has been funded by the NSF, DOE, Sloan Foundation, Engineering Information Foundation, and the NCIIA. She is an associate editor of the *Journal of Engineering Education* and is coauthor of *Total Quality Management, 3rd Edition*.

J. JOSEPH HOEY, IV, PhD, is Vice President for Institutional Effectiveness at the Savannah College of Art and Design. His responsibilities include regional and specialized accreditation, assessment of student learning, institutional research, quality assurance and accountability reporting, and academic program review. Dr. Hoey is Past President of the Southern Association for Institutional Research; is a frequent speaker and presenter on assessment, evaluation, and accreditation issues at regional and national conferences; and serves as an evaluator for the Commission on Colleges, Southern Association of Colleges and Schools. His background includes eight years as the founding director of the Office of Assessment at the Georgia Institute of Technology and a further five years in University Planning and Analysis at North Carolina State University. His published research focuses on academic program review, alumni and employer feedback, validation of student engagement research, community college transfer, and evaluation of online academic programs.

MICHAEL S. LEONARD, PhD, is Senior Associate Dean and Professor in the School of Engineering at Mercer University. He has previously served on the faculties of Clemson University, the University of Missouri–Columbia, and Georgia Institute of Technology. Dr. Leonard received the bachelor of industrial engineering, master of engineering, and doctor of philosophy degrees from the University of Florida. He is a Fellow of the Institute of Industrial Engineers, and a registered professional engineer in Missouri and South Carolina. He currently serves on the Board of Trustees for the IIE. Dr. Leonard has served as an ABET Industrial Engineering Program Evaluation Visitor for almost 20 years. In addition, he has served as a member of the ABET Engineering Accreditation Commission and as a representative member of the ABET Board of Directors.

ELEANOR W. NAULT, PhD, is Director of Assessment at Clemson University. After receiving her PhD in educational leadership in 1997 from Clemson, she began to serve the university as the Director of Assessment with her primary role being to further institutional effectiveness and the practice of assessment in all areas of the institution. She served on the ABET-funded national advisory board for the study *Engineering Change: A Study of the Impact of EC2000*, with past service on the NSF SUCCEED Coalition of Engineering Educators. She is currently an evaluator of NSF and EU/FIPSE grants. Dr. Nault is an institutional liaison to the South Carolina Commission on Higher Education and an SACS/COC site visitor. In addition to serving as a consultant and workshop presenter, she continues to participate in professional organizations such as the Association of Institutional Researchers. Her collaborative research has been published in the *Journal of Engineering Education*.

C. DIANNE RAUBENHEIMER, PhD, is Director of Assessment in the College of Engineering and Adjunct Assistant Professor in the Department of Adult and Higher Education at North Carolina State University. She has worked with faculty and administrators in engineering for two years, and previously in the science and education disciplines, on developing and implementing various assessment and evaluation processes. A particular interest is in assisting faculty to develop and implement classroom-based assessment and action research plans to establish the effectiveness of instruction and to use the data to improve teaching and student learning. She is currently working with several engineering faculty assessing the impact of in-class technology use on teaching and student learning. Dr. Raubenheimer has also worked as an education consultant for a number of organizations conducting program evaluations. Her research interests focus on faculty development, the role of technology in teaching and learning, and assessment in higher education.

Other Authors

SHERRA E. KERNS, PhD, is Vice President for Innovation and Research and F.W. Olin Professor of Electrical and Computer Engineering at Olin College. A Fellow of the Institute of Electrical and Electronics Engineers (IEEE) for her technical contributions, Dr. Kerns is the recipient of IEEE's prestigious Millennium Medal and the IEEE Education Society's Harriet B. Rigas Award. She served on the advisory committee for the National Academy of Engineering's Center for the Advancement of Scholarship on Engineering Education and the steering committee for the NAE *Engineer of 2020* Report. She is Past President and a Fellow of the ASEE. She serves as a member of the board of directors of ABET, having previously served on the Engineering Accreditation Commission of ABET and its executive committee. She has served on the faculties of Auburn, North Carolina State, and Vanderbilt Universities and as director of the multidisciplinary, multi-institutional University Consortium for Research on Electronics in Space. At Olin College, Dr. Kerns is pioneering a unique administrative position with responsibility for enhancing faculty intellectual vitality, providing opportunities for students to learn through discovery, and building a culture that rewards innovation and the taking of appropriate risks.

DAVID G. MEYER, PhD, is Professor of Electrical and Computer Engineering at Purdue University. He received his BS (1973) and MSE (1975) degrees in electrical engineering, MS (1979) degree in computer science, and PhD (1981) degree in electrical engineering, all from Purdue University. In 1982, he joined the School of Electrical and Computer Engineering at Purdue, where he is currently a Professor specializing in engineering education research, embedded microcontroller system design, and electro-acoustics. Dr. Meyer is a member of the IEEE, the Audio Engineering Society (AES), and the ASEE. He has won numerous teaching awards during his academic career, including four national awards: the Eta Kappa Nu C. Holmes Mac-Donald Outstanding Teaching Award, the IEEE Undergraduate Teaching Award, the ASEE Fred Merryfield Design Award, and the IEEE Computer Society Undergraduate Teaching Award.

RONALD L. MILLER, PhD, is Professor of Chemical Engineering and Director of the Center for Engineering Education at the Colorado School of Mines (CSM), where he has taught chemical engineering and interdisciplinary courses and conducted education research for the past 20 years. Dr. Miller has received three university-wide teaching awards and has held a Jenni teaching fellowship at CSM. He has received grant awards for educational research from the National Science Foundation (e.g., misconception identification and repair; developing rigorous engineering education researchers), the U.S. Department of Education's Fund for the Improvement of Post Secondary Education (FIPSE) program (multidisciplinary senior design; integrated freshman-year core curriculum; computer software to measure intellectual development), the National Endowment for the Humanities (integrated humanities/chemical engineering introductory course), and the Colorado Commission on Higher Education (enhancement of freshman/ sophomore engineering design sequence) and has published widely in the engineering education literature. Dr. Miller continues to serve as assessment coordinator for the chemical engineering program and serves on the CSM assessment committee.

BARBARA M. MOSKAL, EdD, is an Associate Professor of Mathematical and Computer Sciences at the Colorado School of Mines. She received her EdD in mathematics education with a minor in quantitative research methodology and her MA in mathematics from the University of Pittsburgh. Her research interests include student assessment, K-12 outreach, and equity issues. In 2000, she received a New Faculty Fellowship at the Frontiers in Education Conference, and in 2006 she received the William Elgin Wickenden Award along with her colleagues, Barbara Olds and Ronald Miller.

BARBARA M. OLDS, PhD, is Associate Vice President for Educational Innovation and Professor of Liberal Arts and International Studies at the Colorado School of Mines. She recently returned to Colorado after spending three years at the National Science Foundation, where she served as the division director for the Division of Research, Evaluation, and Communication (REC) in the Education and Human Resources Directorate. Dr. Olds is also currently a Visiting Professor in Purdue University's Department of Engineering Education. Her research interests are primarily in understanding and assessing engineering-student learning. Her current research focuses on development of concept inventories for engineering topics. She has participated in a number of curriculum innovation projects and has been active in the engineering education and assessment communities. She is a Fellow of the American Society for Engineering Education and was a Fulbright lecturer/researcher in Sweden in 1999.

LARRY J. SHUMAN, PhD, is Associate Dean for Academic Affairs at the University of Pittsburgh School of Engineering and Professor of Industrial Engineering. He holds a PhD in operations research from the Johns Hopkins University and a bachelor's degree in engineering education from the University of Cincinnati. His research focuses on improving the engineering educational experience and the ethical behavior of engineers. Dr. Shuman has published widely in the engineering education literature. He is the Founding Editor of ASEE's *Advances in Engineering Education* and served as a senior associate editor and an editorial review board member for the *Journal of Engineering Education*. He has been principal or coprincipal investigator on over 25 sponsored research projects from the National Science Foundation, FIPSE, Health and Human Services, and the Department of Transportation. He was the academic dean for the spring 2002 "Semester at Sea" voyage and is an ASEE Fellow.

LINDA SUSKIE is a Vice President at the Middle States Commission on Higher Education, an accreditor of colleges and universities in the mid-Atlantic states. Prior positions include serving as director of the American Association for Higher Education's Assessment Forum. Her nearly 30 years of experience in college and university administration include work in assessment, institutional research, strategic planning, and quality management. Ms. Suskie is an internationally recognized speaker, writer, and consultant on a broad variety of higher education assessment topics. Her latest book is *Assessment of Student Learning: A Common Sense Guide* (Anker, 2004). Ms.

Suskie has taught graduate courses in assessment and educational research methods and undergraduate courses in writing, statistics, and developmental mathematics. She holds a bachelor's degree in quantitative studies from Johns Hopkins University and a master's in educational measurement and statistics from the University of Iowa.

KARAN WATSON, PhD, is now a Regents Professor of Electrical and Computer Engineering at Texas A&M University, where she joined the faculty in 1983. Dr. Watson is a registered professional engineer and has been named a Fellow of the Institute of Electrical and Electronic Engineers (IEEE) and the American Society of Engineering Educators (ASEE). Some of her awards include the U.S. President's Award for Mentoring Minorities and Women in Science and Technology, the IEEE International Undergraduate Teaching Award, the HPIEEE Harriett B. Rigas Award, the TAMU Provost's Award for Diversity, and the College of Engineering Crawford Teaching Award. In 2003–2004, Dr. Watson served as a senior fellow of the National Academy of Engineers' Center for the Advancement of Scholarship in Engineering Education. Since 1991 she has served as an ABET accreditation evaluator and a commissioner for the engineering accreditation commission of ABET, and she now serves on the board of directors of ABET. In these roles she has directly participated in 22 U.S. and international accreditation visits, with 12 of these based on EC2000 criteria.